MOVIES, SONGS, AND ELECTRIC SOUND

MOVIES, SONGS, AND ELECTRIC SOUND

Transatlantic Trends

Charles O'Brien

INDIANA UNIVERSITY PRESS

This book is a publication of

Indiana University Press
Office of Scholarly Publishing
Herman B Wells Library 350
1320 East 10th Street
Bloomington, Indiana 47405 USA

iupress.indiana.edu

© 2019 by Charles O'Brien

All rights reserved

No part of this book may be reproduced or utilized in any form or by any means, electronic or mechanical, including photocopying and recording, or by any information storage and retrieval system, without permission in writing from the publisher. The paper used in this publication meets the minimum requirements of the American National Standard for Information Sciences—Permanence of Paper for Printed Library Materials, ANSI Z39.48-1992.

Manufactured in the United States of America

ISBN 978-0-253-04039-8 (hdbk.)
ISBN 978-0-253-04040-4 (pbk.)
ISBN 978-0-253-04042-8 (web PDF)

1 2 3 4 5   24 23 22 21 20 19

*This book is dedicated to
the memory of Samnang Thary O'Brien*

CONTENTS

Acknowledgments   ix

Introduction   *1*

1   Movies and Songs in Transition   *18*

2   Electric Sound as New Medium   *46*

3   Voices and Bodies, Direct and Dubbed   *64*

4   Film Editing after Electric Sound   *89*

5   American Film Songs, Inside the Films and Out   *118*

6   Musical Films Made in Germany   *142*

    Conclusion: Songs in Cinema, from Electric to Digital   *164*

Appendix A: Methods of Measurement   173

Appendix B: Samples and Tests   185

Bibliography   189

Index   207

ACKNOWLEDGMENTS

Finishing this book took a long time, which means that there are a lot of people to thank and the risk that an important name will be left out. I'll begin at the beginning with Hans-Michael Bock, Francesco Pitassio, Leonardo Quaresima, Laura Vichi, and others behind the Gradisca Spring School from 2003 through 2005, when the school's focus was on the multiple-version films of the early 1930s. The viewing of archival prints of rare films, along with participation in workshops and conversations with Horst Claus, Nataša Ďurovičová, Joseph Garncarz, Malte Hagener, Anne Jäckel, Ivan Klimeš, Anna Sofia Rossholm, Petr Szczepanik, Chris Wahl, and others, led me to want to write a book on the period's musical films. Special thanks to Hans-Michael for encouraging my work on German cinema by inviting me to Hamburg to give a talk at the CineGraph conference in 2005.

An initial draft of this book was completed while I was senior fellow at the Centre for Advanced Study in the Visual Arts in Washington, DC (2006–7). What a great place. Thanks to directors Elisabeth Cropper, Peter Lukehart, and Therese O'Malley, along with that year's community of fellows, for providing a stimulating and collegial research environment.

Crucial support for the project came from Canada's Social Sciences and Humanities Research Council, which helped fund archival research conducted in Los Angeles, Berlin, Paris, and London at the following libraries and archives: the Library of Congress, the Margaret Herrick Library at the Academy of Motion Picture Arts and Sciences, the UCLA Film and Television Archive, the Warner Brothers Archive at the University of Southern California's School of Cinematic Arts, the Bundesarchiv-Filmarchiv in Berlin, the Deutsche Kinemathek, the Bibliothèque nationale de France, the Bibliothèque du film in Paris, the British Film Institute, and the British Library. Special gratitude to the Wisconsin Center for Film and Theater Research and the Deutsche Kinemathek for permission to use photos from their fabulous collections.

Research related to this book was presented at conferences sponsored by the following scholarly societies: the Society for Cinema and Media Studies (2008, 2014, 2015), the Society for Cognitive Studies in the Moving

Image (2009, 2010, 2011), Studies in French Cinema (2008, 2009), and the Film Studies Association of Canada (2009). Further venues for the presentation of book-related research included the Splendid Innovations screen translation conference organized in London by Jean-François Cornu and Carol O'Sullivan (2015), the Hollywood's Musical Contemporaries and Competitors conference organized by Jeremy Barham at the University of Surrey (2014), the GRAFICS Workshop on Montage sponsored by André Gaudreault and his team at the Université de Montréal (2014, 2016), and the conference on French and British cinema relations organized by Lucy Mazdon and Catherine Wheatley at the University of Southampton (2007).

Participation in 2012 in the stellar one-week German Film Institute at the University of Michigan, which included round-the-clock screenings of rare films, proved extremely helpful. Thanks to the GFI's organizers, Anton Kaes, Johannes von Moltke, and Eric Rentschler, and to the other participants for welcoming someone who came to German film scholarship late in the day.

This book's ideas were developed through my work as a teacher and graduate supervisor in the Film Studies program at Carleton University. Thanks to my students over the years for providing an audience for my ideas and to my faculty colleagues, especially Carol Payne, Aboubakar Sanogo, and Michael Windover, who read drafts in our faculty writers' group. Assisting with the book's statistical analysis were two students in the Film Studies master's program, Kira Vorobiyova and especially Mohsen Nasrin, a creative practitioner of cinemetrics in his own right. Nancy Duff and Jack Coghill performed life-saving work in redoing the book's DVD frames for me while I was living in Florence, Italy, where the Kuntshistorisches Institut and the Biblioteca Palagio di Parte Guelfa provided congenial spaces for daily work sessions.

Thanks also to Yuri Tsivian for encouraging my use of statistical methods and providing a major resource through his creation and maintenance of the Cinemetrics website; to the late and beloved Gunars Civjans for his creation of the cinemetrics tools that enabled the research for this book; and to Rick Altman, whose course on the American film musical at the University of Iowa many years ago sparked my interest in songs in films. I am also pleased to express gratitude to Petr Szczepanik for inviting me in 2012 to Masaryk University in the Czech Republic to teach a one-week course on "songs in cinema," and to Geoff Brown, Colin Crisp, and Malte Hagener for sending me copies of their writings, including unpublished work. Art critic Anja Caspary provided valuable assistance with the German-language texts. Janice Frisch and Kate Schramm at Indiana University Press guided me through the editorial process, and Leigh McLennon contributed astute copyediting.

Countless people have helped me along the way in the work on this book. I apologize to those whose names I missed. Also, any errors or deficiencies in the book are, of course, solely the author's responsibility.

As always, the deepest thanks go to Randi Klebanoff and our daughter, Madeleine, who inspire me more than words can say.

MOVIES, SONGS, AND ELECTRIC SOUND

INTRODUCTION

THIS BOOK EXAMINES AMERICAN AND EUROPEAN MUSICAL FILMS produced circa 1930, when the world's sound-equipped theaters screened movies featuring recorded songs, and filmmakers in the United States and Europe struggled to meet the artistic and technical challenges of sound production and distribution. The challenges were unusually disruptive. New-media upheavals on a global scale have a long history, beginning with the printing press in the fifteenth century and continuing up through the current digital revolution.[1] A peculiarity of electric sound's introduction into cinema was the sense of aesthetic catastrophe. The telegraph did not eliminate an established art, nor did the telephone, phonograph, wireless, or motion picture. Digital technologies are transforming cinema, but in ways that leave the theater experience largely unchanged. The challenge to cinema's identity posed by recorded sound was more radical. Electric sound's introduction into cinema, in the view of many observers, had brought about an artistic retreat. Devotees of the seventh art railed against the talkies. With the sudden presence of "tenors, clowns, masters of ceremonies, and band leaders," wrote critic Nino Frank, the popular-theater traditions banished from cinema in the 1920s had returned with a vengeance, bringing artistic innovation to a halt.[2] Critic Leo Hirsch proclaimed, "Today one cannot deny that the sound film has ceased all experiments in 'abstract,' mathematical, and expressionist cinema, and that there is no longer an avant garde, that one no longer sees new comic forms, and that the pictorial has disappeared from cinema."[3]

The period's musical films, with their stage-derived song-and-dance sequences, took much of the blame. With stars, formats, and techniques culled from multiple extracinematic media, new and old, the song-heavy films of the late 1920s and early '30s responded to pressures that seemed commercial in nature rather than aesthetic. Thick with what critic Daniel Albright called intermedial dissonance, musical films fell short of coalescing into an artistic whole, a unified form.[4] For many observers, the hard-won artistic gains of the past quarter century were being undone by "the new singing and talking films," which, declared film historian Léon Moussinac, had "reduced the cinema to its state in 1905."[5]

The presence of singers in films exerted special pressures on film technique. Musical films were sold in connection with star vocalists whose profiles in multiple media made them always "bigger" than the films in which they appeared. Song sequences seemed designed less to push forward the film's plot than to facilitate the singer's engagement with her or his public. They thus tend to stand apart from the rest of a film, functioning as an interlude in the story rather than a continuation. The inclination toward formal autonomy made song performances anticinematic in the view of composer Kurt London, for whom the profusion of songs in cinema in the early 1930s had "totally destroyed" the "style of the sound film": "The theme-song broke the tension at the most important points in the film, because it held up the action. And the film must never linger without reason, requiring by its very nature, incessant motion."[6]

Negative critical reaction influenced cinema history for decades afterward, as the musical films of the late 1920s and early 1930s were either dismissed as bad cinema or ignored altogether. Their poor reputation was noted in 1977 by critic Andrew Sarris, for whom due appreciation of conversion-era cinema had been hindered by "the cultural guilt assumed by movie musicals as the slayers of silent cinema."[7] Today, long after the demise of the partisanship behind the established historiography, when songs are routine on movie soundtracks, it may be easier to appreciate the inventiveness of the "song pictures" of the late 1920s and early 1930s—a time when the struggle to bring song performances in line with the aesthetics of narrative cinema made virtually any film daringly innovative in one respect or another.[8] A goal of this book is to counter a long history of critical neglect by bringing out the artistic and cultural interest of the period's surviving films, which serve as a major source of documentation for the arguments that follow.

The Musical Film's Transnational Appeal

Songs became omnipresent in sound films because they helped producers meet a major commercial challenge: the retention of the export market for motion pictures in the face of new distribution barriers linked to synchronous speech. Unlike silent movies, whose visual storytelling exerted universal appeal, films with spoken language raised national and regional obstacles to distribution.[9] As the production of synch-sound films escalated, film-industry observers predicted steep declines in export revenue. In November 1928, *Variety* reported that Hollywood's foreign income, which had comprised roughly 40 percent of its total income prior to sound, had fallen to 30 percent of its total income and would likely "show a further decrease of fifteen to twenty percent within two years."[10] Export distribution was also a major concern in the German film industry, Hollywood's main competitor in the early 1930s in the emergent world market for sound films. German films likewise encountered resistance from audiences specifically on account of the politics of linguistic difference. Worrying events included street violence in Prague in September 1930, triggered by the screening of German-language films.[11]

Recorded sound brought with it special cultural-political challenges. If silent cinema had offered a "universal language," "the talkies," stated the editor of *Photoplay* magazine, "have recreated the Tower of Babel. They have also reawakened consciousness of nationality in a manner that can be equaled only by a war."[12] In Hollywood, Berlin, and elsewhere, the endangered foreign market made urgent the need to create sound movies that could circulate irrespective of the cultural barriers imposed by recorded speech. For export-oriented producers in the United States, Germany, and other countries, songs proved essential in meeting challenges to distribution. Operettas, revue films, musical-stage adaptations, opera-singer vehicles, and backstage melodramas traveled well, reliably drawing audiences in the metropolitan centers where sound films were screened. "Hit songs," proclaimed film journalist Sid Silverman, are "universally appreciated" and can "carry a [talking film] around the world."[13]

The same moviegoers who rejected foreign dialogue accepted and even welcomed foreign-language songs. Translation was deemed unnecessary for songs, which did not attract the same cultural-political resistance as recorded speech. Whereas speech required dubbing, subtitling, the projection of title slides onto a second screen ("side titles"), or some other method of translation, songs in export films often played in their native language only.[14] With respect to American popular music specifically, Europeans were said to prefer performances in American dialect by the original artists.[15] Moreover, songs seemed politically innocuous in ways that dialogue was not, to the point that musical films were rumored to receive less scrutiny from censors. In Italy, Mussolini's government required that speech in foreign films be dubbed in Italian but allowed song lyrics to remain untranslated.[16] "There will always be a receptive audience for singing and dancing pictures," whatever the language of the lyrics, observed an American journalist in 1930, while "straight talkies must, of course, be in the language of the country where they are being shown."[17] For the sound-era film industry, songs, stated Erich Pommer, Ufa's chief producer of foreign-language films, provided an "international means of communication and negotiation [*Verständigungsmittel*]" that could overcome "the foreignness of speech."[18]

Song Integration

Including recorded songs in feature films offered great commercial advantages, but it also confronted producers with the vexing artistic problem noted above: the tendency for the typical song sequence to come across as tangential to the film's narrative. Songs in narrative films often seem gratuitous, amounting to "inserts in an action that could have run its course just as well without them," as film theorist Béla Balázs put it.[19] Songs, remarked a critic in Paris, "arrive suddenly like intermissions [*entr'actes*]": "The action comes to a halt, the actor appears in close-up [*en premier plan*] and sings. And then, when he or she finishes, the film begins again."[20]

The need to integrate songs into movies in a "logical" or "natural" manner was invoked frequently in the transatlantic press in the early 1930s and remains an ideal for film critics today. The common approach can be called *narrative integration*, which involves weaving a song into the causal logic of the film's plot, as when the performance fulfills the protagonist's occupation as a professional entertainer. Meeting the challenge of inserting songs "logically" into films often came down to providing a justification in the story. Marlene Dietrich sings in this or that film because she is playing a cabaret singer who works for a living. The common expedient of visually depicting the music's source serves the same end, as in *True to the Navy* (dir. Frank Tuttle, 1930) when the maid in Clara Bow's apartment turns on the radio that announces "There's Only One What Matters to Me," the tune that Bow is about to sing. The radio confirms that the music we are about to hear—not only Bow's voice but the orchestral accompaniment too—comes from inside the film's story world.

Narrative integration can be distinguished from *formal integration*, an alternative or parallel approach informed by a higher and more elusive goal: the extension of the song's musical logic to the design of the entire film, the dialogue scenes included. The ideal of musicalized drama was often invoked by conversion-era critics and filmmakers, as noted in chapter 1, and it was pursued in some of the most ambitious films of the period, notably the musicals directed by Ernst Lubitsch, Frank Tuttle, and Rouben Mamoulian at Paramount; the *Operettenfilmen* made in multiple languages at studios operated by Ufa, Tobis, and other German companies; and the comedies directed by René Clair at Tobis's Paris studio. In extraordinary productions like these, not only do songs move the narrative forward but passages of narrative action exhibit songlike characteristics, as when actors speak in verse or passages of visual action synch with the music's tempo and meter in the fashion of an animated cartoon.

Most producers of musical films, however, stopped short of trying to musicalize the narrative and instead constructed the song performances differently from the adjacent dramatic scenes. Whereas the dramatic scenes are staged and cut to the ebb and flow of the actors' speech and physical movement, the songs' visuals are determined by the music. That song performances tend to come across as relatively self-contained interludes, distinct from the narrative scenes that precede and follow them, is often regarded as an aesthetic flaw, a failure of integration. An alternative view informs this book, where the song sequence's formal self-sufficiency is seen as a strategic response to three constraints faced by conversion-era filmmakers: inherent differences between song form and narrative-film form; the commercial demands of the larger entertainment culture to which musical films, on account of the broad dissemination of film songs via additional, extrafilmic media, necessarily respond; and the special production conditions needed for song performances.

Regarding production conditions, for example, song sequences required extra preparation and rehearsal and the creative input of personnel such as choreographers, composers, conductors, instrumentalists, and dancers who did not work on the film's other scenes. Film credits sometimes list two directors, one for the songs and another for the dramatic scenes. In *Glorifying the American Girl* (1929), for example, John Harkenrider directed the Technicolor Ziegfeld Follies numbers while Millard Webb directed the black-and-white dialogue scenes. *Glorifying the American Girl* is typical of Hollywood's use of two-strip Technicolor almost exclusively for musical films, often in a piecemeal fashion, for a few numbers only.[21] Additional personnel were needed for the Technicolor song sequences, which required special cameras and extra lighting. The division of labor enabled style differences between the song sequences and the film's other scenes.

The Five Hundred Films

The conversion-era musical film is approached in this book through a corpus of roughly five hundred feature films, musical and otherwise, from the United States, Germany, France, and Britain. The large and heterogeneous corpus reflects the nature of the film-song phenomenon in the late 1920s and early 1930s, when the presence of songs extended well beyond those films regarded today as musicals. Filmed singing performances were a transnational phenomenon, popping up in all fiction film genres. *Bulldog Drummond* (dir. F. Richard Jones, 1929), a comic thriller rather than a musical, nonetheless includes three performances by tenor Donald Novis of the ballad "There's the One for Me." *F.P.1 antwortet nicht* (dir. Karl Hartl, 1932), a science fiction film from Ufa, features Allan Gray and Walter Reisch's "Flieger, grüß' mir die Sonne," a song that became a hit record. In choosing films for this project, I sought out musicals, but to cover the extent of the film-song phenomenon, I was open to virtually any narrative feature available, regardless of genre. In establishing a context for the musical films, even films without songs were helpful.

Also essential to the book's comparative project was the inclusion of as many silent films of the time as could be found. Silent and sound cinemas have long been treated as distinct research objects, covered in separate courses, books, conferences, and festivals. The division traces back to the electric-sound transition, when filmmakers and critics loyal to the cinematic achievements of the mid-1920s saw the talkies as an aesthetic disaster, just as sound film producers denigrated silent cinema as an inferior rival. The concept of silent cinema, which today refers to cinema's first three decades, was invented in the late 1920s, when cinema prior to electric sound became defined negatively, as deficient compared with the talkies. The label *silent cinema*, like foreign-language analogues such as the German *Stummfilm* and the French *cinéma muet*, was an artifact of the sound era.

The division between silent cinema and sound was not nearly so clear-cut in 1929–30, when film audiences encountered a variety of moving-picture options. Sound films came in many forms. Some featured recorded vocals while others did not. Hybrids were common, as with the numerous films that included a few synch-sound scenes but otherwise were effectively silent, with only a music-and-effects track and no vocals.[22] Until 1931, sound films, to accommodate the many unwired theaters, were typically also released with the soundtracks replaced by intertitles, so the films played in at least two versions, silent and sound. The inclusion of silent films in this book thus facilitates the reconstruction of the range of aesthetic possibilities found in the song-infused films of the early sound years.

Inclusive coverage entails looking at the film musical from an unusual angle. In the early 1930s, the genre that critics today call the musical, in which song performances serve to advance a romantic-comedy plot, had not yet emerged from the broader matrix of films-with-songs-in-them. "There is a wide difference between films with music and musical films," advised an American critic in 1931, referring to the current array of film-music possibilities.[23] Westerns, slapstick comedies, action films, family melodramas—all were potential vehicles for song, to the point, suggests film historian Donald Crafton, that it is hard to identify a film of the period that was not a musical in some sense of the term.[24] Acknowledging the diversity of the film-song phenomenon, this book's object of study is less "the musical" than "the musical film," a relatively broad and elastic category encompassing the celebrated Hollywood genre along with virtually any film containing multiple song performances.[25] Think of the musical film not as a distinct genre with precise criteria for inclusion but as a radial or cluster category whose members can exhibit varying degrees of belonging. The objective is to cover the spectrum of film-song possibilities circa 1930, when soundtracks were new, songs often fulfilled melodramatic rather than comedic purposes, and the future for sound cinema remained open. The concern, one might say, is with the film musical's prehistory as much as its history.

The German Film Industry's Rivalry with Hollywood

This book takes up an explicitly comparative study of film history in which developments in Hollywood are juxtaposed with those in Europe, especially in Germany, whose film industry was the only one in the early 1930s to rival Hollywood's on the world film market. This book thus aims to contribute to the scholarly writing on sound in Hollywood produced by Donald Crafton, Rick Altman, Jennifer Fleeger, James Lastra, Douglas Gomery, Kathryn Kalinak, Robert Spadoni, Katherine Spring, Steven Wurtzler, Michael Slowik, and others.[26] But it does so by situating Hollywood's sound conversion in the context of the transatlantic rivalry behind sound cinema's emergence as a global phenomenon. Shaping this rivalry was the sound film patent conference in Paris in July 1930, which resulted in "the apportionment of the film world as between the American and German patent holders."[27] While the United States was given exclusive rights to market sound film technology in North America, India, Russia, and Australia, Germany received exclusivity for Germany, Austria, Scandanavia, Switzerland, the Netherlands, and central Europe.[28] France, Spain, and Italy were included among the "neutral" countries that became a ground for Hollywood's struggle with the German film industry for dominance over the European film market. Essential to that struggle were musical films, which comprised the bulk of the export films made in Hollywood and Germany at the time. Many of these films were made in French-language versions.

This book is directed by the expectation that a comparative study of American and German musical films will provide insight into transnational trends in film style, as demonstrated by the role of the German and American film industries in shaping sound cinema in other countries in the early 1930s. Not only did the world's sound-equipped movie theaters play mainly films from the United States and Germany but also American and German film companies had opened studios in France, Britain, and other countries, where they provided training to local production personnel. Tobis, for example, a German Dutch conglomerate with connections to the electricity industry, operated film studios in up to seven European cities in the early 1930s.[29] Tobis's aesthetic impact is indicated by the musical comedies directed by René Clair: *Sous les toits de Paris* (1930), *Le million* (1931), *A nous la liberté* (1931), and *Quatorze juillet* (1932), which were among the most famous films in the world in the early 1930s. Though filmed in France and commonly understood today as masterpieces of French cinema, Clair's films involved a production technique atypical of the French film industry at the time.[30] Whereas filmmaking in France relied on improvised methods, Clair's productions were carefully scripted and rehearsed.[31]

The careful preparation is evident in the *découpages techniques*, or shooting scripts, for *Sous les toits de Paris*—available in Paris at the Bibliothèque nationale and the Bibliothèque du film—that include detailed instructions for each shot. Specifying, for example, whether a particular shot is to be recorded with sound or if sound is to be made separately and then added to the image later, the documents suggest that Clair began shooting with an exact knowledge of how many shots were needed and how the image and sound for each were to be produced. An intent to align the film's visuals precisely with song structure surfaces in the shooting script available at the Bibliothèque nationale, which includes, written in pencil next to song-accompanied shots, numbers designating the measures of music that the shot will match up with. The practice of fitting shot length to musical duration, which was essential to Clair's style, required a level of planning and preparation rare in French filmmaking in the early 1930s but common in German and at studios operated by Tobis particularly.[32] The affinities with German cinema are suggested in the critical reception of Clair's films, which were compared to the *Operettenfilmen* that were the mainstay of German-language film production at the time.[33] Anticipating Clair's dance-like choreography of actors, critics observed, were the "sound-film artistic experiments" vital to the operettas made in Germany.[34] Although Clair's films are not a main focus of this book, the points made in chapter 6 regarding the production techniques and style of the German cinema's operettas can be applied also to Clair's films.[35]

My comparative analysis of Hollywood and German musical films involves a somewhat novel perspective on the German cinema of the late Weimar period. The latter has long been associated with dramatic auteur films with dark themes, such as Fritz Lang's *M* (1931) and *The Testament of Dr. Mabuse* (1932), von Sternberg's *The Blue Angel* (1930), and Pabst's *Die Dreigroschenoper* (1931). In fact, however, the German film industry at the time produced a great many musical comedies, to the point that the latter constituted the German film industry's dominant genre at the time.[36] The musical films have long been disparaged by critics as escapist and even protototalitarian in outlook.[37] This book, through its focus on German musical films relative to their American counterparts, aims to foster appreciation for an important and neglected body of films.

Period Style

An attempt to bring to light song-oriented motion pictures as a transnational stylistic phenomenon involves an investigation into what in art history has been called period style.[38] In the context of this book, *period style* refers to the combination of techniques that films made in one city, country, and continent were likely to share with films made in others at roughly the same time, regardless of the locale of production. Period styles have defined film history since its beginnings, when silent cinema, with its visual storytelling, can be said to have been the first transnational entertainment.[39] Through a focus on the early sound period, when the challenges of distribution weighed heavily on the global film industry, this book brings transnational film style into focus as an object of research.

The emphasis on style brings with it certain methodological entailments. Style analysis, as art historian Richard Neer puts it, entails an *etiology*, an investigation into origins and causation.[40] To analyze a film's style is to say something about how it was made. Connoisseurship in art history and field research in archaeology, where the provenance of artifacts can be identified through formal analysis, are Neer's examples. But his point applies to cinema too. To study a film's style is to explain its look and sound by specifying the processes that caused them. The procedure can be as simple as attributing an "orphan" film to the correct studio, which archivists practice as a routine necessity. But it can also involve a "worldly formalism" sensitive to how a film's conditions of manufacture and reception surface in the world of the film's narrative.[41]

In any case, style analysis ordinarily requires examining not only film texts but multiple extrafilmic contexts. Those examined in this book include broadcast radio, recorded music, music publishing, and the popular stage, all of which featured the same singers and songs appearing in the films. The investigation thus goes well beyond the films per se—but only up to a point, since the commitment to style analysis requires approaching the contexts hierarchically, according to whether they illuminate the particularities of style. A case in point concerns the role in conversion-era cinema of song performances as "product placements" for sheet music and recorded discs. To understand how the films promote music sales requires investigating media-industrial forces and conditions, but in the analysis in this book, the latter are important not for their own sake but insofar as they help illuminate a specific textual attribute: the quasi-independent song sequence.

Transnational Trends

In film studies, style is ordinarily examined with reference to the personal expression of auteur directors. This book is unusual in its attention to transnational trends encompassing hundreds of films. Such a study involves special challenges. Whereas a director's career invites chronological presentation, and thus rendition in narrative form, transnational style trends can be difficult to narrate. The world's film industries all converted to sound at different times, at various speeds and rhythms, and in ways skewed by local circumstance. Insofar as the investigation's geographical scope expands to cover film production in countries like Japan, China, and India, where sound's introduction occurred years later than in the West, additional chronologies seem necessary, thus further complicating the object of study.

The project can be made manageable, however, through an attention to filmmaking's communal dimension. Even the most singular of filmmakers take up artistic problems shared by others. The sense of a common project, a collective effort, became acute during the crisis of sound conversion, when filmmakers around the world, in the face of severe aesthetic and technical challenges, couldn't help but take a keen interest in how their peers, at home and in other countries, were solving common problems. The account presented in the following chapters acknowledges the transnational character of the aesthetic dilemmas faced by filmmakers by locating agency less in the individual filmmaker than in artistic communities whose contours were by no means limited to a specific locale, studio, or national film industry.

Statistical Analysis

To gain a sense of the period's style trends, the analysis practiced in this book takes up a research method rare in film studies: the statistical analysis of film style. The methodological challenges of studying a massive corpus of films motivated this recourse to statistics. Quantitative methods provided an objective means of assessing similarities and differences across hundreds of films and thus helped counteract the limitations of my personal memory of the many films I was viewing as part of the research for this book. I acknowledge that the utility of statistics for film analysis is extremely limited in certain respects. Computations of average shot length reveal a film's form at a high level of abstraction. In film analysis, as in other fields of humanities scholarship, the meaning of a numerical measurement is never self-evident but requires contextualization and interpretation. The statistical study of film style thus inevitably extends into areas of historical investigation that may prove inaccessible to quantitative analysis. The methodological upshot is that shot-length computations and other quantitative techniques cannot replace old-school practices of mindful film viewing and the examination of nonfilmic documentation.

Nevertheless, statistical methods, when used as a supplement to traditional research practices, offer to the study of film history two distinct benefits. One is increased precision. The statistical analysis of artistic style, music theorist Leonard Meyer proposes, is inescapable because "all classification and all generalization about stylistic traits are based on some element of relative frequency."[42] Any claim regarding a work's originality appeals to an idea of how atypical it is—or isn't—relative to other works. Meyer's claim that quantitative methods enable an improved performance of essential tasks refers to the study of music, but it applies just as well to cinema. Indeed, film editing, with its frames and footage, invites numerical assessment. Cinema, Yuri Tsivian states, is a "quantifiable medium."[43] Although statistical research remains rare in the study of film relative to the study of music, this disparity has eroded somewhat as a result of the powerful, easy-to-use tools available through the Cinemetrics website and other sources.[44]

Beyond the benefit of increased precision in the specification of artistic norms (discussed further in appendix A), one can argue that quantitative analysis offers to cinema study a second, more fundamental advantage: it can cast new light on the object of study, bringing out important aspects of films, or bodies of films, that may otherwise go unnoticed. Essential here are the visual displays that numerical data make possible.[45] Charts and graphs, in divulging patterns of evidence that escape the naked eye, can challenge one's perspective regarding how films are constructed. In pushing one to see in new ways, the visualizations made possible by statistical research can stimulate the rethinking of a film or body of films. What may look like a major limitation of quantitative film analysis—its abstraction, its indifference to the viewer's experience of a film—can become a unique and powerful advantage.[46]

Singing Shots

The research conducted for this book provides a modest illustration of this revelatory effect in three shot categories devised specifically for the cinema of the late 1920s and early 1930s: (1) shots with synchronous speech sourced in the image, hereafter designated as *dialogue shots*; (2) shots featuring singing performances, when an actor sings or whistles a song melody, called here *singing shots*; and (3) *action shots*, which make up a broad category comprising shots lacking synchronous vocals, which range from panoramic landscapes to people walking through doorways, trains arriving at stations, and inserts of clocks and signage. I ended up counting hundreds of sound films using the action, dialogue, and singing metric. The results presented in figure 0.1 display the mean averages for the average shot lengths (ASLs) for 354 sound films produced between 1928 and 1934.[47]

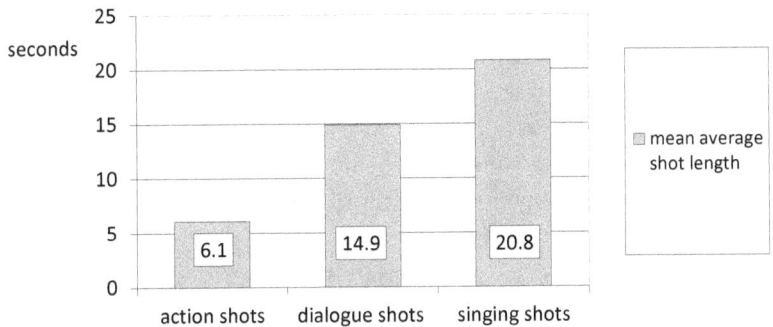

Figure 0.1. Mean ASLs for three shot types in 354 sound films of 1928–34

All shots for all the films were classified as one of the three types. (The intertitles that occasionally surface in early sound movies were excluded from the analysis.) After using the Cinemetrics interface to produce ASLs for each shot type for hundreds of individual films, I then generated "mean ASLs" by producing arithmetical averages for the ASL results for each type.[48] I had settled on the three types after having measured dozens of sound films while experimenting with various shot labels and criteria of category membership (for more on the analysis, including the criteria, see appendix A). Action, dialogue, and singing were chosen as the principal metrics for three reasons. First, these types were consonant with the editing practices I saw in cinema from the late 1920s and early 1930s, when shots with synchronous vocals, in a great many cases, appeared to run relatively long. The decision to distinguish action shots from vocal shots thus responded to the particularities of the films I was investigating.

Second, my shot types imply differences in production practice likely to have entered the filmmakers' awareness. The action shots in sound movies, for example, were often shot "wild," as in the silent period, with the sound added during postproduction. The continuity in production technique perhaps explains why the ASL for the action shots in sound films is almost the same as for the silent: the two were made in the same way.[49] Dialogue and singing shots, however, raised special technical considerations. Unique to sound films, these types were constrained by production methods at the time, when the concurrent recording of sound and image was the norm for shots with vocals. In short, with conversion-era cinema, to designate a shot as involving action, dialogue, or singing is more than an act of description; it points to how the shot was made.

The third justification for the three shot categories is that they were relatively unambiguous and hence easy to distinguish consistently. To test this, I hired research assistants on several occasions to retrace the steps of my analysis by tabulating shots for certain films using the same categories. I wanted to confirm that other scholars following the same procedures would be likely to duplicate my results, and my three shot categories appeared to allow for this. Of the three, the singing shots are the most complex. Most conversion-era films include them, but not all. Of the 354 films comprising my sample, 276 contain singing shots, roughly 78 percent of the total. Relative to the other types, the singing shots exhibit the greatest range and variety in length.[50] They also imposed on filmmakers at the time unique technical challenges, as when, for example, a scene required the presence on the set of an orchestra or a sound system that could reproduce a recording for an actor to lip-synch to. I separated out singing as a distinct category because recorded songs were prevalent in conversion-era cinema, and I was interested in how they functioned. My hunch was that singing shots, like dialogue shots, would run relatively long, on average, and the statistics offered confirmation.

But the numbers also point to something I hadn't expected to find, which is that shots of singers consistently last even longer than shots of speakers. As figure 0.1 indicates, dialogue shots, on average, last roughly twice the length of action shots, while singing shots last nearly triple that duration. The more films I saw from the period, the more consistent the pattern for song performances appeared to be. For any given film of the early 1930s, the longest shot is often a singing shot. These shots may exceed a film's ASL by ten times, as discussed further in chapter 3. The long takes of singers are not unique to Hollywood films but are ubiquitous in the European films of the period.

Singing shots, of course, are defined not only by length but also by other attributes of style. The latter may include a restricted framing, a static camera, a minimalistic mise-en-scène, and a preference for shallow staging, all of which are common during song performances. Explaining such shots necessarily involves considerations of spectator psychology and film-historical context—hence the use of additional, nonstatistical critical methods. The statistical results merely drew attention to the long singing shots. Nonetheless, this flagging of the phenomenon was crucial because it stimulated the line of investigation pursued in this book, where conversion-era cinema is approached through a focus on the song performances that surface in so many films of the period.

A further question concerns whether the long takes depicting singers are unique to the films of the early 1930s. The prevalence of such takes in the films of other times and places seems likely, judging from how song sequences in films are described by critics. Richard Dyer, for example, draws on a wide range of films from different periods and parts of the world to characterize song sequences as relatively motionless, generating a "temporal stasis" unlike the narrative movement of a film's dramatic scenes.[51] As discussed in the conclusion, this similarity between cinema in the 1930s and cinema in other times, including the present, suggests the ongoing relevance of the conversion-era musical film.

Notes

1. On new media as historical phenomena, see D. Thorburn and H. Jenkins, eds., *Rethinking Media Change*; and L. Gitelman and G. Pingree, eds., *New Media*.
2. N. Frank, "Théâtre, music hall, melodrama, opéra," 9.
3. L. Hirsch, "Film sonore et film muet," *La technique cinématographique*, 79. For more on sound's challenge to avant-garde technique, see P. Medina, "Das Ende der französischen Avantgarde?," 7; R. B., "Disappointing International Congress: Avant Garde Dead?," 24; and J. Epstein, "Le cinéma pur et le film sonore," 581.
4. D. Albright, *Untwisting the Serpent*, 29.
5. L. Moussinac, "Un film 'parlant.'" See also remarks by director William Seiter in "Motion Pictures Must Move," 263–65.
6. K. London, *Film Music*, 120.
7. A. Sarris, "The Cultural Guilt of Musical Movies," 41.
8. The term *song picture* comes from E. Schallert, "Sound Waxes International," C16.
9. "Language the Chief American Film Barrier," 57–58; and S. Silverman, "International Show Business," 22.
10. "Sound Eliminates Much Export," 4. See also "Heavy Drop in Sales Abroad on American Films," 6; and "Loss of Foreign Trade," 7.
11. F. Mann, "Language *Barrier* Leads to Conflict"; and C. Wahl, *Multiple Language Versions Made in Babelsberg*, 78–80.
12. J. Quirk, "Close Ups and Long Shots," 30.
13. S. Silverman, "International Show Business," 22.
14. "Operettas with Songs Only Considered Okay for All Over the World," 7. See also the comment from Ufa production head Hugo Correll, quoted in W. Mühl-Benninghaus, *Das Ringen um den Tonfilm*, 227.
15. "Ted Lewis' Walloping Hit in Paris," 58; "French Jazz Composers Lagging," 65; R. Palmer, "Microphone Matters," 8; and M. Gilbert, "Audibility of American Pictures Satisfies Curiosity of Parisians," X6.
16. Regarding the situation in Italy, see the S. Rayment, *Kinematograph Year Book, 1930*, 56; and C. Keating, "'100% Italian,'" 19–20.
17. C. MacDonald, "Demand Talkies in Own Language," 9. Quoted in R. Spadoni, *Uncanny Bodies*, 31.

18. Pommer's remark comes from a 1929 interview on *Melodie des Herzens* (dir. Géza von Bolváry, 1929), the first in a series of operettas by Ufa made in multiple languages. Quoted in W. Mühl-Benninghaus, *Das Ringen um den Tonfilm*, 227, 244.

19. B. Balázs, *Early Film Theory*, 206.

20. P. Autré, "La musique dans les films," iv.

21. Of the seventy-eight Technicolor American features of 1928–33 identified by film historian Richard Haines, sixty-eight appear to have been musical films, most of which used Technicolor for several sequences at most. R. Haines, *Technicolor Movies*, 13–16.

22. On the inclusion of talking sequences in silent films, see the discussion of "goat gland" films in D. Crafton, *The Talkies*, 168–71.

23. "Musical Pictures Again to Be in Vogue," 3.

24. D. Crafton, *The Talkies*, 315.

25. I borrow the distinction between "musical" and "musical film" from R. Altman, "The Musical," 294.

26. R. Altman, *The American Film Musical*; D. Crafton, *The Talkies*; J. Fleeger, *Sounding American*; K. Kalinak, *Settling the Score*; J. Lastra, *Sound Technology and the American Cinema*; D. Gomery, *The Coming of Sound*; R. Spadoni, *Uncanny Bodies*; K. Spring, *Saying It with Songs*; M. Slowik, *After the Silents*; and S. Wurtzler, *Electric Sounds*.

27. The quotation comes from an untitled press release from Will Hays, head of the Motion Picture Producers and Distributors Association. The release, dated July 30, 1930, is available on microfilm in D. Gomery, ed., *The Will Hays Papers*, part 2, reel 4.

28. "Paris Conference Ends with Electrics Dividing World," 3.

29. On Tobis's network of European studios, see M. Hagener, "Unter den Dächern der Tobis." On the British branch, see G. Brown, "The Euro-British Flagship That Sank."

30. C. O'Brien, "*Sous les toits de Paris* and French Film, at Home and Abroad."

31. On the improvised nature of French production practice in the early 1930s, see C. O'Brien, *Cinema's Conversion to Sound*, 129–31.

32. On preproduction planning and rehearsal at the Tobis studio in Berlin, see C. Trask, "Screen Notes from Germany," X6. Regarding preplanning as a hallmark of filmmaking in Germany as opposed to France, see the interview with director Marcel L'Herbier in R. Leclérc, "Marcel L'Herbier über Deutschelands Produktionsmethode," 3.

33. K. London, *Film Music*, 129–30, 133–34. See also the inclusion of *Sous les toits de Paris* as an example of the German operetta's *Puppenspiel-Stil* in "'Einbrecher,'" 2. On the enthusiastic reception of *Sous les toits de Paris* in Germany, see "Interview mit René Clair," 1; J.-P. L., "Auteurs et producteurs allemands rendent homage à 'Sous les toits de Paris,'" 6; and C. Trask, "German Film Notes," 99.

34. Dammann, "'Die Million,'" 2. The same point is made in Hans Feld, "'Es lebe die Freiheit!'" 2; and R. de B., "Les nouveautés d'écran."

35. On the possibility that Clair's films, in fact, provided a model for the contemporaneous German cinema, see K. Trumpener, "The René Clair Moment and the Overlap Films of the Early 1930s."

36. M. Wedel, *Der deutsche Musikfilm*, 267; and "Operettenfilme sind Triumpf: Das Publikum wird überfüttert," 1.

37. The musical films of the late Weimar years are examined in the chapter "Songs and Illusions" in S. Kracauer, *From Caligari to Hitler*, 203–14. On the critical reputation of the films, see B. Currid, *A National Acoustics*, 68–70, 112–13.

38. The concept of period style became important in art historical study in the late nineteenth century. See H. Wölfflin, *Principles of Art History*, 9–10.
39. A. Williams, "Introduction," 1.
40. R. Neer, "Connoisseurship and the Stakes of Style," 3; and J. Gilmore, *The Life of a Style*, 85.
41. The phrase *worldly formalism* comes from R. Neer, "Connoisseurship and the Stakes of Style," 2.
42. L. Meyer, *Style and Music*, 64.
43. Y. Tsivian, "What Is Cinema?," 765.
44. The website's address is www.cinemetrics.lv. For more on the use of cinemetrics, see Y. Tsivian, "What Is Cinema?" 768–75.
45. The importance of visual displays in the statistical analysis of recorded music is noted in N. Cook, "Methods for Analyzing Recordings," in N. Cook et al., *Cambridge Companion to Recorded Music*, 236.
46. On the utility of statistical abstraction in the study of literary history, see F. Moretti, *Graphs, Maps, Trees*, 8–9.
47. The results of hypothesis tests performed on the samples used for fig. 0.1 can be found in table 0.1, appendix B.
48. Of the 354 films measured for fig. 0.1, all contained action shots, 351 included dialogue shots, and 276 had singing shots.
49. The exact figures for the action shots in sound films are $M = 6.11$ seconds, $N = 354$, $SD = 1.92$, and $ME = 0.20$. Those for the action shots in silent films are 5.92 seconds, $N = 67$, $SD = 1.4$, and $ME = 0.34$.
50. The relatively high standard deviation figures in table 0.1, appendix B, indicate the variety in length for the singing shots.
51. R. Dyer, *In the Space of a Song*, 24.

1

MOVIES AND SONGS IN TRANSITION

THE PROBLEMS OF FILM MUSIC THAT AROSE DURING the transition to electric sound were cast in a language with a long history. The project of reconciling the formal patterns of popular music with the demands of dramatic narrative long preceded sound movies.[1] For centuries dramatists had debated options for bringing together music and theatrical narrative, to meld the two into a single form, and this history of music-drama theory informed discussion and debate on the aesthetics of sound films.[2] The main problem for producers of feature-length fiction films was the tendency for the typical song sequence to come across as "an isolated interlude [*isolierte Einlage*] in the film," as a critic in Germany put it.[3] In coming forward as self-contained events, song performances "hindered the natural course of the plot," observed a journalist in London.[4] In the entertainment press, much was made of the need to weave songs into a film's narration. "The introduction of songs seems to be the most acceptable when they further the plot motivation," stated an American journalist.[5]

Narrative integration remains a core desideratum today, when, as in the 1930s, song sequences that can be taken to advance the film's story draw critical praise. Narrative considerations inform the American Film Institute's list of "one hundred greatest film songs," chosen because they "set a tone or mood, define character, advance plot and/or express the film's theme."[6] The narrative motivation practiced by filmmakers, however, is not the formal integration promoted by music-drama theorists, and the latter proved difficult to achieve in the domain of the feature film. Attempts in the early 1930s to extend the tight link between music and image in song sequences to a full-length film through techniques such as the synchronization of actors' movements to the music and the use of verse-like dialogue were relatively rare. For scenes with spoken dialogue, "the abstract time of the musical progression," proposed a critic in Germany, "must be adjusted to the real time of the dramatic action."⁷ The difficulty of this task is suggested in the frequency with which dialogue scenes in early sound films play with no music whatsoever.

Rather than try to render the whole film musical, filmmakers typically interpolated songs as distinct units, different from the film's other scenes. The songs normally have a narrative motivation. A singer's performance is almost always also a story event—an audition, a rehearsal, a revue's opening night, a neighborhood talent show. But once the performance begins, it comes across as somewhat separate from the rest of the film, functioning more as an interlude in the story than a continuation. Filmmakers became adept at assigning the style difference a thematic function, as when the song sequence's formal transcendence suggests a utopian rejoinder to the personal and social deprivations invoked in the film's dramatic scenes.⁸ This is reflected in the critical writing on the American film musical, where the divide between "narrative" and "number," between the music-driven song sequence and the dialogue-based dramatic scene, defines the genre's basic syntax, its characteristic way of organizing scenes and sequences into an overall structure.⁹

The willingness of filmmakers to ignore in practice the ideal of formal integration can be attributed to multiple causes. Later chapters explore the special production conditions needed for song sequences and the commercial pressures of the larger entertainment culture. The focus of the current chapter is on inherent formal differences between songs and narrative films and how these differences factor into how song sequences are constructed. The chapter begins with an overview of how music in sound cinema differed from that in silent films, with an emphasis on the problems and possibilities associated with songs specifically. Illustrating the range of sound-era options are two extremes: the operetta, in which formal consonance between music and image occurs during not only the songs but also the dialogue scenes, and the variety show mix of acts in the revue film, in which intermedial dissonance is allowed full reign.

Film Songs after Recorded Sound

Songs accompanied motion pictures from the beginning.¹⁰ In the late 1920s, however, new technical conditions made them unusually conspicuous. For one, the songs now came exclusively in the form of recordings rather than live performances, which enabled a massive escalation in the showcasing in films of star vocalists known to the film audience through multiple media other than cinema, including the robust new medium of broadcast radio.

The singers' profiles in the media culture at large shaped how song sequences were designed, as is discussed further in chapter 3.

The second technical change concerns the sound-on-film systems from companies such as Fox, Tobis-Klangfilm, and RCA, whose permanent bonding of music and image onto a single celluloid strip allowed visual action and music to work together in powerful new ways. The exact synchronization of music and image had been rare in cinema prior to electric sound, when projection speeds and musical talent varied from one exhibition venue to the next and theater musicians could not be counted on to match music and visual action with precision. In movie houses in the 1920s, observed critic Emile Vuillermoz, "the mismatch [*décalage*] of music and image was the norm and coincidence the exception."[11] The uneven conditions of silent-era film exhibition, film-music scholar Kathryn Kalinak explains, made composers reluctant to "encourag[e] synchronization between the tempo of the action and the tempo of the music." What was favored instead was "the more loosely defined concept of mutual correspondence, in which the structural properties of music (its tempo, rhythm, or harmonics) or its associated powers were loosely matched to the implied narrative content."[12] The Hollywood film scores of the mid-1920s, Kalinak adds, rarely include cues requiring an exact match of music with a film's visual representation.[13]

Film-music practice changed radically with the sound-on-film systems of the late 1920s. In making music-image synchronization not only possible but inevitable, the new systems led to the proliferation of what media scholar Amy Herzog calls "musical moments," which occur "when music, typically a popular song, inverts the sound-image hierarchy to occupy a dominant position in a filmic work."[14] Musical moments were pervasive in cinema around 1930, when songs, for the first time since the nickelodeon era, become the dominant form of film music.

The Ideal of Formal Unity

How did producers of feature-length narrative films respond to the opportunities and challenges of music-image synchronization? One option sought to take the close match of music with visual action characteristic of the period's animated shorts and extend it to an entire film, the dialogue scenes included.[15] The goal, in effect, was to utilize the tight synchronization that the Disney team had achieved in the Silly Symphonies in a feature-length production.[16] This project of rendering musical a full-length film was promoted by theorists and pursued by a small number of ambitious filmmakers. Ernst Lubitsch at Paramount, René Clair at Tobis Films Sonores, and various German directors, such as those working for Erich Pommer's unit at Ufa, are salient examples. But they are also exceptional. The majority of the period's producers were inclined to construct a film's dialogue scenes differently from the song sequences rather than try to unify them within a common, music-based style.

If the maximum integration aimed for by the operettas represents one extreme, then the period's revue films, with their mix of acts featuring diverse singers, comedians, dance troupes, and other entertainers, can be said to illustrate the opposing possibility. Dispensing with narratives altogether, *The Hollywood Revue of 1929* (dir. Charles Reisner, 1929), *The Show of Shows* (dir. John Adolfi, 1929), *Paramount on Parade* (dir. Edmund Goulding et al., 1930), *King of Jazz* (dir. John Murray Anderson, 1930), and *Elstree Calling* (dir. Jack Hulbert et al., 1931) instead present a series of variety show performances introduced by a master of ceremonies. A variant involved framing the performances with a minimalist plot about the making of a variety show, as in *On with the Show* (dir. Alan Crosland, 1929), *Happy Days* (dir. Benjamin Stoloff, 1930), and *Wir schalten um auf Hollywood* (dir. Frank Reicher et al., 1931). Such films fall into the category of narrative cinema, but only barely.

The dissonance inherent to the variety format was most pronounced in the revue films intended for foreign release, where the original American scenes were sometimes supplemented with footage shot in studios outside the United States. Seven foreign versions of *Paramount on Parade*, for example, were assembled at Paramount's Paris studio, where new sequences, added to those made in Los Angeles, featured celebrities and musical acts from France, the Netherlands, Romania, Czechoslovakia, Poland, Italy, Sweden, and Denmark.[17] The four foreign versions of *The Hollywood Revue of 1929* were made in a similar fashion, with, for example, the French version incorporating extra French-language material shot at the Pathé-Natan facility in Joinville near Paris.[18] Acts were added in or taken out depending on how the distributors had assessed the acts' popularity in the version's target market. Continuity, as it were, was provided by an on-screen impresario who introduced the individual acts, "speaking in the language of the country in which the film [was] being shown."[19] Bela Lugosi, soon to star in Universal's *Dracula* (dir. Tod Browning, 1931), played this role in the Hungarian version of *King of Jazz*.

Reproduced below is a promotional still for *Der Jazzkönig*, the German version of *King of Jazz*, in which character actor Arnold Korff introduces the individual acts (see fig. 1.1).

Figure 1.1. A production still for *Der Jazzkönig*, the German version of *King of Jazz* (Stiftung Deutsche Kinemathek)

The footage for Korff's introductions was shot very quickly on small sets whose flat, trompe l'oeil appearance marked a world apart from the sumptuous mise-en-scène of the film's musical sequences.[20] Compare the German version's meager "melting pot of music" (visible in fig. 1.1) with Herman Rosse's lavish original. A further clash in the visual design stemmed from the use of Technicolor for some sequences and black and white for others.[21]

An Artistic Flaw?

While the operettas won praise for their integration of music with drama, the revue films were reviled as a betrayal of cinematic principles.[22] Nonetheless, the blatant stage-derived hybridity did little to undermine the international popularity of *King of Jazz*, *Paramount on Parade*, *The Hollywood Revue of 1929*, and other such films. Indeed, "the revue musicals of the early talkie era were among the most successful exports," Kristin Thompson observes, "even with no translation."[23] The success of the revue films with audiences worldwide suggests that their arrangement of diverse performances in a variety show arc, rather than an aesthetic defect, gave producers of sound films an effective strategy for attracting first-time viewers of sound movies. This alternative understanding informs a countercurrent in the critical writing in which the early musical film's aesthetic dissonance is seen to yield positive artistic effects. Examples include Andrew Sarris, who in the late 1970s attributed the pleasures of the conversion-era musical films to their artistic hybridity: "The very disparateness of the genre's constituents was the guarantor of emotional effectiveness, and woe betide the media purists."[24]

A detailed argument linking the musical film's hybrid aesthetic to a "tradition of the spectacle" in American stage entertainment is advanced by Martin Rubin in his book on choreographer Busby Berkeley, which offers the reminder that "the history of the evolution of the musical is not only the history of relatively integrated forms but also of those elements that pull in the opposite direction, that work to disintegrate and problematize the unity of the discourse of the narrative."[25] Rather than integration, the guiding principle behind many films, proposes Rubin, was aggregation, the interpolation into a film of discrete acts or attractions whose immediate impact as spectacle is likely to exceed the film's narrative requirements.[26]

Anticipating Rubin and Sarris were Hanns Eisler and Theodor Adorno. In their book *Composing for the Film* (1947), Eisler and Adorno, like other critics then and since, described "topical songs and production numbers in musical comedies [as] foreign elements, which interrupted the dramatic context." But this was not a flaw for them because they rejected the critical ideal of formal consonance, proposing instead that "the aesthetic divergence of the media is potentially a legitimate means of expression, not merely a regrettable deficiency that has to be concealed as well as possible." This view led to an unusual assessment of "movie revues," which, for Eisler and Adorno, counted not as a violation of the goal of artistic unity but rather as a frank acknowledgment of the commercial pressures behind the genre. Revue films refuse to "create the illusion of a unity of the two media [i.e., music and cinema] or to camouflage the illusionary character of the whole." Moreover, in flaunting the "aesthetic divergence" inherent in any attempt to combine "pictures, words, and music," movie revues, musical comedies, and other song-loaded films can be deemed "more substantial than motion pictures that flirt with real art." In refusing to conceal the "alienation of the media from one another," such films count for Eisler and Adorno as "aesthetic models of genuine motion picture music."[27]

Film Form versus Song Form

Songs, however, complicated the project of reconciling music with the formal characteristics of narrative cinema. Both songs and narrative films are time-bound media that can be divided into smaller formal units. Songs can be parsed into verses, phrases, and measures and films into scenes, sequences, and shots.[28] But except for song-accompanied moments, when the visual action is staged, shot, and cut in conformity with the music, the units of music analysis rarely match up to those of film analysis. Composers seeking musical models for film scores, advised Kurt London, must recognize that "most of the traditional musical forms are useless."[29] Songs were especially problematic on account of their excessive redundancy. While music ordinarily involves formal repetitions exceeding anything analogous in narrative cinema, the hook-laden popular songs in conversion-era films are repetitive to the utmost. The pulse and meter of the typical film song stays fixed across the song's duration, and the same melodic and rhythmic motifs cycle through the tune. Entire sections repeat, including within an individual chorus, as in the 32-measure AABA scheme common in American popular music at the time.[30] The simultaneous resolution within each 8-measure section of melody, harmonic progression, and lyrics enhances the sense that the song is composed of discrete sections: verse, chorus, A-section, bridge, and so on.

The self-sufficient form yields distinctive cognitive effects, especially with regard to memory. Songs are often recalled in blocks, with a single extract capable of evoking the whole.³¹ Adding to the potential for recall were the lyrics, which, research in music psychology suggests, provide "memory retrieval cues for the music associated with them, and vice versa."³² Just as lyrics may invoke the melody, even instrumental versions of a tune call to mind the lyrics. The capacity for lodging itself in the filmgoer's consciousness was an essential attribute of the typical film song of the early 1930s, for better or worse. "Before we leave [the theater], we've got it—or rather it's got us," observed a critic apropos of the title song from *The Broadway Melody* (dir. Harry Beaumont, 1929). "We may hate the tune even while we hum it."³³

A song's presence in a film is salient in ways that orchestral accompaniment ordinarily is not.³⁴ Orchestral music does not so much accompany the film image as saturate it, merging with it to yield a unified sound-image gestalt. The viewer encounters not an image with music added but a single music-image percept.³⁵ Adding to the indivisibility are the conventions of film scoring, which instruct composers to "sneak in" orchestral cues at moments when sound effects or lines of speech mask the music's entrance.³⁶ No surprise that film viewers—including trained musicians—find it difficult to recall when orchestral music in a film begins and ends or even that it is heard at all.³⁷

Songs function differently. Far from being surreptitious, songs tend to impose themselves on the viewer's consciousness. They often begin emphatically, exuding a sense of occasion. "You ain't heard nothin' yet!" promises the jazz singer. Once underway, a song may elicit bodily responses from the auditor such as toe tapping, humming, or singing. The familiar notion that successful film music remains "unheard," shaping the film experience subliminally, presupposes that the music in question is an orchestral composition rather than a popular tune.³⁸ In August 1931, Martin Boones, music director at MGM, refuted complaints about the absence of music in sound films by stating that music was, in fact, more present now than in recent years but that it tended to pass unnoticed because it no longer came as songs only but increasingly as orchestral underscore.³⁹

One reason songs draw notice is because they recall other times when they were heard, as filmmakers became keenly aware. Composer Max Steiner reported in 1932 that at RKO, producer David Selznick complained that "when a tune has been heard before, the people in the audience search their memories. They say, 'Where did we hear that before? Just what is that melody?'"⁴⁰ To avoid sparking memories irrelevant to the film, producers were known to prefer original compositions for their soundtracks rather than familiar songs. As stated by Arthur Franklin, music head at First National and Warner Brothers, "We cannot use music that is too familiar, or the hearer will lose track of the picture and concentrate on what its title is, and where he has heard it before."[41]

Songs and Stasis

A further peculiarity of song accompaniment is the sense of stasis it can generate. Unlike the forward movement characteristic of the sort of orchestral music commonly used for film accompaniment, songs can seem caught in a loop. Suggesting this sense of eternal recurrence is the idea that songs exhibit a "pictorial" character. According to Daniel Albright, "The very familiarity, the commonness of common chord progressions, tends to de-temporalize the music: we know what is going to happen before it happens. The unity of consonant music . . . seems static, rather pictorial."[42] The dominance of space over time provides the theme for Richard Dyer's book on songs in film, where songs are said to imply "a much weaker sense of movement than in more elaborated musical forms."[43] When inserted into a film, songs, Dyer says, convey "a sense of temporal stasis, of not going anywhere," and "this allows for that feeling of time being suspended, standing still, that can inform song sequences." "When musical numbers appear or disappear in a musical," observes film historian Katie Trumpener, "there is often a perceptible shift in the atmosphere, the emotional 'weather' of a movie. The action of the film slows to a dreamlike halt—or shifts to a different tempo."[44]

The sense of stasis drew notice in the 1930s, as in Erwin Panofsky's observation that music in the Disney cartoons came up less like an event in a sequence than a tableau: "The purest form of a phenomenon in time, music, seems actually to be converted into a spectacle in space (for instance: a series of soap-bubbles of different sizes which, when pictured, emit sounds exactly corresponding in height and volume to the relative size of the bubbles)."[45] The result, Panofsky suggested, is a "spatialization of time."[46] Sound cinema, with its capacity for matching the moving image to a song's structure with razor-like precision, actualized this picturelike quality as never before. Whether this was a good thing depended on the context. Though fascinating in an animated short, a picturelike sense of stasis could create a problem in a feature-length narrative by adding to the song sequence's digressive effect. In impeding the sense of forward movement essential to narrative cinema, song sequences, judged Kurt London, were "anti-cinematic": "In a film the music must never be allowed to become stationary or to hold up the general movement. It must flow on its even course even when the visual images are apparently standing still."[47]

Song-Determined Editing

The impact on film style of a song's musical structure is evident in how song sequences are edited, which differs from editing of a film's dialogue scenes. Dialogue editing ordinarily conforms to the rhythm of the actors' performance, as when cuts occur between lines of speech (see chap. 4). Song sequences, however, exhibit a different dynamic, whereby cuts in the image coincide with developments in the song's verse-chorus structure. Typical is Rudy Vallee's brief, one-minute "Vagabond Lover" performance in *Glorifying the American Girl* (dir. Millard Webb and John Harkenrider, 1929). In shot 1, Vallee, in medium long shot, sings the opening verse and first chorus of "Vagabond Lover." As soon as the chorus ends, the cut to shot 2 reveals Vallee and the band in an extreme long shot, where they perform an instrumental break. Once the break concludes, the cut to shot 3 returns to the medium long shot framing of shot 1, where Vallee concludes the performance by repeating the chorus. Each of the performance's three main shots thus match up to a basic unit of musical form.

An extreme variant of song-driven cutting involves what Eisenstein called "metrical montage," in which shot lengths follow a mathematical scheme that fits exactly with the lengths of the song's basic musical units. Such sequences are prevalent in European films. Among the many examples that can be cited are the frenzied nightclub scene near the end of *Einbrecher* (dir. Hanns Schwarz, 1930), when the African dancers perform to "Ich laß' mir meinen Körper schwarz bepinseln"; Martha Eggerth's Hungarian folk dance in *Leise flehen meine Lieder* (dir. Willy Forst, 1933); the reprise of "Ein guter Freund" in the factory scene near the end of *Die Drei von der Tankstelle* (dir. Wilhelm Thiele, 1930); the battle-of-the-bands sequence in *Walzerkrieg* (dir. Ludwig Berger, 1933), when the teams supporting the opposing orchestras alternately thrust their signs in the air; the flood of close-ups of faces and musical instruments during the performance by the mountain villagers in *Der weiße Rausch* (dir. Arnold Fanck, 1931); and the manic folk dance in the brothel in *Der Mörder Dimitri Karamasoff* (dir. Fritz Kortner, 1931).[48] Béla Balázs's description of the "kitchen symphony" sequence in *Zwei Herzen im Dreivierteltakt* (dir. Géza von Bolváry, 1930) suggests the powerful pulse-like effect generated by such cutting: "A great banquet is in preparation. A series of sound and image closeups follows in rapid rhythm. Wood is sawn. The saw rasps. Wood is chopped. The axe thrums. Fire is kindled in the hearth. It crackles. Sugar is pounded. Cream is whipped. And boiling water bubbles. Then the same sound images, repeated in rhythm phrases. Everyday sounds composed into a work of art. A symphony of noise comes into being."[49]

Less obtrusive than the strict metrical approach described above is the practice of placing the sequence's principal cuts in line with the first quarter note in a measure. With this technique, "the jump from one 'shot' to another," explained director John Murray Anderson with respect to his work on *King of Jazz*, "is accomplished always on the downbeat of the accompanying music."[50] The shot change may happen exactly on the downbeat, or it may occur up to a beat and a half early, so that what falls on the downbeat is not the cut itself but the action or gesture that opens the new shot. I will use the term *downbeat cut* to refer to both since in either case the cut serves to emphasize what happens visually on the first quarter note of the measure. Justification for the technique can be found in research in the psychology of music, which suggests that the listener's attention is most acute at strong metric positions and at the downbeat especially. The essential factor, states music psychologist David Huron, is the downbeat's predictability: "The downbeat isn't merely that moment when events are more likely to occur in music. The downbeat sounds nice. . . . Since the downbeat represents one of the most predictable of event-moments, events that fall on the downbeat tend to evoke positive feelings."[51]

The "Florida by the Sea" number at the beginning of *The Cocoanuts* (dir. Joseph Santley and Robert Florey, 1929), Helen Morgan's delirious performance of "I've Got a Feeling I'm Falling" in *Applause* (dir. Rouben Mamoulian, 1929), and Kitty Kelly's raucous "I Got Rhythm" song-and-dance act in *Girl Crazy* (dir. William Seiter, 1932) are among the countless examples of song sequences where most cuts happen either on the downbeat or in slight anticipation of it. Even when downbeat cuts make up only a minority of the total for a sequence, they tend to be the most important structurally, providing the pivot for the overall visual and sonic design. Illustrations include the scene in *The Broadway Melody* in the apartment when Eddie (Charles King) introduces his new song, "The Broadway Melody," to the two sisters, Hank (Bessie Love) and Queenie (Anita Page). In this sequence—as in many others in a wide variety of films—a few downbeat cuts bring music and image into alignment at key moments. Such cuts create what Kevin Donnelly calls "isomorphic cadences," where passages in the song that

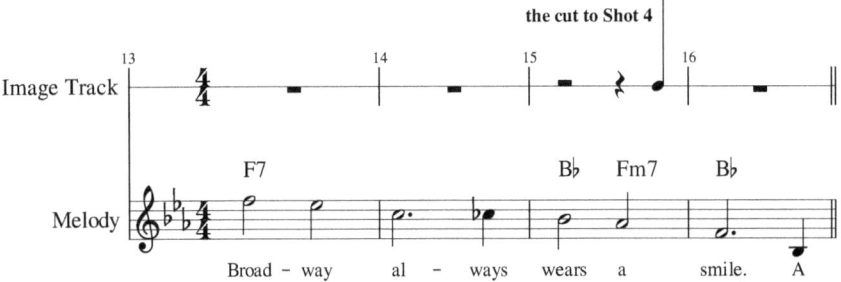

Musical Example 1.1. The first sound-image cadence in *The Broadway Melody* performance in the hotel room

suggest movement toward the song's harmonic center are accented visually through techniques of editing and camerawork.[52]

Musical example 1.1 illustrates the first of the sequence's sound-image cadences.

The position of the cut relative to the song's melody is marked by the quarter note on the image track, which happens on the fourth beat of measure 15, just before the downbeat of measure 16. The cut, of course, is instantaneous; but rendering it as a quarter note captures the rhythmic effect, which comes from the cut's anticipation of the gesture at the beginning of shot 4: Queenie's smile. The gesture occurs one quarter note later, on the downbeat of measure 16 (see the stave for "Melody" in musical example 1.1), conforming to one of the most common rhythms in popular music, in which the fourth beat in one measure gives way to the first beat in the next.

The cut to shot 4 occurs at a pivotal moment in the song's form, exactly halfway into the chorus, at the beginning of the final measure of the song's B-section. To understand how the cadence works, it is useful to look at the shots that lead up to it. The sequence begins with Eddie framed in a medium shot, preparing to sing, and then continues through the first 10 measures of the song's 32-measure form. As is typical of conversion-era singing shots, shot 1 is a long take whose fixed "medium shot" camera position, long duration, and shallow focus offer little to look at beyond the singer, whose face and hands provide the main expressive cues (see fig. 1.2).

Bolstering the singer's centrality is the clarity of the scenic space. Eddie's position between the two sisters, with Hank on the left and Queenie on the right, had been established in the preceding shots. Thus, when Eddie at the end of shot 1 glances off to the right, the subsequent cut to the shot of Queenie is expected.

Figure 1.2. A frame from shot 1 (screen capture, *The Broadway Melody*, 1929): "Your trou - bles there"

Figure 1.3. A frame from shot 2 (screen capture, *The Broadway Melody*, 1929): "are out of style"

Figure 1.4. A frame from shot 3 (screen capture, *The Broadway Melody*, 1929): "for Broad - way al - ways wears a . . ."

The cut to shot 2 does more than confirm the actors' positions; it initiates a pattern whereby shot changes occur during long notes in the melody, thereby bringing the shot lengths into conformity with the lengths of the melody's main phrases (see fig. 1.3).

For example, the cut to shot 2 falls near the second beat in measure 10, between the words "there" and "are" in the line "your trou - bles there / are out of style," and hence between two distinct four-note phrases. The sequence's visual flow thus lines up with the song's melodic motion.

The cut to shot 3, a close-up of Hank, lands, as far as I can tell, slightly after the third beat of measure 12 (see fig. 1.4).

The cut anticipates a major development in the song's form: the 7-note descending phrase "Broad - way al - ways wears a smile," which begins on the downbeat of measure 13 and then moves stepwise down the (slightly altered) E♭ major scale, covering a full octave, from F to F.[53] Scalar declination of this sort, Huron argues, is extremely common in both Western and non-Western music, where "phrases and works have a statistical tendency to fall in pitch toward the end."[54] Once the decline begins, the listener expects

Figure 1.5. A frame from shot 4 (screen capture, *The Broadway Melody*, 1929): "... smile."

further downward movement for the remainder of the phrase's duration, which, in this case, pushes the viewer or auditor to the end of the first half of the chorus.

Reinforcing the musical trajectory is the placement of the cut to shot 4 on the fourth beat of measure 15, one quarter note prior to the F that concludes the descending phrase (see musical example 1.1). The cut thus propels us to the memorable finish, with Queenie beaming precisely when Eddie sings the word *smile* (see fig. 1.5).

The coincidence of the gesture with the word suggests the tight music-image causality familiar to song sequences: more than react to Eddie's invocation of Broadway's "smile," Queenie's facial expression seems to incarnate it. Adding emphasis are two musical devices besides the downbeat: First, Queenie's smile coincides with the F that finishes the melodic descent. Second, the chord changes from F minor 7 to B♭ major, so that the harmony declines by a fifth, the most common cadence in popular music. The cadence creates a "before-after" effect typical of song sequences: once Queenie smiles, the sequence seems to start over.[55]

Nonetheless, the closure that comes from the cut to shot 4 is not as strong as it might be.[56] The song is in the key of E♭, which makes the chord heard at this moment, a B♭, imply something less than a full finish. Partial resolution is suggested also in the final F in the descending melody, which belongs to the E♭-major scale but not to the E♭ major triad that defines the song's harmony. Reflecting the musical incompletion is the image track, which returns not to the medium shot of Eddie but to the close-up of Queenie. The suggestion—musically and visually—is that the interaction between Queenie and Eddie remains ongoing.

The chorus is indeed only half over. In the sixteen bars yet to come, formal patterns introduced at the beginning of the sequence continue to play out, beginning with the cut to shot 5, which happens on the third beat in measure 18, just after the start of the chorus's second half (see fig. 1.6).

With the framing of shot 5 repeating that of shot 1, the cut, in effect, enacts a visual reset: just as the music returns to the beginning of the song's form, so does the visual composition. Also like shot 1, shot 5 is relatively lengthy, covering over 12 measures of music. Whereas shot 1 spans most of the chorus's first half, shot 5 encompasses most of the second. As with the first half, the closure effect is strongest at the end, when Charles King, in shot 6, sings the song's final syllable, the "- dy" in "that's the Broad - way mel - o - dy" (see fig. 1.7).

The syllable begins on the third beat of measure 31 and then carries over to the first quarter note of the next measure, the final measure of the chorus. So, we have a second sound-image cadence. This time, however, the musical resolution is stronger. The concluding note is E♭, the root for the song's key, and it lasts for a whole note plus a quarter note, making it the longest in the song. Also, the music at the end of shot 6 undergoes a slight ritardando before quickly picking up again for the second chorus. Mirroring the musical closure is the distant shot composition, where—for the first time in the sequence—all three actors appear in the frame. The three friends then go on to dance to instrumental versions of a further verse and chorus, and the song's end has the strongest visual closure: the trio freezes in place in a tableau-like pose, with Eddie and Queenie looking straight out to the camera. The sequence thus exhibits an overall pattern of development, whereby the closure effect increases incrementally as the sequence unfolds, with the most powerful resolution reserved for the very end.

Figure 1.6. A frame from shot 5 (screen capture, *The Broadway Melody*, 1929): "a million hearts beat quicker"

Figure 1.7. A frame from shot 6 (screen capture, *The Broadway Melody*, 1929): King sings the final syllable

Songs in Dialogue Scenes

The Broadway Melody, an MGM production with a large budget, is an exceptional film in important respects. But the pattern whereby changes in the visuals match up to the song's structure is extremely common. "Musical performances naturally take over and structure a film's timeline, superimposing the music's design on the scene," James Buhler, David Neumeyer, and Rob Deemer propose. A fascinating aspect of this momentary musical dominance is that it holds not only for singing performances featuring star vocalists but also for virtually any song-accompanied moment in a sound film, including dramatic scenes where songs provide an unobtrusive sonic background. Even when a diegetic café band performs at low volume during a dialogue exchange, Buhler, Neumeyer, and Deemer report, "classical practice tends to situate articulations of scene segments and music together."[57]

A scene in Hitchcock's *Blackmail* (1929) suggests that this convention arose early in sound film history. The scene takes place in the Corner House restaurant, where shopgirl Alice (Anny Ondra) dines with boyfriend Frank (John Longden) until they are interrupted by the arrival of the interloper Crewe (Cyril Ritchard). Underscoring the drama is a well-known song of the period, Sunny Clapp's "Girl of My Dreams" (1927). Throughout the scene, dialogue and the blocking of the action match up with the song's main shifts in form.

The scene begins with Alice and Frank taking their table in medium long shot just as an unseen house orchestra begins playing the "Girl of My Dreams." When Frank departs briefly to retrieve Alice's glove, the tune's bridge begins. Next comes the main dramatic development: the arrival of Crewe, with whom Alice exchanges surreptitious glances. The cutaway to Crewe's entry into the restaurant happens the instant the song's bridge ends and a new chorus begins. Marking the moment is a close-up of Crewe, who nods his head in Alice's direction during a brief pause in the music. The musical hiatus both underlines Crewe's conspiratorial gesture and allows the film's editor to reset the relation between music and image. Immediately after Crewe acknowledges Alice, "Girl of My Dreams" begins again and continues until the conclusion of the chorus, which happens at the end of the scene at the precise moment when the door closes behind Frank, who, breaking off the dinner date, has left the restaurant early. The dialogue and the actors' movements thus conform to the song's structure, even though the "Girl of My Dreams" is incidental to the scene and, in fact, is at times barely audible.

Song Spotting

So far, I have focused on the construction of individual song sequences. What about the insertion of songs in the film as a whole? A song's placement in a film, entertainment-industry personnel agreed, could greatly color a viewer's judgment of both the song and the film. Music publisher J. J. Robbins, responsible for the ambitious international campaign to promote MGM's songs, described a song's association with the film's narrative as decisive to its commercial success: "The most essential item in popularizing a number is 'spotting' it in properly. This means that it must be played or sung at the [proper] psychological moment in the film."[58] For Robert Crawford, music head at Warner Brothers and First National, "the identification of a song with a definite emotional scene increases its popularity enormously."[59]

So much did a song's link to the film image aid its commercial success that even an objectively weak tune, it was claimed, could become a massive seller if properly spotted.[60] "A fair song spotted in a good picture will easily outsell a good song not in a picture," *Variety* announced in 1930.[61] The megasuccess of "Sonny Boy," allegedly written in a single half-hour work session, was attributed not to the song's intrinsic quality but to its role in *The Singing Fool* (dir. Lloyd Bacon, 1928).[62] Likewise, Axt, Mendoza, and MacDonald's "I Love You Now as I Loved You Then" was said to have become a bestseller not on its own merits but through multiple placements in MGM's *Our Dancing Daughters* (dir. Jack Conway, 1928).[63] The causality went in the opposite direction, too, with inept soundtrack placement thwarting even a strong song's career, as music publishers charged when a film song sold poorly.[64] The high stakes made "the 'spotting' of songs . . . among the most important contingencies discussed at story conferences," reported a journalist in 1929.[65]

Songs in conversion-era films are rarely heard only once. They often repeat, in whole or in part, up to a dozen times over a film's duration. "No picture . . . should have more than four songs," stated songwriter Irving Berlin, "but these four should be sung often."[66] Nacio Herb Brown, the composer of "Singin' in the Rain," "The Broadway Melody," and other MGM themes, commented in 1932 on spotting technique as follows: "The best method . . . is to use a short melody that people can remember. This appears early in the picture. Then later it shows up sung by a character. If possible, the tune is used again, even though in an obscure way, before the final fade out."[67] Brown's remarks suggest Hollywood's so-called "rule of three," the screenwriter's maxim according to which characters' names and other bits of narrative information are repeated three times to ensure retention even for inattentive viewers.⁶⁸

Theme songs in Hollywood films, in fact, are often performed three times. Such is the case with Charles King's rendition of the title song in *The Broadway Melody*, Nancy Carroll's performance of the "Swanee River" number in *The Dance of Life* (dir. John Cromwell, 1939), tenor Donald Novis's performance of "There's the One for Me" in *Bulldog Drummond* (dir. F. Richard Jones, 1929), and Chevalier's singing of "You Brought a New Kind of Love to Me" in *The Big Pond* (dir. Hobart Henley, 1930). Likewise, *Pointed Heels* (dir. Edward Sutherland, 1929) features three on-screen performances of its theme "I Have to Have You," and in *Tanned Legs* (dir. Marshall Neilan, 1929) Oscar Levant's "With You, With Me" is sung three times. But a song's presence in a film typically goes beyond the singing performances. *The Singing Fool* contains thirteen separate cues for "Sonny Boy" outside of the three times that Al Jolson sings the tune. A further example, discussed below, is the title song for *The Broadway Melody*, which includes, besides Charles King's three performances, eight additional cues for the song.

The repeated use of melodies from a few commercial pop songs is not unique to American films but occurs also in films made in Germany, where the strategic repetition of song melodies in multiple forms likewise became standard practice. Masters of the technique included Ufa's Werner Richard Heymann, who claimed that forty minutes of the music-accompanied running time of *Bomben auf Monte Carlo* (dir. Hanns Schwarz, 1931) derived from the melodies of the film's four main songs.⁶⁹ The tune "Das ist die Liebe der Matrosen" is heard eleven times on the film's soundtrack in one form or another, by my reckoning. In *Die Drei von der Tankstelle*, the nine occurrences on the film's soundtrack of the theme song "Ein guter Freund," another Heymann composition, add up to over nine minutes of running time, more than 10 percent of the film's total.

Song Repetitions

Assessing a song's use in a film requires examining not only the singing performances proper but also the many additional cues involving the same melody. Each recurrence invites the viewer to recall previous times when the melody is heard as well and primes her or him for subsequent acts of audition. While the plot's chain of cause and effect implies forward movement, song cues expand the song's range of story associations by suggesting parallels between nonconsecutive scenes, thus adding thematic depth and complexity to the film's narrative. "By reprising the same song at different points in the film's action," observed a critic in France, "one can create, destroy, and re-create ambiances, and evoke memories and circumstances."[70]

The title tune for *The Broadway Melody* offers an example of how songs can shape a film's narrative. Prior to the apartment performance analyzed in this chapter, the song is heard twice in the opening scene in the music agent's office, first when Eddie teaches it to the piano player and second when he sings it for the impromptu audience of show people. After the third cue in the apartment (analyzed above), the song is performed eight additional times, including four times during the rehearsal, twice during the dress rehearsal, and once at the after-hours party, where the title is mentioned in the dialogue. During the final dialogue scene, an instrumental rendition of the melody swells up as the final "The End" appears. The song thus comes up in the film a total of eleven times, to comprise some fourteen minutes of screen time. Moreover, the cues are dispersed throughout the film's running time in a manner that implies a narrative function, with "The Broadway Melody" dominating in the film's first half, where nine cues occur within the first forty minutes, but then giving way in the second to the romantic ballad "You Were Meant for Me." The shift midfilm from one song to the other coincides with a change in story focus, away from the friendship of Eddie, Hank, and Queenie and toward Eddie and Queenie's romance.

Any cue is potentially important structurally because, as noted earlier, a few seconds of a melody are enough to prompt the auditor's recall of the entire tune, regardless of changes in key, tempo, and orchestration. Conversion-era filmmakers understood this. To the chagrin of music publishers, they were known to truncate songs in odd ways, reducing the standard 32-bar chorus to short fragments, secure in the knowledge that the song would remain recognizable.[71] An example occurs in the melodrama *Millie* (dir. John Francis Dillon, 1931) in the brief scene in the taxi that follows the party in the nightclub, where a vocal trio's performance of the title song commemorated the heroine's birthday. Afterward in the cab, Millie (Helen Twelvetrees) offhandedly sings a line from the song: "I'm a red-headed woman." It's only a single, four-second phrase, but enough to recall the nightclub scene and add to the song's thematic associations. With certain repetitions too brief and incidental to draw the viewer's notice, the total number of cues likely will be higher than the viewer remembers. Song cues can motivate a song's presence in a film simply by enhancing the song's familiarity for the film's viewer, even subliminally, as is suggested in chapter 4 regarding the cues for "I'm Daffy over You" in *Monkey Business* (dir. Norman McLeod, 1931). In breaking songs into bits and pieces, submitting them to new arrangements and orchestrations, and inserting them here and there into the soundtrack, film-industry song spotters adhered to aesthetic principles unknown in the music industry.

Songs as Underscore

The capacity for music listeners to recognize melodies despite changes in tempo, key, and instrumentation makes possible an essential film-music technique: the appropriation of the melody introduced in a diegetic song performance for use as nondiegetic orchestral accompaniment.[72] The transposition of song melodies into orchestral themes was already commonplace in the early Vitaphone features, where the melodies from song performances surface also in "silent" scenes with orchestral accompaniment. An example from *The Singing Fool* is what I will refer to as the "gray skies" motif from "Sonny Boy" notated in musical example 1.2.

This short, descending phrase has a prominent role in the song's unusual 40-measure structure. It surfaces just after the opening eight-measure verse, at the start of the song's chorus. It then recurs twice and always at the beginning of an eight-measure section. The repetitions feature different lyrics—"Friends may for - sake me" and "[When] I'm old and gray, dear"—but in keeping with the diminished harmony, the melancholy remains.[73]

The gray skies motif is one of the very first musical passages heard on the film's soundtrack, where it comes up at the start of the opening credits. It isn't heard again until the scene in which Al sings the tune to Sonny before bedtime, which occurs roughly halfway into the film. Then, during the final thirty minutes, the motif recurs eight times as nondiegetic orchestral music. The first repetitions come when Al visits Sonny in the park, and then directly afterward, when Al, visible through the car window, is left behind as the limousine containing Sonny departs. The third happens when Al, in his dressing room, receives a note from the hospital informing him that Sonny is ill. The fourth and fifth cues occur later at the hospital, when Al learns that Sonny has died and then immediately afterward when, too late, he dashes into Sonny's room. The seventh cue comes near the film's conclusion when Al, after performing "Sonny Boy" to an auditorium of fans, collapses behind the curtain, and the eighth a moment later, prior to the closing title. In all cases, the phrase marks a moment of crisis, a spike in the melodrama consonant with the gloomy lyrics.

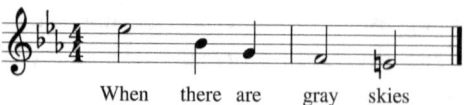

Musical Example 1.2. The "Gray Skies" motif from "Sonny Boy"

The gray skies motif in *The Singing Fool* points to an oddity of song accompaniment: the lyrics for a song cue remain relevant even for an instrumental version. Such relevance was a given for a song as widely distributed as "Sonny Boy," which, as noted in chapter 5, set sales records for sheet music and recorded discs, including in countries where languages other than English were spoken. A similar situation held for the scene in *Blackmail* described earlier in this chapter. Though heard in the film in an instrumental version, "Girl of My Dreams," critic Jack Sullivan suggests, was familiar enough to the film's audience for its lyrics to provide an ironic commentary on Alice and Frank's relationship.[74]

Music/Image Associations

The task of song spotting required that filmmakers grapple with how aural and visual perception interact. Humans classify sounds according to the spatial location of a sound's presumed source, with the essential information about location provided through vision.[75] Sounds are recalled along with the accompanying images because the brain is inclined to associate the two for purposes of memory retrieval, which gives music a special capacity for forming associations with the coincident visuals—and vice versa.[76] A song can recall for a film's viewer an accompanying image, just as an image can trigger recollection of music and lyrics. Filmmakers often try to forge specific visual associations across a song's various cues. Take the scene from *The Broadway Melody* described in this chapter. When Charles King, in shot 5, places his hand on his heart (see fig. 1.6) while singing the word *hearts* in the line "a million hearts beat quicker there," he performs a gesture that he has already enacted twice when performing "The Broadway Melody" in the music agent's office. King will make the hand-on-the-heart gesture during the song again later in the film, during the dress rehearsal. The association of the gesture with the film's main theme creates a motif that makes possible a telling departure roughly halfway into the film's running time, when King clasps his hand to his breast while singing a new song for Queenie alone, the romantic ballad "You Were Meant for Me." The transfer of the gesture from the dance tune to the ballad marks the film's main narrative development: Eddie and Queenie's realization of their romantic attraction to one another.

An additional factor, considered further in chapter 5, concerns how promotional materials circulating in the culture at large can inform how song sequences are constructed, as when song sequences accommodate a performer's characteristic poses. Consider the cover of the sheet music for "Sonny Boy" (see fig. 1.8).

The photo references the first of Al Jolson's performances of "Sonny Boy," when he sings Sonny to sleep after returning home from a night's work at the Clicquot Club. The scene's staging and shot composition establish an iconography that informs two subsequent scenes: in Central Park when Al cradles Sonny on the bench and in the hospital during the second "Sonny Boy" performance. In all cases, Sonny appears in the lower left of the frame and Al in the upper right. Finally, the bedroom scene is cited again in Jolson's third performance of "Sonny Boy" in the crowded auditorium, when Sonny, wearing pajamas, appears via a superimposed image. The intent to recall the bedroom scene during the public performance is indicated in notes dictated by producer Darryl Zanuck during a preview screening of *The Singing Fool*, which include the following order: "Double expose through Al singing, so that we dimly see Al rocking—big figure of baby in arms—lap dissolve of baby in bed scene."[77]

The pietà-like composition shown in figure 1.8 is not limited to *The Singing Fool* but is reproduced also in similar scenes in other films. It turns up, for example, in the next film in Warner Brothers' Jolson cycle, *Say It with Songs* (dir. Lloyd Bacon, 1929), which includes a similar scene in which Jolson, via a recording, comforts his ailing son, played, once again, by child actor Davey Lee (see the frame reproduced in fig. 3.1). As in *The Singing Fool*, Jolson and Lee appear in a medium shot, with Lee in the left foreground, cradled in Jolson's arms. This image became so iconic that even films unconnected with Jolson and Warner Brothers emulated it. Examples include *Glorifying the American Girl*, when Buddy (Ed Crandall) comforts the bedridden Barbara (Gloria Shea), and *A Bedtime Story* (dir. Norman Taurog, 1933), when Maurice Chevalier sings "Goodnight Monsieur Baby" to the infant that his womanizing character, improbably enough, ends up caring for. The first example is melodramatic and the second comedic, but both cite the iconography of *The Singing Fool*.

42 | *Movies, Songs, and Electric Sound*

Figure 1.8. The sheet music illustration for "Sonny Boy"

Iconographic citations can give a song sequence an allegorical quality that lifts the performance out of the flow of the film's narrative and thereby adds to the sense that the story's time has slowed down or stopped altogether during the song. They also illustrate how the impact of a song sequence can depend on not only the music and lyrics but also the association of the lyrics with particular images. That a singer's image is likely to appear also in other films and in the culture at large feeds into the concern, mentioned earlier in this chapter, that a song's presence in a film might recall for the viewer experiences that are irrelevant to the film's story. Such a concern is relevant not only to conversion-era films but also to films of other periods, including the present. In the next chapter, the focus shifts to issues specific to the late 1920s and early 1930s with an investigation into changes in film exhibition, the domain in which the sound cinema's novelty was most imposing—sometimes distressingly so.

Notes

1. An overview of the history of music-drama debate can be found in P. Kivy, *Introduction to the Philosophy of Music*, 160–81.

2. On the relevance to cinema of the history of music-drama theory, see S. Paulin, "Richard Wagner and the Fantasy of Cinematic Unity," in J. Buhler, C. Flinn, and D. Neumeyer, *Music and Cinema*, 58–84. On film music in the early 1930s, see the quotations from composer Constant Lambert (1934), musicologist M. D. Calvocaressi (1935), composer George Antheil (1936), and composer Carlos Chavez (1937) in F. Steiner, "What Were Musicians Saying about Movie Music during the First Decade of Sound?" 89–90.

3. "Musik-Kritik zum 'Lied einer Nacht,'" 2.

4. S. Rayment, "Year Two of the Revolution: The Story of 1929," in S. Rayment, *Kinematograph Year Book, 1930*, 11.

5. "Musical Pictures Again to Be in Vogue," 3.

6. "AFI's 100 years . . . 100 Songs," American Film Institute, accessed March 22, 2017, http://www.afi.com/100years/songs.aspx.

7. H. Angel, "'Die verkaufte Braut,'" 2. "Ton und Wort, die abstrakte Zeit des musikalischen Ablaufs und die reale Zeit des Sprachablaufs dem Handlungsablauf anzupassen."

8. On the utopian aspect of the song sequences, see R. Dyer, "Entertainment and Utopia."

9. On the centrality of the narrative/number dichotomy to studies of the Hollywood musical, see K. Spring, *Saying It with Songs*, 5–6; R. Altman, *The American Film Musical*, 106–7; and M. Rubin, *Showstoppers*, 11–14.

10. The history of song usage in silent cinema is examined in R. Altman, *Silent Film Sound*, 220–78.

11. The remark from Vuillermoz is quoted in E. Toulet and C. Belaygue, eds., *Musique d'écran*, 76. The "extremely vague synchronization" in movie exhibition in the 1920s is noted in K. London, *Film Music*, 69.

12. K. Kalinak, *Settling the Score*, 58–59.

13. K. Kalinak, *Settling the Score*, 56.

14. A. Herzog, *Dreams of Difference, Song of the Same*, 7.

15. On music-image synchronization in the animated shorts of the early 1930s, see D. Goldmark, *Tunes for 'Toons*, 19–20. On enthusiasm for Disney, see, for instance, remarks by director René Clair in "Un enquête à Londres: l'avenir du film parlant," 3; cinematographer Eugen Schufftan in "Probleme der Tonfilmgestaltung," 5; director Sergei Eisenstein in M. Segal, "The Future of Film," 143; producer Karl Ritter in "Micky," 365–66; and music publisher Francis Salabert in "Une visite aux studios Salabert," 521.

16. The importance of short films, animated and otherwise, to Hollywood's use of recorded songs in films is taken up in J. Fleeger, *Sounding American*, 13, 22–25.

17. On the foreign versions of *Paramount on Parade*, see H. Waldman, *Paramount in Paris*, 28, 147, 185, 200, 207, 229, 233. The Dutch version is discussed in K. Dibbets, *Sprekende film*, 99–100, 102.

18. On the making of the French version of *The Hollywood Revue*, see "Foreign Competition," 6.

19. "Nine Versions of *King of Jazz* Made by Universal," 58.

20. The introductory sequences for the nine foreign versions of *King of Jazz*, which involved up to twenty actors and emcees, were all filmed in a mere two days. See the detailed account of the production of the foreign versions in J. Layton and D. Pierce, *King of Jazz*, 215.

21. All sequences in *King of Jazz* were filmed in Technicolor, but to cut costs on the foreign release, some prints were printed in black and white. See J. Layton and D. Pierce, *King of Jazz*, 207. At least some of the *Der Jazzkönig* prints circulating in Germany included black-and-white sequences, it seems. See "'Der Jazzkönig,'" 2.

22. On the critical response in the United States to the revue films, see E. Schallert, "Revues Stir Controversy," B11, 22.

23. K. Thompson, *Exporting Entertainment*, 159.

24. A. Sarris, "The Cultural Guilt of Musical Movies," 41.

25. M. Rubin, *Showstoppers*, 13.

26. M. Rubin, *Showstoppers*, 14–18.

27. H. Eisler and T. Adorno, *Composing for the Films*, 73–74.

28. J. Buhler, D. Neumeyer, and R. Deemer, *Hearing the Movies*, 131–33.

29. K. London, *Film Music*, 154.

30. On the ballad structure common in the American popular music of the 1920s, see K. Spring, *Saying It with Songs*, 31–34, 37–38; and H. Laing, "Emotion by Numbers: Music, Song and the Musical," 9.

31. O. Sacks, *Musicophilia*, 212.

32. A. Cohen, "Film Music," in J. Buhler, C. Flinn, and D. Neumeyer, *Music and Cinema*, 368.

33. H. Grace, "Dance Music: A Short Life and a Gay One," 693.

34. On songs as film accompaniment versus orchestral music, see R. Altman, "Cinema and Popular Song," 19–30.

35. M. Chion, *Audio-Vision*, 3–24.

36. R. Bellis, *The Emerging Film Composer*, 71–72.

37. On the difficulty of consciously attending to film music, see R. Bellis, *The Emerging Film Composer*, 71; and R. Stilwell, "Sound and Empathy," 183n.

38. On the distraction caused by songs on movie soundtracks, see Dr. F. H., "Das Musikproblem im Tonfilm: Los vom Schlager!" 11.

39. Martin Boones is quoted in M. Merrick, "It's In, So It Can't Be Out," B11. On orchestral music in Hollywood films, see also P. Scheuer, "Musical Picture Quietly Undergoes Renaissance," B9.

40. The quote from Max Steiner comes from "Classical Composers Banished from Films," B10. See also J. Wierzbicki, *Film Music*, 129.

41. Arthur Franklin's remark is cited in P. Scheuer, "Musical Picture Quietly Undergoes Renaissance," B9.

42. D. Albright, *Untwisting the Serpent*, 18.

43. R. Dyer, *In the Space of a Song*, 24.
44. K. Trumpener, "The René Clair Moment and the Overlap Films of the Early 1930s," 39–40. Quoted in R. Spadoni, *Uncanny Bodies*, 28.
45. E. Panofsky, "Style and Medium in the Moving Pictures," 127.
46. E. Panofsky, "Style and Medium in the Moving Pictures," 124.
47. K. London, *Film Music*, 132.
48. Composer Karol Rathaus's work on *Dimitri Karamasoff* is examined in "Bildmontage nach einer primären Musik," 5.
49. B. Balázs, "The Sound Film," 201.
50. The quote from Anderson comes from P. Scheuer, "Jazz Spectacle Sets Pace in Novelties," 19.
51. D. Huron, *Sweet Anticipation*, 97.
52. K. Donnelly, *Occult Aesthetics*, 94–122.
53. The scale is a descending E♭ major scale with a passing tone added between the sixth and fifth degrees of the scale, commonly known today as the E♭ bebop major scale.
54. D. Huron, *Sweet Anticipation*, 97.
55. On the potential in sound-image synchronization for a before-after effect, see J. Buhler, D. Neumeyer, and R. Deemer, *Hearing the Movies*, 138–39.
56. On the attributes of musical "closure," see B. Snyder, *Music and Memory*, 59–67.
57. J. Buhler, D. Neumeyer, and R. Deemer, *Hearing the Movies*, 181.
58. J. J. Robbins is quoted in P. Scheuer, "Picture-Lyric Trend Queried," B13.
59. Robert Crawford is quoted in P. Scheuer, "Picture-Lyric Trend Queried," B13.
60. A. Green, "Words about Music," 96.
61. "Non-Film Songs Don't Class with Picture-Songs," 73.
62. P. Scheuer, "Picture-Lyric Trend Queried," B13.
63. A. Green, "Words about Music," 96; and "Theme Song Interjection into Pop Music Industry Keeps Trade Topsy-Turvy," 71.
64. S. Silverman, "'29 and Talkers—1930 and Wide Film," 78. On the problems associated with improper spotting, see "Picture Songs Pushing Trade into Heavy Overproduction," 57; and "Operettenfilm = Krise in USA," 9.
65. S. Silverman, "'29 and Talkers—1930 and Wide Film," 78, 93.
66. The quotation from Irving Berlin appears in "Talking of the Talkies," 128.
67. Nacio Herb Brown is quoted in C. Hall, "Hollywood Turns to Music in Films," X4.
68. D. Bordwell, J. Staiger, and K. Thompson, *The Classical Hollywood Cinema*, 31.
69. W. Heymann, "Musik nach Maß," 2.
70. R. Champfleury, "Vive la chanson!"
71. "Picture Songs Pushing Trade into Heavy Overproduction," 57.
72. D. Levitin, *This Is Your Brain on Music*, 133–34, 137–38, 149.
73. An additional lyric surfaces in Jolson's third performance of "Sonny Boy" in *The Singing Fool*: "[And then the] an - gels grew lone - ly."
74. In J. Sullivan, *Hitchcock's Music*, 5.
75. In B. Stein et al., "Crossmodal Spatial Interaction," 28.
76. See D. Levitin, *This Is Your Brain on Music*, 39.
77. Zanuck's notes on the preview screening, dated August 1, 1928, can be found in a dossier of materials on *The Singing Fool* in the Warner Brothers collection at the Cinematic Arts Library at the University of Southern California.

2

ELECTRIC SOUND AS NEW MEDIUM

Electric sound's reception by the public can be compared to that of the "new media" of other times, when an initial moment of astonishment likewise soon gave way to adjustment and habituation. Like the telegraph of the nineteenth century or the smartphones of the twenty-first, sound cinema, radio, and the electric gramophone initially impressed observers as absolutely novel in certain respects. Within a few years, however, these media had receded into the background of everyday routine. In the United States in 1930, sound cinema, a journalist noted, was now referred to in the past tense: "Sound came so fast (it became 'natural' so soon) that practically nobody (and least of all the movie critics) realized what was happening until it happened."[1] In 1932, after two years of industrial sound film production in Europe, a swift familiarization was likewise apparent. "It's been barely two years since the silent film has given way to the talking film," observed a critic in Paris, "but we so easily become accustomed to miracles that the prodigious perfection achieved by the talkies no longer astonishes us."[2]

Electric sound's short-lived state of novelty offers a context for making sense of the period's musical films. Cinema's interactions with cognate media created a media-historical dialectic whereby sound films promised to improve on established stage entertainments, just as the latter retooled in response to audience expectations linked to sound cinema, broadcast radio, and the electric gramophone.[3] Symptomatic of the process was the neologism *silent cinema*, and analogues in other languages such as the German *Stummfilm* and the French *cinéma muet*, which reconceived cinema history in light of the emergent electric-sound norm.

This chapter focuses on developments in film exhibition around 1930, when Hollywood, while centered on the production of sound films, continued to release silent editions for screening in movie theaters in countries around the world, the majority of which were not yet sound ready. In Europe, for example, where only fifteen hundred of the continent's twenty-five thousand movie venues were estimated to be wired for sound, the market for silent films remained strong, and audiences were acutely aware of the novelty of sound cinema.[4] The entertainment press of the period abounds in commentary on how the sound-movie experience differed from the silent. References in 1930 to the concept of "live music" distinguished the on-site performances in movie theaters by musicians in the flesh from the sound cinema's recorded accompaniment. Conditions for innovations in terminology included film soundtracks with long, music-free stretches; the modernized acoustics of sound-era movie theaters; and, most importantly, the banishment from film exhibition of live entertainment in favor of recorded. A survey of allusions in the period's musical films to earlier media suggests electric sound's effects on the motion picture experience. Through filmic representations of theater orchestras and other entertainment institutions that sound movies had helped obliterate, musical films tried to compensate for the loss of the live-performance component of silent-era exhibition. The films thus commemorate their media predecessors strategically, highlighting their own novelty in ways that imply continuity with attractive aspects of the antecedent media.

Change and Continuity

The film industry's adoption of electric sound has long been understood as a radical change from one type of cinema to another.[5] Shaped by publicists who described sound cinema as a leap forward from silent cinema as well as critics who believed that the talkies were killing the art of film, the story concerns the old giving way to the new. The association of new media with historical progress has a long history. Cultural historian Gregory Downey cites "the development of long-distance telephone, the replacement of analogue with digital technology in the movie industry, and the privatization of public broadcasting" as examples of how "over and over we have celebrated our 'new' media and tried to bury the 'old,' such that our very notions of media, modernity, and even 'progress' have tended to unfold hand-in-hand."[6] Ensuring sound cinema's status as a full-blown new-media development was its reliance on the vacuum-tube electronics vital to radio and long-distance telephone, the technological marvels of the day. An ultramodern achievement, sound movies seemed to arrive from the future, which had the effect of instantly consigning "silent cinema" to the historical past.

A shift in thinking was enacted in the years after World War II by the film theorist André Bazin, who challenged sound-era film historiography by positing aesthetic continuity between sound cinema and silent. The key point concerned editing and scenography in Hollywood sound films, which, Bazin observed, featured essentially the same découpage as their silent forerunners.[7] Bazin's affirmation of deep aesthetic continuity across silent and sound periods anticipated the accounts of sound-era Hollywood formulated by film historians in the 1970s and 1980s. Barry Salt, for example, in the first edition of his book *Film Style and Technology: History and Analysis*, proposed that "the trend in the early 'thirties in mainstream cinema [can be characterized] as an attempt to return to the main features of the last silent films, 1928 vintage, as soon as the various technical constraints on putting a film together were relieved."[8] A similar idea informs the epic study of classical cinema by David Bordwell, Janet Staiger, and Kristin Thompson, who stress the enduring commitment in sound-era Hollywood to principles of style and narration that were already in place as early as the 1910s.[9] "Differences between silent and sound visual style," Bordwell proposes, "can be seen as issuing in large part from attempts during the years 1928–1931 to retain the power of editing in the classical style."[10] In sum, while electric sound's overhaul of the technology of cinema disrupted filmmaking practice, the ground rules behind the artistic use of the technologies, the basic aesthetic principles, remained unshaken: sound-era filmmakers were still staging, shooting, and editing scenes according to continuity rules established ten years before.

Another important argument in favor of historical continuity across silent and sound eras was advanced by Douglas Gomery, who in his PhD thesis and subsequent writings argues that electric sound was far less disruptive to the motion picture industry than is suggested in much of what has been written on the topic.[11] The familiar emphasis on "the supposed chaos on the studio lots," Gomery charges, has fostered a distorted view of the period by obscuring long-term continuities in media-industrial history.[12] Though Gomery is concerned with economic and industrial developments rather than the aesthetic currents stressed by Bazin, Salt, and Bordwell, Staiger, and Thompson, he likewise looks at the period in retrospect, free from the passions of the time and with the hindsight of trends that became clear years, if not decades, after the fact.

In identifying underlying conditions and forces whose impact may have escaped notice at the time, these historians demonstrate the benefits of looking at the period in a manner unavailable during the period itself. A potential drawback for a study of the period's song-oriented cinema, however, is that a focus on continuity can occlude the important changes that did occur. One such change concerns the preferences of the audience, whose volatility during the first years of sound cinema had powerful effects on the period's musical films.[13] An exemplary instance is the American film audience's rejection of musical films in mid-1930, after having embraced the genre over the preceding two years. In this chapter, audience tastes are approached through a focus on film music, where ambivalence regarding sound was especially strong. The investigation rests on two methodological choices whose net effect is to emphasize changes occasioned by sound cinema: First, conversion-era musical films are examined through period testimony, with an emphasis on beliefs and concerns operative in the early 1930s. Second, the focus is on the sphere of film exhibition, where the impression of radical change was especially strong. An emphasis on contemporary accounts of changes in exhibition can enable a better understanding of the period's musical films by clarifying some of the conditions and forces behind them, including those that, in retrospect, may appear unique to the period and hence fleeting in importance.

"Live" Music versus Recorded

The erasure of the local culture of live entertainment that had hitherto defined motion picture exhibition was perhaps the most profound change in the sound film experience. In any country that had begun to convert over to sound cinema, musicians, dancers, comics, jugglers, magicians, acrobats, and other artistes who had been a familiar presence in movie venues quickly disappeared. The effects on popular music were profound. In North America, by the summer of 1931, reports historian James Kraft, half of the approximately twenty-five thousand members of the American Federation of Musicians who earned their principal income from movie accompaniment had lost their jobs.[14] In other countries, too, employment for musicians vanished once theaters became sound ready. In the summer of 1930, the first year of industrial sound film production in Germany, fully half of the twelve thousand musicians employed in movie theaters prior to the release of sound movies were out of work, reported the Berlin Chamber of Commerce.[15] In Canada, by September 1929, some 350 Canadian theaters had wired for sound, more than four times the number predicted, and "theatre orchestras were extinguished with abandon."[16] In Britain, twenty thousand movie-house musicians nationwide—four thousand in London alone—faced unemployment, according to music-industry historian Cyril Ehrlich.[17]

The expulsion of musicians and other entertainers from movie theaters unmistakably altered the cinema experience. Changing characterizations of sound cinema in the contemporary press, where the introduction of new terms and concepts signals changes in understanding and adjustments in perception and awareness, are symptomatic. An example is the use of the adjective *live* or *living* to distinguish performances by musicians in concert halls, cafés, and movie houses from recordings. The *Oxford English Dictionary* lists as the first use of the word *live* to refer to a performance "heard or watched at the time of its occurrence, as distinguished from one recorded on film, tape, etc." as an item in the BBC Year Book of 1934 that distinguishes between the broadcasting of "live material" and "recorded."[18]

This distinction between the "live" and the recorded, I discovered through the research conducted for this book, was prevalent already in 1930 in the film press, where it differentiated the emergent regime of movies with soundtracks from the residual practice of music performed by on-site entertainers. Examples include the campaign of the American Federation of Musicians to oppose "the elimination of living music from theatres" and references in the London-based film daily the *Bioscope* to "'live' music" and "live [movie-house] showmen."[19]

Analogous terminological innovations in entertainment-trade publications in other languages signal the transnational nature of the change. In Berlin, orchestras at theaters that continued to show silent films were commended for providing "living art [*lebendige Kunst*]" as opposed to sound cinema's recorded music.[20] French examples include the assertion by the orchestra director at the six-thousand-seat Gaumont-Palace in Paris that "there is a much greater life [*vie*] and variety in a living orchestra [*orchestra vivant*]" than in music recorded and reproduced on a film's soundtrack.[21] As with their English-language analogues, German and French invocations of liveness distinguish the new sound cinema from its "silent" rival.

The "Realism" of Electric Sound

The motion picture community's invention in 1930 of the concept of a live performance raises a question of media historiography. Recorded music was not new in the late 1920s; it had been a major international industry since the mass marketing of Berliner's gramophone at the turn of the century.[22] By 1910, with the record business now centered on the production of discs rather than cylinders, "recorded sound had become the first nonprint mass medium," as noted by media historian Lisa Gitelman.[23] Around the same time, recorded music became a component of commercial film exhibition, particularly in Germany, where films screened with sound-on-disc accompaniment. *Tonbilder*, as they were called (literally "sound-images") were essential to the economics of the national film industry.[24] In sum, recorded music was not new in 1930, nor was its use as film accompaniment. Why did the notion of live music (as distinct from recorded music) emerge only with electric sound, some thirty years after the creation of an international record industry and the first wave of sound-on-disc films? Put another way, why didn't the notion of liveness turn up decades earlier, when music recordings and home players were first mass distributed and recorded music was first employed in film exhibition?

The answer perhaps lies in electric sound's simulation of musical performance, whose improvement in quality over the earlier acoustic technologies struck listeners as revelatory. "Discs that have been electrically recorded disconcert us with their extraordinary purity," stated a critic in France, alluding to the broadened technical capacity of the electric systems.[25] The sonic spectrum for acoustic recording covered between two hundred and two thousand cycles per second, a small fraction of the human ear's range of twenty to twenty thousand cycles.[26] The gamut for electric sound, however, ran from one hundred to five thousand cycles or more, thus opening new thresholds at both the high and low end.[27] The improvement was immediately evident to consumers of recorded music. Bass tones inaudible on acoustic recordings, such as the low notes on a grand piano, were now easily heard, adding new ballast to the sound. Also apparent was a boost in the high frequencies, which enhanced the effect of liveness and presence essential to electric sound's "realistic quality."[28] The effects on voices were astonishing. Sibilants and other speech inflections registered on electric recordings with startling clarity (as is discussed further in chap. 3). In narrowing the phenomenal gap between a musical performance and its technological reproduction, electric sound inaugurated the period when "the relationship between live performance and recording was arguably at its closest," state the editors of the *Cambridge Companion to Recorded Music*.[29]

Immediate and permanent changes in popular music were the result. For one, the range of voices featured on recordings quickly expanded. In nearly doubling the pitch span for recorded music, lifting it from three octaves to five and a half, electric recording was friendly to a much wider range of vocal talent. Female vocalists, who were said to record poorly on the acoustic systems, featured routinely in the popular music circulating via radio, the electric gramophone, and sound movies.[30] Also, new options for instrumentation became available. String instruments that had been difficult to record acoustically—violins, harps, banjos, and guitars—became prominent on electric recordings. Violins and pianos no longer had to be physically modified to make them loud enough to register. Nor were musicians required to cluster around a recording horn. Instead they could disperse in the recording studio much like on the concert stage. Session orchestras increased in size, with up to three times the number of violins used for electric recordings than for acoustic.[31] Symphonic works were now recorded by the large ensembles they had been written for. In the mid-1920s, discs featuring orchestral music performed by large symphonies found their way onto the bestseller lists for the first time.[32]

Adding to the realism was electric sound's inscription of place.[33] More than just capturing the music, the microphone registered the room tone, the volume of air in the space where the music had been made. With the new technologies, reported *Gramophone* magazine, "the 'sound' of whatever recording apartment has been used, were it studio, theatre, or hall, is conveyed to the listener almost as unmistakably as the music itself."[34] Record companies exploited the new spatial registration by recording choirs and orchestras in churches and other historic performance venues.[35] With electric sound, proposed a journalist, "the 'atmosphere' of the concert hall [is] brought right into even our small dens; comfortably cuddled in our armchairs, we can shut our eyes and—we are there!"[36] Recorded music's capacity to substitute for a performance perhaps made necessary the invention of a term like *live* to distinguish the original from the reproduction.

Robot Music

Comparisons between live and recorded music arose insistently regarding motion picture exhibition, where recordings replaced flesh-and-blood musicians on a massive scale. The change sparked resistance from audiences. The orchestras were a major attraction at certain theaters, which, in fact, were reputed to attract moviegoers as much for the in-house musicianship as for the films.[37] Cinema musicians did more than accompany the film: they responded to the ambience of the event of performance, reflecting as well as shaping the audience's mood. Motion picture music was human and empathic, an effect of the musicians' interaction with an audience in real time. The term *live* suggests as much. In comparison, the recorded music used for sound films—robot music, the musicians' union called it—came across as empty of human rapport.[38] "The discriminating picture-goer," reported a critic in London, "sickens of the poor mechanical reproduction of music sooner than he tired of music badly played by human performers."[39] Patrons of the picture palaces regarded recorded music as an inferior substitute. "No five violins amplified from a record are going to top the same number in the [movie-house orchestra] pit," announced *Variety* in January 1929.[40] In Dallas, Texas, where in 1930 the average resident was believed to go to movies twice per week, a poll of film patrons showed that 92 percent of the respondents preferred a "human orchestra" over a recorded music track.[41]

The entertainment press circa 1930 is thick with evidence of the disappointment that audiences felt over the loss of the musicians. As late as January 1931, after the majority of American theaters had wired for sound, the *Motion Picture Herald* reported that audiences in American cities understood that compared with the music on a soundtrack, "the house orchestra [would] be easier on the ear even if the score [wasn't] as appropriate or well-constructed."[42] The same disenchantment caused by the loss of the orchestras became evident in other countries. Electric sound's "abolition of the orchestra," protested a journalist in London in 1930, had removed "practically the last trace of human contact between the audience and the entertainment. This is a fact not lightly to be dismissed."[43] "I want, and want badly, the return of the real orchestra or real musicians," wrote a movie fan in London. "There are plenty of cinema-goers who agree with me."[44] Film audiences in Spain were said to object to "the substitution of good orchestras by mechanical music."[45] In Munich in December 1929, *Variety* reported, "the American synchronized version" of *Submarine* (dir. Frank Capra, 1928) "had to be taken off after three days, owing to audience dissatisfaction. Patrons compared it unfavorably with the former 35-piece orchestra at the Emelka Palast."[46]

The Reduction in the Amount of Music

In accounting for complaints regarding the sound-era movie experience, two additional factors merit consideration. One is a crucial style difference between silent and sound movies: the reduction in sound films of the amount of musical accompaniment. Unlike silent films, which ordinarily were accompanied entirely by music, beginning with the opening studio logo and continuing through to the concluding "The End," sound films (as discussed in chap. 4) usually employ music intermittently, reserving it for certain passages and avoiding it for others. Indeed, some sound films include no music at all except for what is heard during the opening and closing titles. Figure 4.2 is indicative, showing that in 1929–30, at the height of Hollywood's theme-song fad, more than 50 percent of the average feature film's running time was music-free. In 1930–31, when the Hollywood companies began removing songs from films, the "no music" figure climbs to over 70 percent of a film's running time. Even musical films normally give around half of their running time to shots that include no music.[47] In sum, sound movies did more than replace live music with recorded. They also, for long stretches, replaced live music with silence. The disquieting effect of the absence of music on how certain scenes played presumably fed into the impression that the silent-film experience somehow had been richer and more transcendent.[48]

Changes in Theater Acoustics

Also contributing to the experiential change were the major architectural modifications required by electric sound. Established film exhibition venues, and especially the luxurious picture palaces of the 1920s, were too reverberant for sound screenings.[49] The echo appropriate for a motion picture orchestra compromised the intelligibility of recorded dialogue. Wiring a motion picture venue for sound thus required more than installing amplifiers and speakers; it meant reducing reverberation through sound-absorbent building materials, upholstered seats, and air conditioning. These changes, media historian Emily Thompson explains, were integral to an architectural trend associated with the period's sound media, whereby theaters, concert halls, and other public buildings were remade in accordance with electroacoustic principles drawn from the same Bell Laboratories research behind broadcasting, public address, long-distance telephone service, and sound movies.[50] In the new buildings, sound acquired phenomenal characteristics that seemed abstract, unrelated to the site's particularities. Driving the acoustic standardization was the emergence in the 1920s of a "sound conscious" generation of Americans who, Thompson reports, sought built environments whose sonic properties were consonant with the decontextualized sound associated with the electric-sound media.[51] Cinema, in fact, via the acoustic makeover of tens of thousands of theaters, first in the

United States and then in other countries, played the key role in normalizing the new sound for the broad public.⁵²

The "modern sound" described by Thompson may have factored into complaints circa 1930 regarding the "cold and distant feeling" in sound-era movie theaters.⁵³ The *Oxford English Dictionary* lists as an additional meaning for the word *live* a reference to room acoustics, dating from 1930, that mentions specifically studios for "radio broadcasting and sound pictures." Here the adjective *live* characterizes "a room or enclosure having a relatively long reverberation time, as opposed to dead."⁵⁴ Something like this live-or-dead distinction seems to inform dramatist André Antoine's remark that "even the poor piano in the small movie house animates the room," where liveness defines not just the music but the space in which it is heard.⁵⁵ In any case, the changes in room acoustics needed for sound film projection distinguished the ambience of the sound film theater, for better or worse.

A Reversal in Theater Policy

The relatively quick and total replacement of silent cinema has made sound cinema look like a media-industrial steamroller that left its predecessor flattened in its wake. But the situation on the ground was complicated. In London, Paris, Munich, Madrid, Sydney, and other cities around the world, motion picture exhibitors, struggling to retain their clientele after wiring for sound, went as far as to revert to programs with live, acoustic music, which in some cases meant rehiring orchestras that had been let go just a few months before.⁵⁶ In England the conglomerate Gaumont British announced in October 1930 that it had "decided to reintroduce human orchestras in many of its theatres. This means that upwards of 200 halls in the group's chain will be providing 'live' music."⁵⁷ While sound movies provided the feature presentation, orchestras were retained for prologues, overtures, intermissions, and supplemental acts. Even in the United States, where the process of conversion unfolded relatively quickly and relentlessly, large theaters in the urban centers often maintained a capacity for live entertainment.⁵⁸

The retention of live entertainment defined sound-era film culture in countries such as France, where movie exhibitors pursued what *Variety* called "the vaudfilm policy," whereby movie exhibition was combined with stage entertainment, with the same actors featuring in both. "Whereas people hesitate to go and see a straight picture show, having found that the talkers currently shown are not always up to standard, they patronize plentifully those houses where besides a film there is stage entertainment."⁵⁹ Live entertainment in French film exhibition endured well beyond the conversion years to affect the style of French films, which were described as "filmed theater" into the late 1930s.⁶⁰

Allusions to the Conditions of Exhibition

Musical films invoke exhibition conditions in an unusually explicit fashion. Narrative films are not known for encouraging their viewers to think about how they were made. In fact, the viewer's immersion into a film's story world—its unified, self-sufficient complex of characters, settings, and actions—has been said to depend on how film conceals its conditions of manufacture. But as critic Jane Feuer has pointed out, the many conversion-era films that "take for their subjects the world of entertainment—Broadway, vaudeville, the Ziegfeld Follies, burlesque, nightclubs, the circus, and, to a lesser extent, mass entertainment media in the form of radio or Hollywood itself" amount to something of a special case.⁶¹

The self-referential aspect is blatant in films whose stories refer to sound cinema's threat to stage entertainment. In *Happy Days* (dir. Benjamin Stoloff, 1929), for example, a young couple struggles to save Colonel Billy Bachelor's minstrel show from the bankruptcy looming due to the public's preference for the talkies. The film's heroine, Margie (Marjorie White), a singer in the show and fiancée of Colonel Billy's grandson, offers a frank assessment: "How can we go into a town and compete with these talking pictures? We soak them a dollar for this terrible show and for half that they can see a million-dollar picture." The irony is that *Happy Days*, with its large all-star cast, simulated stage performances, and use of Fox's seventy-millimeter widescreen Grandeur system for prints projected in large theaters, is exactly the sort of "million-dollar picture" that was driving the country's few remaining traveling shows into financial ruin. The sound cinema's displacement of the popular stage is explicit also in in other films. In Universal's *Once in a Lifetime* (dir. Russell Mack, 1932), the first lines of dialogue are spoken at an empty vaudeville house, where the customer asks at the ticket window, "Where's all the customers tonight?" The man answers, "Must be over in New York looking at those talking pictures." *Footlight Parade* (dir. Lloyd Bacon, 1933) begins with show producer Chester Kent (James Cagney) realizing that "people aren't paying for shows no more. Talking pictures is what they want."

These films, whatever their differences, are typical of the period's musical films in two respects. First, their stories culminate in a reconciliation whereby the initial antagonism between sound cinema and its stage predecessor gives way to a symbolic merger of the two media. In *Happy Days*, Margie winds up saving Colonel Billy's minstrel show by recruiting famous film stars to join the cast. In *Footlight Parade*, Chester modernizes the live-entertainment prologues of silent-era exhibition in a manner appropriate to sound cinema's stepped-up demands. In *Once in a Lifetime*, the ex-vaudevillians, their total incompetence notwithstanding, become pillars of the Hollywood community. In all cases, new and old media accommodate one another in ways that benefit everyone. Second, in these films, sound movies pose a threat not to silent cinema but to the sort of popular stage entertainment that had been crucial to the motion picture experience prior to electric sound. For the moviegoing public at the time, cinema had become inseparable from what had recently become known as live performance. Audiences regretted the loss not of silent movies per se but instead of the stage entertainment integral to silent-film exhibition.

Filmic Representations of Old Media

The musical film's self-referential dimension further manifests in sentimental depictions of the entertainment practices that the electric-sound media were pushing to the cultural margins. Many conversion-era film heroes earned a living through song plugging, the repeated performance of a song either to stimulate retail music sales or to entice a producer to contract the song to a show. Essential to the American music industry in the first decades of the twentieth century, song plugging declined quickly in the late 1920s, when the electric-sound media, and sound cinema especially, began serving the same function more effectively.[62] "In the old days," specified a journalist, "a music firm needed four months to plant a number with 100 big time acts, [which was] considered an excellent showing if accomplished. Today the screen outlet means that 100 Jolsons, 100 Chevaliers, 100 Dennis Kings, 100 Ramon Navarros, 100 [Lawrence] Tibbetts, etc. are plugging a song in that many cities the first week a picture is released. Where thousands heard [the songs] before, millions of people are hearing and humming the new melodies within the space of a very few months."[63]

Sound films had made song pluggers redundant in the United States, except in large movie theaters, where discs and sheet music for film songs were "vended regularly on a grind by the military uniformed ushers."[64] Nonetheless, representations of song plugging became a staple of the period's musical films, which frequently open with a scene in which the main character hawks a song to a small audience. In *The Broadway Melody* (dir. Harry Beaumont, 1929), for example, singer-songwriter Eddie (Charles King) pitches his song in the music company office to a small gathering of theatrical agents, performers, and onlookers. In *Glorifying the American Girl* (dir. Millard Webb and John Harkenrider, 1929), clerk Gloria (Mary Eaton) sings the latest hits to customers at the department store's music counter. In *Sous les toits de Paris* (dir. René Clair, 1930), street singer Albert (Albert Préjean) passes out lyric sheets in the local quartier to the passersby, who gather around. Supported by a blind accordionist, he leads the people in communal song. A likely inspiration for Clair's nostalgic depiction was the opening scene of Paramount's *The Battle of Paris* (dir. Robert Florey, 1929), which begins in a similar manner, with Georgie (Gertrude Lawrence) and Zizi (Charlie Ruggles) plying their trade on the corner, handing out sheet music for Vincent Scotto's "Sous les ponts de Paris" to an impromptu gathering of locals and tourists. As in Clair's film, while the singer performs, the pickpocket works the crowd.

Depicting a face-to-face manner of audience engagement that the electric-sound media had set in decline, these scenes recalled an era in entertainment history prior to sound movies, when interaction between performer and audience seemed more natural, spontaneous, and intimate than what was becoming the norm. Nothing has been lost by the replacement of live with recorded music, such scenes suggest; viewers accustomed to the live entertainment of "silent" cinema can still enjoy the same pleasures.

Filmic Simulations of the Stage Experience

The emulation of live entertainment was essential to the many musical films intended as low-cost alternatives to stage shows. Such films not only represent stage-entertainment practices but also simulate theatrical modes of spectatorship, as if to offer an experience comparable to that of a stage show. This practice of "virtual Broadway," as Donald Crafton calls it, rested on strong financial incentives.[65] In 1929, a ticket for a quality New York stage show cost around $4.40, whereas a ticket for a film cost a mere $0.75. With this disparity in price, the cinema could substitute for the stage, provided that the filmmakers were able to properly model the stage experience—which required, a journalist proposed, bringing "the camera close enough to make the ensemble seem to be in the same theatre."[66]

Figure 2.1. A production still for *Glorifying the American Girl* (Wisconsin Center for Film and Theater Research)

The idea that the film's performers ought to share the same space as the movie-theater audience informs the many films of the period that mimic the live-music ambience of the silent-era picture palace. Filmic simulations of the theater orchestra include the lengthy Ziegfeld Follies sequence in *Glorifying the American Girl*, where the orchestra intermittently becomes visible in the lower portion of the frame, as in the production still reproduced in figure 2.1.

Center stage in the photo is Mary Eaton, onetime "Ziegfeld Girl" and recent Broadway star, who enacts in this 1929 film the same signature pirouette she had made famous on the stage. Visible below and in front are the pit musicians, who occupy a space that seems to reach out beyond the image and into the space occupied by the movie-theater audience. A further invocation of the stage experience comes with the insert that isolates the $27.50 tickets for the Ziegfeld show. The insert was perhaps intended less to promote ticket sales for the Follies than to remind the filmgoer of the relatively miniscule cost of a ticket to the movies, which provided, hypothetically, the identical entertainment.

The same composition—where a theater proscenium, filmed straight on, implies a viewer positioned in a large theater at around row ten, with the orchestra partly visible at the bottom of the frame—can be found in similar simulated theater sequences in other films. Examples include the Follies sequences in *Dance of Life* (dir. John Cromwell, 1929) and *On with the Show* (dir. Alan Crosland, 1930); Jolson's performance of "Tomorrow is Another Day" at the end of *Big Boy* (dir. Alan Crosland, 1930); and MGM's *The Hollywood Revue of 1929* (dir. Charles Reisner, 1929), during the opening credits and at other moments in the film when the pit orchestra is shown playing. Adding to the effect of liveness was the direct-sound production method, which attributes the music heard on the film's soundtrack to the orchestra visible on screen: the bows of the violins move exactly when the music tells us they should. *The Hollywood Revue of 1929* even includes a virtual intermission. Covered in a single shot that runs more than three minutes, the intermission happens halfway into the film's running time. As with the orchestras visible in *Dance of Life*, *Glorifying the American Girl*, and *Big Boy*, the camera position implies the vantage point of a spectator seated toward the front of a theater auditorium, and it remains fixed throughout the shot's duration. During the shot's first forty-five seconds, some two dozen players of the MGM Symphony Orchestra enter the pit, pick up their instruments, sit, and tune up. Next, conductor Arthur Lange waves the baton, and the orchestra goes on to play three songs featured elsewhere in the film. The curtain behind the musicians, which had also appeared during the film's opening credits, remains closed for the intermission's duration.

In simulating the live-music format of silent-era exhibition, films such as *The Hollywood Revue of 1929* responded to the legions of filmgoers described by an exhibitor in Ohio: "They want to see the orchestra as it enters the pit, just as they used to do in the old days. They long for the thrill of the opening overture, the flourish of the baton, and all the other appeals which they have so long associated with living musicians who can be seen as well as heard, and who can interpret the theme of the picture in a human way, and without the many defects which exist under the present mechanical conditions."[67] Offering the assurance that nothing has been lost by the replacement of live with recorded music, conversion-era films simulate the very movie-music experience that Paramount, MGM, and the other Hollywood majors at the time, in wiring their theater chains, were hastening to eliminate.

In examining electric sound's transformation of film exhibition, this chapter illustrates the ambivalence of audiences toward the new regime of recorded music. The predominant factor was sound cinema's expulsion of musicians and other entertainers from movie theaters, which, in the view of numerous commentators, diminished the quality of the movie experience. The sense of loss quickly became manifest in the period's musical films. Moviegoers did not have to wait for the cartoons and MGM musicals of the 1940s and 1950s to find filmic expressions of nostalgia for the silent cinema's live stage entertainment, whose bond with audiences had come to seem, in retrospect, natural and authentic.[68] The sense of regret was apparent already in 1929, when the conversion-era musical film was both emulating and supplanting the audience-performer interaction characteristic of sound cinema's predecessors.

Notes

1. "Color and Sound on Film," 124, 127.
2. "Au studio: les maîtres du son."
3. The process invites comparison with the media interaction and redefinition theorized in J. Bolter and R. Grusin, *Remediation*.
4. The figure of fifteen hundred theaters is cited in "Sound Rapidly Replacing Silents Abroad, Gov't Finds," 32.
5. See the discussion of this point in D. Crafton, *The Talkies*, 1–4.
6. G. Downey, *Technology and Communication in American History*, 3.
7. A. Bazin, "The Evolution of Film Language."
8. B. Salt, *Film Style and Technology*, 1st ed., 286.
9. D. Bordwell, J. Staiger, and K. Thompson, *The Classical Hollywood Cinema*, 294–308.
10. D. Bordwell, J. Staiger, and K. Thompson, *The Classical Hollywood Cinema*, 308.
11. See, for example, D. Gomery, "The Coming of Sound to American Cinema"; and D. Gomery, *The Coming of Sound*, 1–6.
12. D. Gomery, *The Coming of Sound*, xvii.
13. On the audience's unpredictability during the first years of sound cinema as "one of the great mysteries of this part of film history," see A. Williams, "Historical and Theoretical Issues in the Coming of Recorded Sound to the Cinema," 129.
14. J. Kraft, *From Stage to Studio*, 38, 50–58.
15. "German Film Industry in May: Berlin Chamber of Commerce Report," 7. See also "German Musicians Protest Officially against Sound Pictures," 73.
16. W. Gladish, "The Year in Canada," in S. Rayment, *Kinematograph Year Book, 1929*, 35.
17. See the quotation from Ehrlich in R. Philip, *Performing Music in the Age of Technology*, 13.
18. *The Oxford English Dictionary*, 2nd ed., s.v. "live." Available also in the dictionary's online edition. On the *OED* definitions of "live" sound, see P. Auslander, *Liveness*, 51–52.
19. With respect to the American Federation of Musicians, see "Living Music Defenders Get Votes," 69. Regarding the *Bioscope*, the first of the references to "live music" appears in

"Back to Orchestras? Gaumont Revert to 'Flesh and Blood,'" 18; and the second surfaces apropos of an advertising campaign for films from British International Pictures in "Cash Prizes for Live Showmen," 14.

20. See, for instance, references to "lebendige Kunst" and "lebendigen Musikbegleitung" in "Die Musiker und die Tonfilmfrage," 3; and the reference to "der Verbindung von Film und Varieté lebhaft" in H. Wins, "Kommt des Orchester im Lichtspielhaus," 11.

21. R. Régent, "La musique enregistrée supprimera-t-elle les orchestras?" 2.

22. P. Gronow and I. Saunio, *An International History of the Recording Industry*, 9.

23. L. Gitelman, *Always Already New*, 59.

24. On recorded music in silent film exhibition, see C. O'Brien, "Sound-on-Disc Cinema," 42–51. Further discussion of the *Tonbilder* can be found in chap. 6.

25. G. Clair, "Disques et cinéma," 432.

26. On differences in sound quality between acoustic and electric technologies, see T. Day, *A Century of Recorded Music*, 9–16; and M. Chanan, *Repeated Takes*, 56–60.

27. On the "frequency characteristics of recording systems," see P. Wilson, "Cornucopiae: A Study in Gramophone Theory," 477. On film sound specifically, see D. Morton, *Sound Recording*, 96.

28. The phrase *realistic quality* comes from P. Wilson, "Acoustic versus Electric," 453–54.

29. N. Cook et al., eds., introduction to *The Cambridge Companion to Recorded Music*, 3.

30. On female vocalists, see, for example, T. Adorno, "The Curves of the Needle," 607.

31. On acoustic versus electric practices for orchestra recording, see S. Chapple, "In the Recording Studio," 289–90.

32. R. Philip, *Performing Music in the Age of Recording*, 21, 35.

33. On characterizations in the 1920s of electric recordings as realistic, see T. Day, *A Century of Recorded Music*, 16–18, 32.

34. H. Warwick, "Concert Hall or Studio?," 9.

35. E. Goossens, "The Gramophone in America," 120.

36. Indicator, "Atmosphere," 11.

37. A. Hoerée, "Essai d'esthétique du sonore," 46.

38. "Canadian Conference on Film Canned Music," 65.

39. D. Robson, "Architects and Sound," iv.

40. S. Silverman, "The Smothering Talker," 17. See also the discussion of audience preferences in S. Rayment, "Year Two of the Revolution: The Story of 1929," in Rayment, *Kinematograph Year Book, 1930*, 9; and "English House Returns to Silence for Summer," 2.

41. The poll is cited in "Dallas Fans' Likes," 53. Comparable poll results are referenced in "Sound or Silent Future," 1.

42. S. Silverman, "Rehabilitation of Flesh-and-Blood in Film Houses Gains Momentum, Survey Shows," 71.

43. "Problems of Presentation," vii.

44. "Back to Orchestras?" 18.

45. A. Cardona, "Spain," 4.

46. "Silent and Sound Facts Revealed by German Exhibs," 4.

47. The no-music estimation for the musical films derives from a sample of forty-nine musical films of 1928–34. The numbers for the no-music category are $M = 51.7$ percent, $SD = 19.4$, and $ME = 5.5$. Compare these to the no-music figures for seventy-two contemporaneous films belonging to other genres: $M = 68$, $SD = 24.1$, and $ME = 5.6$.

48. A. Boswell, "Trials of the Talkies," 53, 113.

49. R. Altman, *Silent Film Sound*, 392.
50. E. Thompson, *The Soundscape of Modernity*, 229–34.
51. E. Thompson, *The Soundscape of Modernity*, 3.
52. E. Thompson, *The Soundscape of Modernity*, 256.
53. On "the cold and distant feeling given off by mechanical music" in movie theaters, see A. Antoine, "Inquiétudes des musiciens," 101. The full quote is as follows: "Il reste . . . évident que la musique mécanique, quelle que soit sa perfection, garde quelque chose de lointain et de froid: là, comme sur l'écran, la présence réelle de l'exécutant est un élément de chaleur et de vie; même de pauvre piano des petites boîtes anime la salle."
54. *The Oxford English Dictionary*, 2nd ed., s.v. "live." The reference comes from an issue of the *Journal of the Acoustical Society of America*.
55. A. Antoine, "Inquiétudes des musiciens," 101.
56. A. Cardona, "Spain," 4; "Same Necessity as in America," 53; "Swing Away in Buenos Aires from Am. S. and D. Talkers—Going for Silents," 7; and "Vaudeville Coming Back," 24.
57. "English House Returns to Silence for Summer," 2. See also "British Cinema Back to Music," 5.
58. "Vaudeville Coming Back," 24.
59. "Vaudfilm Back Abroad," 53.
60. On the French cinema's inclination in the 1930s toward "filmed theater," see C. O'Brien, *Cinema's Conversion to Sound*, 13, 34–35, 54–56, 77, 117, 147.
61. J. Feuer, *The Hollywood Musical*, ix.
62. "Song Plugger Going?" 57. On song plugging in the American music industry, see K. Spring, *Saying It with Songs*, 17–19, 79–80.
63. "Non-Film Songs Don't Class with Picture-Songs, and Why," 2.
64. "Film Houses Work for Song Selling," 57.
65. D. Crafton, *The Talkies*, 63–88.
66. S. Silverman, "'The Broadway Melody,'" 13. On musical films as a substitute for musical theater, see also the interview with director John Murray Anderson in H. Lang, "He Didn't Know How!," 132.
67. "Slams Talkers; Says Audiences Want Orchestras," 28.
68. On nostalgia in the MGM musicals of the 1940s and 1950s, see J. Feuer, *The Hollywood Musical*; on the vaudeville-inspired "memory palace" offered by the cartoons of the same decades, see D. Crafton, *The Talkies*, 265.

3

VOICES AND BODIES, DIRECT AND DUBBED

THE ELEMENT OF FILM STYLE WHERE THE AESTHETIC impact of electric sound was immediately evident was acting. As soon as recorded speech entered movies, actors' performances, it was plain to see, started to change. "Actors, when they . . . switch from the mute film drama to the oratorical, oftentimes transform their style and even their type," stated a journalist in 1929.[1] Established acting technique was at odds somehow with the expressive potential of the new technology. Scenes in talkies, exhibitors reported, didn't play like scenes in silent films. Depictions of romantic passion, for example, now accompanied by recorded speech rather than instrumental music, reportedly drew laughter from audiences.[2] Established stars, their careers threatened, signed up for elocution lessons in a desperate effort to repair their style, but there was no consensus on how to do so.[3] Furthering the disruption was the quick influx into motion pictures of singers, vaudevillians, and other stage entertainers with minimal, if any, film experience. The new stars' face-to-face manner of engaging the public was difficult to reconcile with current narrative-film technique, which required that actors perform as if unaware of the movie audience's presence. This was especially true of the singers, whose stature in media other than cinema, including the powerful new medium of broadcast radio, made them seem always bigger than their film roles. Rather than ignore the audience, singers tended to engage with it. Practices of scene construction were adjusted to accommodate singers, whose sudden omnipresence in motion pictures added to the intermedial dissonance—the sense of aesthetic incoherence and incompletion—associated with the period's musical films.

A survey of sound-related revisions in the craft of film acting brings out the problems and possibilities associated with using singers in movies. Singers held a peculiar status in narrative cinema, and circa 1930, singing technique itself changed in response to pressures from the electric sound media, cinema included. Aesthetic effects and strategies derived from the potential in the new media for the singer's voice to be heard separately from her or his image. One technical innovation with major consequences for film-song performance was the "playback" or "prescoring" method, whereby the vocals were recorded separately and then played back on the set while the singer, lip-synching to the recording, was filmed. More than yielding improvements in sound quality and lip synchronization, playback altered a scene's emotional valence by making the act of singing seem physically effortless, which helped give song sequences an ethereal, transcendent quality that further separated them from the rest of the film. As with the dubbing of actors' voices in films intended for foreign release, playback was developed first in Hollywood, and it was used most extensively there. A different approach, involving the simultaneous recording of voice and image, remained the norm for musical film production in Germany, as is argued in chapter 6.

Changes in Acting

Sound cinema, it was understood, required from actors something other than the customary way of relating to the camera. Unlike the poetic, dreamlike experience associated with silent cinema, sound films, stated a theater manager in the United States, came "weighted down with realism."[4] Actors in a "talking picture" evince a unique sense of presence, proposed one critic: "When characters speak from the screen, they become more intimate, more real; speech intensifies life."[5] Synchronous voices made the motion picture experience, by some accounts, more like a stage show. Audiences for the Vitaphone shorts, for instance, were reported to applaud at the end, as if the featured artists were there in person.[6] Singers in films were said to elicit the sort of response appropriate for a singer onstage. When Jolson sings in *The Jazz Singer* (dir. Alan Crosland, 1927), proposed a critic in Paris, "brusquely one forgets that one is in the cinema. One adopts the mentality that one brings to the musical-hall or concert."[7] Cinema had become more like everyday life, proposed film director René Clair, who observed of "people leaving the cinema after seeing a talking film" that "they talked and laughed, and hummed the tunes they had just heard. They had not lost their sense of reality."[8]

The peculiarities of electrically recorded speech further motivated the attribution of realism to sound cinema. In contrast to the abstraction of the silent cinema's intertitles, electric technologies registered speech accents and other vocal subtleties specific to each actor's body. The microphone, in the words of cultural historian Steven Connor, captured "a whole range of organic vocal sounds which are edited out in ordinary listening; the liquidity of the saliva, the hissings and tiny shudders of the breath, the clicking of the tongue and teeth, and popping of the lips."[9] Actors in speaking parts now came with precise regional and class identities. The fine-grain personal and social inscription made sound film acting comparable to stage acting, and sound movies, in fact, often featured stage-trained talent. But the stage analogy was limited by electric sound's capacity for taking in vocal gradations inaudible to a theater audience.[10] Hence the emergence in the late 1920s of an additional comparison, according to which the microphone's detailed registration provided an aural complement to the visual device of the close-up.[11] Just as the close-up, the most cinematic of film techniques, registered infinitesimal shifts in facial expression, the microphone captured the materiality of speech, the grain of the voice, down to the slightest inflection. A further media analogy with long-distance telephone likewise alluded to the increased proximity: while the telephone, Donald Crafton explains, "made it possible to converse 'close up' at great distances," sound cinema brought up close not only the actor's voice but his or her body too.[12]

The sense of nearness allowed actors to explore psychological and behavioral nuances unique to sound cinema. Actors on the legitimate stage had already begun scaling down their gestures, moving away from histrionic convention and toward psychological realism, and sound cinema allowed for radical experimentation in this regard.[13] As James Naremore puts it, the soundtrack "furthered a movement toward invisible acting, inviting us beyond outward display, as if voices were letting us in to private regions, and revealing the 'natural' traits of individuals."[14] Adding to the naturalism were restrictions in cinematography and lighting. For films with spoken dialogue, a filtered, soft-focus look seemed inappropriate, observed a critic in *Variety* in March 1929: "Sound has virtually wiped out all demand for positive film of soft characteristics. Reason for this is that it is not convincing to see a fuzzy, ethereal portraiture in close-up joined with speech. Portraiture that carries a vocal accompaniment must be sharply defined rather than soft focused if the dialogue is expected to carry conviction."[15]

The realism elicited ambivalence from critics such as Alexander Bakshy, for whom talking films, however wondrous their technology, had brought about a "shrinking of the actor's personality."[16] Unlike the silent cinema's potential for grandeur, the naturalistic performances in the talkies seemed less transcendent—"smaller," as Gloria Swanson famously declared in *Sunset Boulevard* (dir. Billy Wilder, 1951). At the same time, film actors in speaking roles exhibited a degree of self-possession that suggested independent agency. The actors appeared able somehow to break free from the films in which they appeared. By some accounts, the presence of speaking actors had troubled the established hierarchy of film personnel, tipping the balance of power away from the director and toward the actor. Remarked Jean Renoir in 1931 apropos of *La chienne* (1931), his first major sound film, the key difference between sound cinema and silent concerned the actors; in sound films, "the film's director no longer completely possesses them."[17] Likewise emphasizing the irrepressibility of the sound-era actor was the critic Molly Haskell, for whom the introduction of spoken dialogue had served to empower female actors and enable an improvement in female roles: "The silent woman was more often a projection of the director's fantasies, an object manipulated into a desired setting, whereas the talking woman might take off on her own."[18]

Singers in Films

The peculiarity of sound film acting stemmed also from the personnel appearing on the screen, who now included many entertainers new to cinema. In Hollywood, observed a journalist, "studio contract lists have been changed, with practically every company now carrying many former stage favorites and those who have had stage and musical comedy training."[19] Singers were an exemplary case. Songs had been sold with reference to celebrity vocalists for decades, and this practice escalated with the electric-sound media.[20] With the same recording artists featured in cinema, radio, the gramophone, and public performance, singers in films, rather than incarnating fictional roles, seemed to arrive from another world, their identities already formed through their work in other media.

The frequency with which singers retained their first names for their film roles signals their unusual status. Among the many examples that can be cited are Bing Crosby in *Reaching for the Moon* and *The Big Broadcast* (dir. Frank Tuttle, 1932); Fanny Brice in *Be Yourself* (dir. Thornton Freeland, 1930); Al Jolson in *The Singing Fool* (dir. Lloyd Bacon, 1928), *Mammy* (dir. Michael Curtiz, 1930), and *Wonder Bar* (dir. Lloyd Bacon, 1934); Eddie Cantor in *Palmy Days* (dir. Edward Sutherland, 1931), *The Kid from Spain* (dir. Leo McCarey, 1932), and *Roman Scandals* (dir. Frank Tuttle, 1933); and Chevalier and MacDonald in *Love Me Tonight* (dir. Rouben Mamoulian, 1932). European illustrations are likewise easy to come by, beginning with Ufa's prototypical *Die Drei von der Tankstelle* (dir. Wilhelm von Thiele, 1930), in which Lilian Harvey plays "Lilian" and Willy Fritsch plays "Willy." A visitor from another realm, "the musician [*Musiker*] shows up as a foreign body [*Fremdkörper*]," observed a critic Germany in 1930 regarding the numerous singers now appearing in narrative films.[21]

Practices of staging and cutting that treated singers differently from other actors added to the incapacity of singers to merge into their characters in the manner of ordinary actors. An indicator is shot length. Singing shots in cinema, as demonstrated in chapter 1, run much longer than the other shot types on average, with shots during singing performances often exceeding a film's ASL by ten times or more. In any given film, the longest take typically occurs during a song sequence, as in *Der schwarze Husar* (dir. Gerhard Lamprecht, 1932), an *Operettenfilm* from Ufa, which includes singing shots featuring Mady Christians that last up to 165 seconds; in *Animal Crackers* (dir. Victor Heerman, 1930), when Harpo Marx whistles "Why Am I So Romantic?" during a take that runs over three minutes; and in *Arm wie eine Kirchenmaus* (dir. Richard Oswald, 1932), which has a nearly four-minute shot that begins with Trude Hesterberg singing an up-tempo cabaret song and ends with a hypnotic spoken song by comedian Fritz Grünbaum.[22]

Beyond the unusual length, shots of singers tend to exhibit additional peculiarities. The framing is often tight rather than wide, the staging and range of focus shallow rather than deep, the mise-en-scène minimalistic, and the camera stationary. Singing shots, their excessive length notwithstanding, give the viewer relatively little to look at beyond the singers themselves. Conversion-era filmmakers seemed to understand that singers, during the act of singing, invite the viewer's undivided attention. Hence the impression, discussed in chapter 1, that story time seems suspended during song sequences. A wonderful illustration is the 166-second take in *Dance of Life* (dir. John Cromwell, 1929), when veteran hoofer Skid (Hal Skelly), in the middle of his vaudeville act, lies down on the stage and, framed in medium shot, sings/whispers "True Blue Lou," intermittently puffing on a cigarette.

A further oddity of singing performances in films are the occasional acts of direct address, when the singer looks out toward the camera, as if striving to engage directly with the movie-house audience. At such moments the film offers no longer an actor playing a role but a celebrity addressing her or his public. An example occurs in the talent-show scene in *Sunny Side Up* (dir. David Butler, 1929), when Janet Gaynor performs the film's title song for the assembly of Yorkville residents. At one point, Gaynor faces the camera and exhorts the audience to participate: "We'll all sing a chorus of 'Sunny Side Up.' What do you say?" Her plea is ostensibly aimed at the gathering of inner-city neighbors and friends, but her frontal approach to the camera seems to reach out beyond the film's story world to an implied auditorium of moviegoers. The audience acknowledgment enacts a momentary alteration of the actor's status, transforming her from the character Molly Carr into Fox Pictures star Janet Gaynor.

The practice of direct address reaches a limit in *Big Boy* (dir. Alan Crosland, 1930), the screen adaptation of Al Jolson's stage hit of 1925, in which Jolson plays to the camera throughout. While the other actors are positioned in the fashion conventional for narrative cinema, at an angle oblique to the camera, Jolson faces forward, and not only during the songs but for the dramatic scenes too. Further marking off Jolson from everyone else is the blackface makeup, motivated by his role as a "Negro jockey."[23]

The strange framing and makeup anticipates the film's unusual ending: a four-minute coda during which Jolson steps out of character to offer his public a song performance. The inaugural moment comes just after Jolson's character, amazingly, has won the Kentucky Derby, thus ending the film's story. As Jolson, in close-up, spins around in a 360-degree turn, the movie set, via a composite image, is replaced by a new stage set, which leaves Jolson standing in front of a microphone, out of costume, and without the blackface worn in all previous scenes. Flanking him on the stage are the film's other actors, who appear in formation in neat, symmetrical rows, still in costume but motionless. Visible in front is a pit orchestra and the backs of the people occupying the front rows in a packed theater. The represented space, in the manner of the musical-theater simulations described in chapter 2, suggests an extension out into the implied space of the real-world movie theater. Speaking into the microphone, Jolson hails the crowd: "I hope you enjoyed the story of the picture as much as I had fun in making it." Reminded by an attendee that "no Jolson show would be complete without a Jolson song," Jolson sings the film's theme, "Tomorrow is Another Day," to the auditorium of fans, surrogates for the film's movie-theater audience.

Big Boy ends still outside the film's story world, with Jolson onstage, facing the orchestra and audience.

Changes in Vocal Performance

The singers who entered motion pictures en masse during the conversion years did so at a time when the practice of singing was itself mutating under pressure from the electric-sound media. More than reproduce performances, the new media helped create new audiences for singers. As the concert experience was remade according to norms inspired by sound movies, radio, and electrically recorded discs, vocal technique changed accordingly.[24] The artistic effects were comparable to what happened with electric sound's transformation of film acting. In both cases, the technology seemed to bring the singer unusually close to the audience, well beyond what had been possible onstage, thus enabling, in the words of music historian Daniel Leech-Wilkinson, "intimacy as a new or reinvented dimension of musical expressivity."[25]

The microphone-dependent performance styles associated with radio offer an example of electric sound's potential for an enhanced sense of intimacy. The "crooning" associated with American radio singers like Bing Crosby, Rudy Vallee, Russ Colombo, and Nick Lucas made use of a condenser microphone held close to the singer's mouth, which captured the voice while excluding the spatial characteristics of the recording site. The absence of room tone creates the illusion that the singer's voice is aimed straight at the individual auditor alone, who feels personally and intimately addressed, even when the singer is broadcast from a radio studio in a distant city. Adding to the effect were adjustments in demeanor. Singers facing the radio microphone were advised to scale down their vocal mannerisms by imagining they were performing not for an auditorium of fans but for a single auditor in a domestic setting.[26]

The effects on singing style drew protests from concert-hall traditionalists, who complained that the microphone exempted singers from the traditional performance challenge of projecting their voices out to the last row of the house.[27] By some accounts, crooning's illusion of intimacy brought the (male) singer too close to the (female) auditor—indecently or obscenely close.[28] Aggravating the transgression was the new style's undeniable popularity. In September 1929, shortly after the release of *The Vagabond Lover* (dir. Marshall Nielan), RKO's vehicle for NBC star Rudy Vallee, sheet music for the film's title song became the nation's top seller, and Vallee featured on four of Victor's six top-selling discs for the month.[29] The high sales ensured widespread adoption of the new vocal technique, whatever the critical judgments against it.

The new vocal techniques helped spur changes in songwriting. The range for vocabulary and diction expanded as lyricists exploited electric sound's capacity for capturing "the sharp pronunciation of final consonants," observed composer Kurt London, which freed writers and singers from the need always to end song lyrics with vowel sounds.[30] Lyrics became more personal, playful, urbane, and euphemistic, as ballads displaced the minstrel songs, novelty tunes, and marching-band fare that had been popular in the 1910s.[31] Enabling the intimacy, Philip Furia and Laurie Patterson suggest, were technical developments in sound-era Hollywood, where so many songwriters had found employment.[32] As sound film technique evolved, so did the songwriting. An example concerns the use of playback for vocal performances, which relieved singers of the need to sing while facing the camera. In separating off the task of singing, playback opened new possibilities for acting performances during song sequences; further, it also, Furia and Patterson propose, "changed the rules of songwriting," allowing for vowels to become shorter, alliterative consonants to proliferate, and rhythms to become more complex.[33]

Electric-Sound Stardom and the Disembodied Voice

Conditions for the new vocal styles included the technology-enabled likelihood that the listener would encounter the singer's voice independently of her or his image. Voice-image separation was not new in the 1920s. It had already become common in the late nineteenth century with the emergence of the international recording industry, not to mention communication technologies like the telephone and the Dictaphone. But it took on new salience with electric sound's naturalistic reproduction of voices, which triggered public interest in the singers' personalities. At issue was a dialectic, proposed the editor of *Gramophone* magazine: just as the electric-sound media provoked in music consumers "a lively interest in the appearance and behavior of the people who record their cabaret or music hall songs," an "acquaintance with [the performers'] appearance [stimulated] appreciation of their records."[34]

For singers who reached their public through radio and gramophone, ordinary vocal technique seemed insufficient. Contemporary singers, wrote

Theodor Adorno in 1927, were inflecting their voices with added expressive emphasis, as if aiming to inscribe into the sonic reproduction the resonance of their physical bodies.[35] Compton MacKenzie, founder of the monthly *The Gramophone*, proposed in 1930 in a piece on radio drama that the actors' invisibility required a more emphatic vocal expression: "The very lack of the visual appeal over the wireless, the absence of colour and movement and perfume, makes it more imperative to heighten and differentiate the voice in every possible way."[36] The radio singer, advised radio star Virginia Rea, famous as Olive Palmer of the *Palmolive Radio Hour*, must learn "to project personality through the voice alone."[37]

Electric sound's potential for voice-image separation carries implications for vocal performance given that listeners tend to depend on the singer's demeanor in interpreting the singer's expressive intent. Research undertaken by psychologist Jane Davidson shows that bodily gestures such as swaying motions or a hand lift, and changes in facial expression like a raised eyebrow, provide the listener with essential cues for both musical structure and the performer's expressive intent.[38] The strictly aural media of radio and gramophone, in excluding this crucial visual information, would seem burdened with a severe artistic limitation. The situation with these media was complex, however. Certain vocalists were said to appeal to audiences more successfully through electric mediation than personal appearance. In their 1929 book *Le phonographe*, André Coeury and G. Clarence cite numerous anglophone jazz artists who had become popular in France solely through imported recordings. From Sophie Tucker to the Revelers, Paul Robeson, and Ethel Waters, the new "stars of the phonograph" offered an appeal that rested on their voices alone.[39] When these stars tour Europe, Coeury and Clarence advise, they ought to devise their performances in accord with audience expectations raised by the recordings—by, for example, eliminating from their act broad comedy at odds with the sentimentality of their hit ballads.

The performer's visual absence could even count as a plus, with the electric-sound simulation improving on the artist in the flesh, as in radio-saturated North America, where vocalists lacking charisma in person achieved singing stardom anyway. Exemplifying the new celebrityhood was Rudy Vallee, an obscure performer who quickly became famous through his presence on broadcast radio. With this star, "the voice is all that matters!" the advertisement declared.[40] It was enough to hear Vallee sing to imagine what he looked like. In fact, some critics warned, it was best that fans *not* see him on the grounds that Vallee, bland and diffident in public appearances, would fail to come across as the magnetic "blond giant" of the publicity. As a reporter observed in 1929, Vallee's "stature with women listeners who have not seen him in person is not short of remarkable."[41]

The paradox of an electric-sound simulation strong enough in its affective force to supersede the performer in the flesh was a period phenomenon, extending beyond North America and encompassing performers whose stage charisma exceeded Vallee's. A singer's stage appearances were now judged in light of the films. In a 1930 report on a stage performance by Maurice Chevalier in London, a journalist confessed, "I got considerably less kick out of seeing him on the boards than I did out of his most recent screen performance in *The Big Pond*" (dir. Hobart Henley, 1930). The singer incarnate, oddly enough, came across as less "real" than the filmic simulation. "I found myself watching, over a sea of heads, this real Chevalier singing the songs I heard from the screen. But to me he was much less real than he had been on the screen: a mere marionette figure in the place of the great sunny-faced comedian who has made himself my screen favorite."[42] Chevalier's success as a film star might even undermine his stage career insofar as fans bring to the stage performances film-derived expectations: "All the ladies will love to meet the Maurice of their dreams. I can only hope that they will come away feeling that flesh and blood has rewarded them."[43]

The power of a recording to substitute for the artist in person is essential to the climactic scene in *Say It with Songs* (dir. Lloyd Bacon, 1929), where Jolson plays Joe Lane, an absent, ex-convict father, whose healing powers over his injured son become manifest when Kitty, the boy's mother, plays Joe's hit recording of "Little Pal," the film's theme song. After Kitty starts up the family disc player (see figs. 5.1 and 5.2), Jolson's image, via a series of cinematographic dissolves, materializes above the boy's bed (see fig. 3.1)

In this song performance, the ordinary causality is reversed: instead of the body producing the voice, the voice, assisted by electric-sound technology, conjures the body. The impact of the instant when Jolson materializes rests on a judicious use of the song synchronization techniques surveyed in chapter 1. For one, Jolson first materializes at a key moment in the song's development, at the change from verse to chorus. Moreover, in the manner of the "downbeat cut" in musical example 1.1, the fade-in for the dissolve begins, it seems, on the fourth quarter note in the final measure of the verse, and it ends on the chorus's first downbeat. The rhythm adds to

Figure 3.1. A frame from the "Little Pal" performance (screen capture, *Say It with Songs*, 1929)

the moment's sense of inevitability. As noted in chapter 1, the shot's composition, in which Jolson appears on the right, looking down on the ailing child in the lower left, conforms to other images of the star, both in *The Singing Fool* and in the relevant film-song publicity. At one point, Davey Lee—the same child actor who plays the boy in *The Singing Fool*—reaches up to Jolson in a manner that replicates the composition of the photo used for the "Sonny Boy" sheet-music cover (see fig. 1.8). For the moviegoer who contemplates purchasing one of the recordings of "Little Pal," a hit song in 1929, the familiar iconography offers a tacit promise: the recording alone is enough to bring the artist to life.[44] Moreover, just as Vallee, Chevalier, and other singers may seem more compelling in movies than in person, the virtual Jolson has occult powers unavailable to ordinary mortals: immediately after the song ends and the saintly apparitions vanishes, the boy, miraculously, is cured of his injury.

Mistaken Identities

The "Little Pal" scene from *Say It with Songs* is typical of the ingenuity with which the uncanny aspects of the period's trends in musical performance were explored in sound cinema, with its many possibilities for voice-image disconnection. Rife with what Michel Chion calls "acousmatic voices," whose reproduction occurs without the visual depiction of the speaker-singer, conversion-era films often feature characters whose true identities are masked by false voices.[45] Think of the many crime films where villains escape detection through voice substitution, such as *Murder!* (dir. Alfred Hitchcock, 1930), *Studio Murder Mystery* (dir. Lowell Sherman, 1931), *The Canary Murder Case* (dir. Malcolm St. Clair and Frank Tuttle, 1931), *The Testament of Dr. Mabuse* (dir. Fritz Lang, 1932), and *The Phantom Broadcast* (dir. Phil Rosen, 1933).

Mistaken identities enabled by the electric-sound media come up often in the musical films' comedy-of-errors plots. In *Vagabond Lover* (dir. Marshall Nielan, 1929), singer Rudy Bronson (Rudy Vallee) can impersonate bandleader Ted Grant (Malcom Waite) because the latter became famous mainly through radio. In *Ein Lied geht um die Welt* (dir. Richard Oswald, 1933), Ricardo (Josef Schmidt), an opera singer known through his voice alone, is unable to win over record-store clerk Nina (Charlotte Andres); while his rich tenor voice attracts her, his "ugly" (*hässlich*) appearance supposedly repels her.[46] In *Das Lied einer Nacht* (dir. Anatole Litvak, 1932), con man Koretsky (Fritz Schulz) can substitute for star tenor Enrico Ferrara (Jan Kiepura) because Ferrara's music is known mainly through radio and recorded disc.

Such substitutions illustrate what became known in the late nineteenth century as "the ventriloquism effect," which results when a spoken voice combined with the sight of a puppet's mouth leads the beholder to attribute the voice's origin to the puppet.[47] Scenes that turn on the difficulty of distinguishing the actor who appears in the image from the voice's actual source are abundant in European films.[48] In *Das Lied einer Nacht*, Koretzky serenades Mathilde (Magda Schneider) in a moonlit garden, his voice "dubbed" by Enrico, who hides in the shrubbery. Later in the same film, Mathilde, who listens in the adjacent room, is misled by Enrico's imitation of a recording of his own voice, down to a skipping needle. In *I Sing for You Alone* (dir. Mario Bonnard, 1933), a film made in Rome also in French and Italian versions, Marcello, an accomplished but shy singer played by tenor Tito Schipa, surreptitiously provides the voice for a handsome but talentless imposter. In *Der Herr auf Bestellung* (dir. Géza von Bolváry, 1930), trickster Willy Forst, concealed from the story-world audience, dubs the stage-frightened Paul Hörbiger in scene after scene. Revelation of the truth often comes through technical breakdown, as in *Moritz macht sein Glück* (dir. Jaap Speyer, 1930), when Siegfried Arno, in blackface, mimics Al Jolson with astonishing accuracy until the skipping needle gives away the trick; in *Monkey Business* (dir. Norman McLeod, 1931), when Harpo performs Chevalier's "You Brought a New Kind of Love to Me" with the assist of a portable disc player and the gag ends with the machine's malfunction; and in *Je t'adore, mais pourquoi* (dir. Pierre Columbier, 1930), a film made also in English, Spanish, and Italian versions, when the gigolo entertains the errant society lady with what turns out to be a mechanical piano and the ruse is exposed when the man's gestures fail to match up with the music.

The film's viewer is often the first to fall prey to the ventriloquism effect, as in the numerous conversion-era films that begin with a gag in which moving lips divert attention from a sound's true source. In the theatrical agency in *Viktor und Viktoria*, for example, an offscreen soprano voice is heard while the camera tracks down the hallway, revealing actors waiting for their auditions. When the camera at last stops to frame a woman with an open mouth, she, we discover, is only yawning. The same gag surfaces in *Das Lied einer Nacht*, where the operatic voice of Enrico Ferrara (Jan Kiepura) accompanies the extreme close-up of an open mouth before a camera pulls back to reveal a dentist drilling into a patient and the true source of Enrico's voice: a radio set located in the dentist's office. In *Die verliebte Firma* (dir. Max Ophuls, 1932) a singing voice continues to be heard even though the apparent singer has stopped, which motivates the cut to the extrawide shot that unveils the actual vocalist: the film's heroine, her voice echoing from a nearby mountaintop. Such visual gags self-consciously invoke the sound cinema's technical conditions.

Anempathetic Voices

The potential in sound cinema for a singer's voice to float free from her or his body opened possibilities for thematic development through a variant of what Michel Chion calls "anempathetic sound," which occurs when an inexorable song suggests the presence of impersonal forces indifferent to the hero's plight.[49] In conversion-era films, electric-sound mediation often adds to the anempathetic impact, as in *Gloria* (dir. Hans Behrendt, 1931), where Maria (Brigitte Helm) and her young son learn through an emergency radio bulletin that her aviator husband (Gustav Frölich) is attempting a dangerous transatlantic flight. When the broadcast returns to a program of recorded music (*Schallplattenkonzert*), the distraught Maria, at the sound of the singer's voice, covers her ears.

Figure 3.2. A frame from the "Je n'ai qu'un amour, c'est toi" sequence (screen capture, *Prix de beauté*, 1930)

Technology-enabled anempathy reaches its zenith in the final scene of *Prix de beauté* (dir. Augusto Genina, 1930) when, in the screening room of International Sound Films, beauty-contest winner Lucienne, played by Louise Brooks, witnesses her own on-screen appearance in a short promoting her new song, "Je n'ai qu'un amour, c'est toi." The subsequent event of Lucienne's murder by the jealous boyfriend (Georges Charlia) ends with one of the most iconic motion picture images of the period, the famous composition in which Brooks appears twice: in the foreground as murder victim and in the background, in the projected screen image of the film-within-the-film, as singing star (see fig. 3.2).

The striking moment when "the picture on the screen continues talking, and those still in the room go on hearing the voice of the one who has just died," was singled out at the time as an "entirely new" effect, distinctive to sound film.[50] What seemed new was perhaps the interpretive potential opened by the juxtaposition of the recorded singing voice with the image of the murdered singer. The song had already played in the film's first scene, but in the murder scene, as film historian Kelley Conway explains, it yields new meanings.[51] The "you" (*toi*) of the title "I have only one love, it's you" (*Je n'ai qu'un amour, c'est toi*) no longer refers only to the boyfriend, last seen stalking the studio hallway, but also designates the broad media-consuming public to whom Lucienne offers herself via her new career in musical films. Moreover, the voice is not Brooks's but another performer's, a voice double, thus splitting the identity of the "I" of the song's title between Brooks, Lucienne, and the vocalist, reputed to be Hélène Regelly, a star singer herself.[52]

An intriguing aspect of the scene is how the thematic complexity seems to coalesce at the cut to the composition reproduced in figure 3.2. The composition features in a shot that lasts only six seconds. What makes it capture the viewer's attention? What makes it so memorable? The striking graphic design provides only part of the answer. Also essential is the skillful editing. The cut intervenes at a key moment in the song's form, just as the refrain is about to repeat, at the beginning of the seven-note phrase "ne sois pas ja - loux, tais-toi," the whole of which is covered by the shot. As in the earlier examples from *Say It with Songs* and *The Broadway Melody*, the cut slightly anticipates the phrase, so that what falls on the downbeat is not the cut itself but the image of Brooks singing the first word. Also, the phrase is perhaps the most familiar in the song. After playing at the opening, it repeats twice during the verse, so that by the time the shot in figure 3.2 arrives, the melody has been heard three times already. The shot's appearance thus entails a complex temporality. On the one hand, the arresting composition counts as a new event; on the other, the coincident music suggests that something familiar is starting up again.

Connecting the Actor's Voice to the Body On-Screen

Filmic references to the technology-enabled separation of voices from bodies allude to a major technical concern in the film community at the time, which was to ensure that viewers attribute the actors' voices to characters in the film's story world rather than to their immediate source, the loudspeakers in the movie theater.[53] Debates during the period regarding the proper location for speakers centered on two incompatible solutions to the problem. The choice came down to the sort of sound emitted, with the essential distinction drawn between nondiegetic music, on the one hand, and dialogue and source music, on the other. For nondiegetic music, the best loudspeaker position was below and in front of the screen, the place closest to the pit, the musicians' customary location. Described by Ufa's head of production Hugo Correll as "ghost music [*Geistesmusik*]," or "underlying mood music that one knows not where it comes from," this sort of sound did not require localization in the world on-screen.[54] But for reproducing speech and source music, locating the speakers below the screen was problematic because it created a sound source separate from where the actors appeared. If the voices seem to come from the pit rather than from the lips moving on the screen, then the audience's attention might turn away from the film's story and toward its technological support, the theater's sound system. As stated succinctly in *Variety*, "For talking pictures . . . horns any place other than near the screen tend to destroy the dialogue illusion."[55]

In Hollywood, where the "dialogue illusion" was paramount, the consensus by 1930 was that the speakers ought to be installed behind the screen. A related development was a new policy for visual representation, which held that the sources for a scene's sounds, including all musical sounds, ought to be represented on-screen. Voices, the axiom went, should be accompanied by the image of the actors' moving lips, and musical performances ought to refer to a source visible in the film's story world—whether a singing actor, jazz ensemble, spinning gramophone disc, public-address loudspeaker, or radio set. Composer Max Steiner reported that at the RKO studio beginning in 1929 and continuing for the next few years, pit music in the accepted silent-era sense was no longer allowed: the producers had "decided that you could not have background music unless you showed the source. In other words, you had to have an orchestra on view, or a phonograph or performance, so that people would not wonder where the music was coming from."[56]

Such an approach is indeed evident in RKO films from the time. In *Mexicali Rose* (dir. Erle Kenton, 1929), the instrumental music for a three-minute dialogue scene between Rose (Barbara Stanwyck) and Bob (Sam Hardy) is attributed to a disc player started up by the bartender. More labored is the moment later in the same film when a band of street musicians is shown waiting outside the hacienda to play a love song for the couple. Inside, the offscreen music—performed by an ordinary orchestra rather than the street band—prompts the following dialogue exchange: "Who's that?" "Just some street musicians." MGM was another studio in which deliberate efforts were taken to assign a diegetic source to a song that, in fact, functions as pit music. In *Chasing Rainbows* (dir. Charles Reisner, 1930), in the early scene in Bessie Love's apartment, Charles King's heartfelt apology is supported by the ballad issuing from the gramophone player he has started up.

Such practices endured for several years. In *Roman Scandals* (dir. Frank Tuttle, 1933), Busby Berkeley's fantastic "Build a Little Home" production number begins when Eddie Cantor drops the needle on a spinning gramophone disc.[57]

The Challenge of Close-Ups

The task of visualizing the music's source encountered special obstacles when it involved singing, whose physical and psychological demands were known to interfere with the singer's ability to act.[58] The challenges of sound filmmaking went beyond what singers faced on the stage. Singers in films typically had to perform in close-up, where fluctuations in facial muscles were magnified far beyond what was visible for a stage performance. Also disconcerting were the film-production methods of the early 1930s, when the music, vocals, and visuals for song performances were ordinarily recorded concurrently. Singers had to perform in the presence of not only a microphone but also other actors, a film crew, and an orchestra. Jeanette MacDonald's biographer claims that the transition to movie roles made the young star "worried about looking ugly while singing on-screen," which led her in the summer of 1929 to spend "long nights rehearsing her numbers for *The Love Parade* [dir. Ernst Lubitsch, 1929] within eyeshot of oddly positioned mirrors specially installed throughout her Beverly Wilshire suite."[59] Albert Préjean, the star of *Sous les toits de Paris* (dir. René Clair, 1930), *L'opéra de quat' sous* (dir. G. W. Pabst, 1931), and other musical films of the period, flagged close-ups as a special source of anxiety: "One can't imagine how difficult it is to sing before the camera. Onstage the space between the audience and the performer erases the actor's tics and grimaces. The public is distant. But here, in a film studio as silent as a church, one must vocalise while posing. When the results are projected onto the screen, it becomes evident that one has twisted one's mouth and become as ugly as an opera tenor. For a close-up, the result is a disaster."[60]

To ease the difficulty of shooting song sequences, close-ups were often produced separately from the scene's other shots and from the vocal recording. One procedure was to record the music, vocals included, on the set with the singer and dancers in long shot and then shoot close-ups of the singer separately. The vocalist (or vocalists) and orchestra would perform again for the close-ups, but only the music recorded for the long shot would be used for the finished scene. Such a process is summarized in a report on the making of MGM's *The Hollywood Revue of 1929* (dir. Charles Reisner,

1929): "Whole scenes then were photographed, and then the close-ups were made by moving the camera nearer while the selected player or players repeated the action required. Their voices already had been recorded."[61] Similar measures were taken for dubbed films, where close-ups were likewise set aside for special treatment.[62] Given the production challenges facing singers, producers of musical films were known to avoid close-ups altogether.[63]

The Postsynchronized Voice in American Films

A crucial development in the handling of close-ups with vocals was the technique of playback, which falls under the heading of what sound engineer J. P. Maxfield called "pre-scoring," an approach "where the sound record is made first, and the scene photographed synchronously with the playing of the record."[64] The numbers featuring the Paul Whiteman band in *King of Jazz* (dir. John Murray Anderson, 1930) provide an example. "The music," explained a journalist, "is recorded in advance, and the performers go through the motions only while the camera is being ground. The music is played back while they enact this silent drama, thus enabling the securing of proper synchronization."[65] This method, director John Murray Anderson explained, allowed for technical improvements in the music and made it easier to plan the visuals.[66] Whiteman's music, however, is primarily instrumental and thus did not require lip synchronization. The same is true of the "Wedding of the Painted Dolls" sequence in *The Broadway Melody* (dir. H. Beaumont, 1929), often cited as an example of playback since the music features vocalist James Burrows and was prerecorded and then played back on the set when the dancers were filmed; but Burrows himself never appears on-screen, thus obviating the need for lip synchronization.[67]

Playback's most powerful effects concerned voices, as became evident after 1931, when multitrack technologies and methods were introduced in the studios and the production companies adopted dubbing as the main means of preparing films for foreign distribution. Playback, in short, was integral to a system-wide change in Hollywood filmmaking informed by a counterintuitive principle: the separation of sound production from image production. Demonstrating playback's improvement in lip synchronization is the opening scene of *Love Me Tonight* (dir. Rouben Mamoulian, 1932), where Maurice Chevalier performs Rodgers and Hart's "That's the Song of Paree." The shots of Chevalier singing in his apartment appear to have been recorded direct, with an offscreen orchestra providing the accompaniment. But the subsequent shot of him running out into the street, where he continues to sing while hailing his neighbors ("Mrs. Bendix, how is your appendix?"), was recorded via playback. Playback shots blend seamlessly with those recorded direct, making the difference in production method effectively undetectable. (I had to watch the exterior shot four times before spotting the telltale moment at the end when Chevalier's lips fail to move despite his voice being heard.)

The aesthetic result of playback, Altman argues, went beyond the "obvious function of providing a cleaner, more technically perfect recording" to generate powerful and novel effects.[68] The key point is that playback "disguises breathing and other signs of effort, and in general creates an eerie, far-off effect, an injection of the ideal world into the real," enabling what Altman refers to as "the notorious American penchant for singers who sing effortlessly." Such performers "look like movie singers, who, having left their physical efforts in the recording room, can act out the spiritual side of singing for the camera, and never let on that producing the sound cost them any effort."[69] In the scene from *Love Me Tonight*, for example, the impression of physical transcendence enabled by playback amplifies Chevalier's comic persona as carefree, charming, and personable.

A Controversial Technique

Playback's status today as a run-of-the-mill practice makes it easy to forget how controversial it and other voice-replacement techniques were circa 1930 when MGM, Paramount, and other studios began standardizing them. More than an ordinary, ethically neutral production technique, the act of grafting one actor's voice onto another's body provoked accusations of impropriety and dishonesty, as is suggested in the use of terms like *faking* and *duping* to describe it.[70] The revelation that the performances of certain stars had been created via voice transfer, though the advertising had indicated otherwise, provoked outrage from fans.[71] An example concerned the sheet music and publicity for *Weary River* (dir. Frank Lloyd, 1929), which refers to the theme song "as sung by Richard Barthelmess" when, in fact, a playback artist had provided the voice.[72] Voice-substitution disclosures in *Photoplay* and other fan magazines were said to alienate audiences from sound movies.[73] Joan Crawford was among the Hollywood stars who tried to ward off dubbing-related controversy by stating publicly that they insisted on doing their own singing in their films.[74] The same concerns surfaced in England apropos of Anny Ondra's voice in Hitchcock's *Blackmail* (1929), which, it turned out, had been supplied, uncredited, by another actor. Responding to critics, a representative of British International Pictures protested, "Hollywood used to double hands, legs, and even whole bodies, and never gave screen credit to doubles. Why the squawking on voices?"[75] Voices, in fact, *were* different somehow. To replace an actor's voice seemed morally offensive.

The controversy reached a fever pitch regarding the dubbing of films for foreign release. No one in 1930 spoke in defense of dubbed films, my examination of the film trade press suggests. In fact, denunciations were the norm. "The talking picture in the foreign market has quite enough to contend with apart from the entirely intense feeling which may easily be worked up against the practice of dubbing," stated the publisher of *Exhibitors Herald World* in the summer of 1930.[76] The dubbing of foreign voices, claimed a critic in January 1930, was a "failed expedient for getting around the American difficulty" of exporting movies to places where languages other than English were spoken.[77] Regarding Germany specifically, it was proposed in *Variety* that "to synchronize American talkers with German dialogue would be a joke."[78]

In the transatlantic film world of 1930, the conviction was widespread that films for foreign-language markets were best produced in that target market's language with actors who were native speakers. The *Motion Picture Herald* summarized the consensus: "Nowadays, if a producer wishes to cater to another big market, he has to produce in that market's language. He has to hire a director, a writer, a cast, a whole national unit of the other market, and he has to invest in a production which he can use there and there only."[79] Dubbing was seen as viable only for markets where there were too few theaters to justify the making of full foreign-language films.[80] In March 1930, Universal announced that its Spanish-language films would not be made in separate versions but instead would be dubbed "solely for the reason that there are not more than fifty theatres in the world wired for sound that use Spanish spoken pictures."[81] At the beginning of 1931, the policy of multiple-version production looked secure at the top American studios. A British journalist reporting from Hollywood stated, "'Dubbing' is becoming more and more a thing of the past."[82]

Change, however, was already underway. In February 1931, MGM canceled contracts for seventy-five actors, scenarists, and directors whose principal jobs involved foreign-version production.[83] The studio was now dubbing its films for foreign release. In the summer of 1931, blocks of dubbed films from MGM and Paramount were released in Europe to a surprisingly favorable reception. Some fourteen dubbed movies were sent to France, a famously difficult market, where they ended up doing far better than expected.[84] Audiences in the French provinces were said to prefer dubbed imported films over subtitled.[85] A country-by-country survey of the European film trade in 1931 conducted by the US Department of Commerce noted the success of dubbed American films in Italy, Belgium, Germany, Romania, Yugoslavia, and other countries.[86] By the end of 1931, Hollywood, by and large, had abandoned the making of multiple versions and instead began relying on dubbing as the main method for preparing films for foreign distribution. In 1932 the Paramount studio complex in Saint-Maurice-Joinville curtailed the making of French-language shorts and features and instead began dubbing films shot in the United States.

How is this change to be explained? A key factor appears to have been pressures related to Hollywood's massive investment in the promotion of stars. Hollywood films were sold through their stars, both at home and abroad. Sound film audiences in Europe, announced a report from the Department of Commerce, wanted "the old-time well-made 'movie' with box-office names."[87] For countries where languages other than English were spoken, Joan Crawford dubbed was better than Crawford entirely replaced, body and voice, by a foreign-language actor with no Hollywood star power.[88] "People don't go to see an American film," reported a critic in France. "They go to see a film featuring this or that star. They go to see Chevalier in *The Big Pond*."[89] The strategy of making additional versions with foreign-speaking actors, explained a journalist, did not allow the studios to "cash in on the established box office power of the former English-speaking silent stars."[90] As a consequence of Hollywood's reliance on export versions starring foreign actors, "well-established star values [were] crumbling overseas."[91] It is no surprise that the studio concerned to improve dubbing technique "to almost uncanny perfection" was MGM, the so-called home of the stars.[92]

Hollywood's use of playback and other postsynchronization methods for song sequences was a US-based development in film technique with crucial aesthetic implications. Such methods were used in European films too, as is further discussed in chapter 6. But they were developed first in Hollywood and used more extensively there. The American film musical, "more than any other type of film," proposes Rick Altman, "has resorted to dubbing, rerecording, looping, post-synchronization, and other [such] techniques."[93]

In injecting "the ideal into the real," voice transfer techniques like playback created a sort of magic unique to a film's musical sequences and thereby helped foster the narrative-and-number syntax that would come to define the American film musical.

Notes

1. E. Schallert, "Jazz King Will Turn Comedian," B23.
2. "Kidding Kissers in Talkies," 1, 63; and A. Boswell, "Trials of the Talkies," 53, 113.
3. See, for example, S. Eyman, *The Speed of Sound*, 229–30, 304–7.
4. J. O'Connell, "Talkers 'Producers' Rattles' Says Pioneer," 117.
5. H. Franklin, "Talking Pictures—the Great Internationalist," 18. Comments on the realism of sound film acting also appear in R. Fonjallez, "Défense du cinéma muet"; G. Stuart, "Le retour au bon sens"; and E. Roux-Parassac, "En écoutant le parlant," 223.
6. On audience response to the Vitaphone shorts, see D. Crafton, *The Talkies*, 120–21.
7. The quotation appears in an unidentified clipping included in a dossier of French newspaper reviews from 1929 of *The Jazz Singer* in the Rondel Collection at the Bibliothèque nationale in Paris.
8. R. Clair, "The Art of Sound," in E. Weis and J. Belton, *Film Sound*, 92.
9. S. Connor, *Dumbstruck*, 38. Quoted in J. Smith, *Vocal Tracks*, 84.
10. J. Smith, *Vocal Tracks*, 82.
11. The analogy with the close-up crops up in remarks from French producer J. Haïk in "M. Jacques Haïk nous donne son opinion sur l'avenir du film parlant français," 13. See also J. Smith, *Vocal Tracks*, 84.
12. D. Crafton, *The Talkies*, 34–35.
13. On links between changes in vocal technique in American theater in the 1920s and the "rise of modern sound media," see J. Smith, *Vocal Tracks*, 89–96.
14. J. Naremore, *Acting in the Cinema*, 48.
15. "Changes Forced by Sound," 60.
16. A. Bakshy, "The Shrinking of Personality," 590.
17. M., "Quelques minutes avec Jean Renoir. "
18. M. Haskell, *From Reverence to Rape*, 139.
19. W. Greene, "Old Reliables Wobble," 18.
20. On the importance of star vocalists to the history of song marketing, see K. Spring, *Saying It with Songs*, 24–29.
21. E. J., "Musik zu 'Zwei Herzen im Dreivierteltakt,'" 2.
22. The exact length of the shot in *Der schwarze Husar* is 165 seconds, in *Animal Crackers* it is 188 seconds, and in *Arm wie ein Kirchenmaus* it is 223 seconds.
23. M. Hall, "Mr. Jolson in Black-Face," 17.
24. See, for example, M. Katz, *Capturing Sound*; and R. Philip, *Performing Music in the Age of Recording*.
25. D. Leech-Wilkinson, "Recordings and Histories of Performance Style," in N. Cook et al., *Cambridge Companion to Recorded Music*, 258. See also the remarks from Michael Jarrett and Simon Frith quoted in J. Smith, *Vocal Tracks*, 93–94.
26. T. Day, *A Century of Recorded Music*, 158.

27. G. Giddins, *Bing Crosby*, 117–18.
28. See the discussion of the critical reception of the crooners in A. McCracken, *Real Men Don't Sing*, 208–63.
29. "Coast Music Survey," August 14, 1929, 70.
30. K. London, *Film Music*, 180.
31. On changes in ballad style in the 1920s, see K. Spring, *Saying It with Songs*, 30–31.
32. P. Furia and L. Patterson, *The Songs of Hollywood*, 64.
33. P. Furia and L. Patterson, *The Songs of Hollywood*, 8.
34. C. Stone, "Listener's Corner," 90.
35. T. Adorno, "The Curves of the Needle," 607.
36. C. MacKenzie, "You Are Making Robots out of Your Actors," 303.
37. O. Palmer, "Requirements of the Radio Singer," in T. Taylor, M. Katz, and T. Grajeda, *Music, Sound, and Technology in America*, 335.
38. J. Davidson, "Communicating with the Body in Performance," and J. Davidson, "Bodily Movement and Facial Actions in Expressive Musical Performance by Solo and Duo Instrumentalists: Two Distinctive Case Studies."
39. A. Coeury and G. Clarence, *Le phonographe*, 57–63.
40. The advertisement appears in *Variety* 94, no. 7 (March 27, 1929), 12.
41. "Radio's Many Money Names," 69. See also the appraisal of Vallee in "'The Vagabond Lover,'" 519.
42. Observer, "'Maurice' Becomes—a Marionette!," 25.
43. In addition to Observer, "'Maurice' Becomes—a Marionette!," see the remark on the superiority of Chevalier's film roles over his stage presence in G. Bauër, "Maintenant que le cinéma a parlé."
44. The "Little Pal" discs on Victor and Brunswick ranked among the top sellers in August, as did the sheet music editions. See "Coast Musical Survey," 58. Edwin Bradley claims that "Little Pal" topped the national sales lists for over a month that summer, in E. Bradley, *The First Hollywood Musicals*, 52.
45. M. Chion, *The Voice in Cinema*, 126–31.
46. I say *supposedly* because the Charlotte Anders character's rejection of Schmidt may refer to Schmidt's Jewishness, which had factored into his film roles. Schmidt (1904–42), the son of a cantor, fled the Nazis in 1938 and eventually died in an internment camp. See S. Prawer, *Between Two Worlds*, 189–90; and Rabbi G. Shisler, "Joseph Schmidt," Music and the Holocaust, accessed March 28, 2017, http://holocaustmusic.ort.org/places/camps/josef-schmidt/.
47. On the "ventriloquism effect," see C. O'Callahan, *Sounds*, 172.
48. For further instances of voice-body separation in German films of the early 1930s, see T. Elsaesser, "Going 'Live.'"
49. M. Chion, *Audio-Vision*, 8–9.
50. C. Stenhouse, "A British Eye on Paris," 511. The novelty of this same scene is noted also in A.-P. Richard, "Le film sonore entre le théâtre et le cinéma," iii.
51. K. Conway, *Chanteuse in the City*, 167–73.
52. T. Dwyer, "Mute, Dumb, Dubbed: Lulu's Silent Talkies," 180–83.
53. R. Altman, "Moving Lips," 67–79.
54. The quotation from Correll comes from a 1933 memo cited in R. Rother, "Zwischen Parodie und poetischem Wachtraum," 275.
55. "Chicago's Canned Applause Making 'Em Warm Up," 1. See also J. L. Dixon, "How the 'Talkies' Work," 18.

56. M. Steiner, "Scoring the Film," 76.
57. On explicit references in conversion-era films to the music's source, see K. Spring, *Saying It with Songs*, 98–117. Criticism of the practice surfaces in D. Mendoza, "Problems of Recording Music," 11, 30–31.
58. J. Maxfield, "Technic of Recording Control for Sound Pictures," 422; and T. Cohen, *Playing to the Camera*, 13.
59. E. Turk, *Hollywood Diva*, 78.
60. The quotation from Albert Préjean comes from George Stuart, "Dans une vieille rue de Paris . . . à Epinay."
61. "'The Hollywood Revue,'" X4.
62. On the separate treatment of close-ups at MGM, see "Europe Off Dubbing," 7.
63. See, for example, C. Wahl, *Multiple Language Versions Made in Babelsberg*, 43, 283n.
64. J. Maxfield, "Technic of Recording Control for Sound Pictures," 421–22.
65. E. Schallert, "Ghosting Songs Now Favored," B13.
66. H. Lang, "He Didn't Know How!" 75, 132.
67. In, for example, P. Furia and L. Patterson, *Hollywood Film Songs*, 35; and K. Lewis, "'Broadway' Playback."
68. R. Altman, *The American Film Musical*, 64.
69. R. Altman, *The American Film Musical*, 151.
70. N. Ďurovičová, "Local Ghosts: Dubbing Bodies in Early Sound Cinema," 86–87.
71. See, for example, M. Larkin, "The Truth about Voice Doubling," 32–33, 108–10.
72. M. Babcock, "Song Doubling Now in Discard," B13. The phrase "as sung by Richard Barthelmess" appears on the cover of the *Weary River* folio published by J. Albert and Son.
73. "Exposure of Talker-Making by Film Fan Mags," 17.
74. Also notable is Lon Chaney's insistence, conveyed by notarized deposition, that he had performed all the voices for the five characters he played in *The Unholy Three* (dir. Jack Conway, 1930), as noted in R. Spadoni, *Uncanny Bodies*, 38.
75. "Ghosting and Doubling in Talker Publicity," 2. See also the remarks on the *Blackmail* controversy in H. Matthews, "London Film Notes," X4.
76. M. Quigley, "Dubbing," 16. See also "Plan of Dubbing Foreign Lines in English Versions Being Discouraged," 41; C. Belfrage, "Hollywood's Multi-Lingual Quandary," 20; and C. North and N. Golden, "Sound Film Competition Abroad," 757.
77. J. D. Williams, "Overhaul the Quota!" 38.
78. "Germans See the End of U. S. Film over There," 5.
79. H. Fraenkel, "Can Industry Stay International?" 58, 64.
80. See, for instance, "M-G Off Dubbing," 4.
81. "Universal Takes Lead in Foreign Version Films," 26.
82. C. Belfrage, "Hollywood's Multi-Lingual Quandary," 20.
83. "Hollywood stoppt die Versionen," 1.
84. The figure of fourteen dubbed films is derived from "The Motion Picture Industry in Continental Europe in 1931," 34. On dubbed films in France, see R. Lehmann, "A propos de 'dubbing,'" 2; L. M., "Il faut mettre au point la question du 'dubbing,'" 2; and J. Morienval, "Le doublage, ses nécessités et ses limites," 158.
85. See the report on the findings of a poll of French film viewers taken by a "large regional daily" in "In Frankreich: Große Tätigkeit im Dubbing," 5.
86. "The Motion Picture Industry in Continental Europe in 1931," 14, 37, 47, 73.
87. "The Motion Picture Industry in Continental Europe in 1931," 11.

88. The Joan Crawford example comes from P. Harlé, "La margarine peut-elle remplacer le beurre?," 11.
89. G. Bauër, "Maintenant que le cinéma a parlé," 1.
90. "Dubbing Tough Routine but Cheaper," 6.
91. G. Kann, "Foreign Troubles Mean Domestic Troubles, Too," 52.
92. "Dubbing's Comeback on Coast," 4.
93. R. Altman, *The American Film Musical*, 64.

4

FILM EDITING AFTER ELECTRIC SOUND

CHANGES IN THE CRAFT OF FILM EDITING SIGNALED how deeply electric sound transformed film technique. Synch-sound shots failed to join together in familiar ways, and editing practices prominent in silent cinema immediately became rare in sound films. As talkies began proliferating, the range of editing techniques narrowed radically, as if the inclusion of spoken dialogue allowed for only one way of cutting a film. Editing-related limitations proved devastating for modernist and avant-garde filmmakers, whose "culture of montage," warned Sergei Eisenstein in 1928, had come under threat.[1] For commercial producers, editing a sound movie was "one of the most difficult problems ... to solve," declared the general manager of Warner Brothers' studio in 1930.[2] Indicating the difficulty was the steep increase in shot duration, with shots in sound films running twice as long, on average, as those in silent films. At the limit were the singing performances, whose unique technical and aesthetic challenges manifested in the extreme length of the typical singing shot as well as in the music-determined editing evident during virtually any song-accompanied passage in a film.

It is thus worth revisiting considerations regarding the editing of song sequences (first taken up in chap. 1) in the wider context of trends in editing generally, which includes techniques relevant not only to song performances but to other scenes, especially dialogue scenes. The peculiarities of sound-era distribution had certain effects on editing—for example, it required completion of a film, the editing included, prior to its release. Additionally, editing trends affected film music. The amount of screen time devoted to musical accompaniment brings to the fore two differences from silent cinema: the radical reduction in the amount of music overall and the near-total replacement of the nondiegetic orchestral music customary in silent cinema with source music and with songs especially. Sound-era changes in editing technique are illustrated through an analysis of the cycle of musical comedies produced at Paramount featuring the Marx Brothers, with a focus on the artistic possibilities opened by Hollywood's adoption in 1931 of multitrack recording and mixing. These new technologies allowed the American musical film to develop in a somewhat unique direction by furthering Hollywood's tendency to distinguish song performances from other scenes and, beginning in 1930–31, to use songs mainly in comedic rather than melodramatic contexts.

Editing after Sound

Sound-era distribution had imposed on filmmakers technical and financial obstacles unimaginable during the preceding decades, when films were prepared for release quickly, at a low cost, and by various agents other than the films' producers. Shots deemed problematic, whole scenes even, were removed altogether and replaced with intertitles. Titles were rewritten, scenes deleted, the scene order shuffled, and a film's story thereby revised.[3] Adding new intertitles into a feature film cost as little as several thousand dollars, thus allowing a film's language to be replaced swiftly and cheaply. "With the silent film," reported economist Howard Lewis, "it was comparatively inexpensive to retitle a picture in any language; it probably required $2,500 to cover the average cost of such adaptation. But it has cost somewhere between $30,000 and $50,000 to make a foreign version since sound pictures made their appearance."[4] The process of foreign-market distribution required expensive new translation procedures, announced the *Motion Picture Herald* in January 1931: "Gone are the times when [the producer] just had to have some other titles put in to exploit the same negative in a dozen different countries."[5]

Adding to the challenge was the need to consider in advance solutions to the problems of sound-era distribution. Rather than finish a film and then decide how to distribute it, one had to settle on plans for distribution at the outset, prior to shooting. If a film required an extra full-length version with a foreign-language cast, for example, then considerable planning had to occur. With sound movies, proposed playwright Bertolt Brecht in his commentary on the film adaptation of *Die Dreigroschenoper* (dir. G. W. Pabst, 1931), a German film made also in a French version, it was "no longer a matter of how a particular artwork . . . can be made marketable, but rather of the way in which an artwork must be constructed from the commercial perspective."[6]

Preparing sound films for export required exceptional technical expertise. With silent films, language replacement and story revision were undertaken not only by producers but also by distributors, censors, and even exhibitors, who routinely altered films after distribution had already begun. Virtually anyone with scissors and glue could delete a scene. Editing a sound film, however, was a complex task, beyond the technical and financial wherewithal of anyone but trained specialists, who completed the editing in advance of the film's release. The same was true also of other postproduction tasks, such as lab work. Whereas silent films were sent out as negatives and the release prints struck only after the film had arrived at the distribution site, sound films were routinely sent out as positive prints only.[7] "The original negative never reaches this country," observed a technician in Britain regarding the American talkies of 1930.[8]

The difficulty and expense of altering sound movies once distribution was underway raised new dangers regarding censorship. With sound films, film historian Ruth Vasey explains, it became "economically imperative to ensure that anything likely to lead to censorship action or public protest [be] removed at the point of production."[9] Otherwise, if the censor ordered cuts, and if these were enacted by someone without the necessary skill, then the film might end up damaged as a result. The need to stave off censorship threats that could imperil Hollywood's competitiveness on the emergent world market for sound films motivated the Motion Picture Production Code of 1930, which stipulated that "the history, institutions, prominent people and citizenry of other nations shall be represented fairly."[10] Required to anticipate the censor's demands as never before, sound-era filmmakers, in effect, censored themselves. The inclusion of songs in films was symptomatic of this issue, as songs seem to have been judged by censors as less ideologically contentious than speech (as noted in the introduction).

The Period Trend in Editing

Musical films ordinarily include song sequences along with the same sort of dialogue scenes found in virtually any feature film. To understand how musical films were edited, it is thus necessary to consider sound's impact on editing generally. A starting point is provided in figure 4.1, whose shot length figures for 1927–34 for both silent and sound films yield an overview of the main sound-related trend: a steep increase in shot length, with the

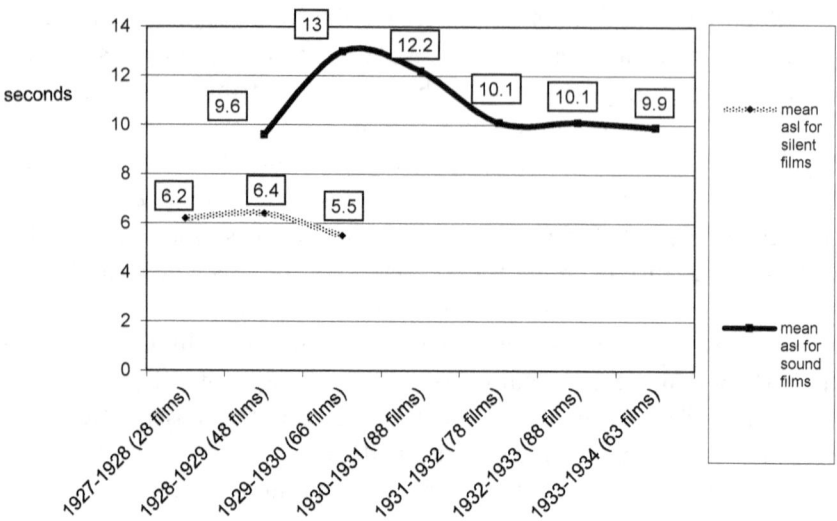

Figure 4.1. Mean ASLs for 73 silent films and 396 sound films of 1927–34, by season

ASL for sound films registering at roughly double that for silent films released in the same year.[11]

Figure 4.1 adds new detail to our understanding of film history by showing the size of the increase and when it began surfacing in films. Standing out is the 1929–30 film season, when the mean ASL for sound films comes in at thirteen seconds—three seconds higher than the season before and more than double the figure for the season's silent productions. The dramatic increase for the sound films provoked a reaction in both Hollywood and Europe, where producers set out to devise ways of reducing shot length. The effects became evident in the 1930–31 season, when, figure 4.1 reveals, the mean ASL for American and European cinema drops almost a full second. The decline, continued into the next four years, when shot lengths—while longer, on average, than in silent films—became progressively shorter, to the point that, at the end of the four years, the figure was around 25 percent less than at the outset. The trend toward brevity lasted through 1937, when, Barry Salt's research suggests, the mean ASL for Hollywood and European films reached bottom and "a new trend towards longer takes was just starting to emerge."[12]

A more fine-grain assessment of sound's effects on editing becomes possible when specific shot categories are examined. Especially relevant are shots involving dialogue, whose excessive length drew notice as a worrisome departure from established practice. With dialogue shots in sound films running much longer, on average, than action shots (see fig. 0.1), the choice between dialogue and action carried implications for a film's editing: a decrease in dialogue, all things being equal, meant a reduction in a film's ASL. Sound-era filmmakers were said to face a choice between speech, on the one hand, and visual action, on the other, with more of one meaning less of the other. This dialectic is indicated in figure 4.1, in the high ASLs for the sound films, which can be ascribed both to long dialogue passages and the small proportion of running time dedicated to action shots, which tend to run much shorter than dialogue shots. For 354 sound films of 1927–34, the mean for the action shots works out to 30.1 percent of a film's running time, whereas for 66 American and European silent films of 1927–30, the mean for the same shot type is 86 percent.[13] In short, the sound films devote, on average, two-thirds less of their running time to action shots. This vast disparity alludes to the reality behind the frequent complaint at the time that sound movies were deficient in visual action. What they had instead was recorded dialogue, and "every line of dialogue put into a picture takes its toll in slackened tempo," stated an exhibitor in 1930.[14]

Further evidence of the impact of spoken dialogue on editing can be found when the ASLs for the dialogue shots in sound films are juxtaposed with those for dialogue intertitles in silent films (not listed in fig. 4.1).[15] Figures drawn from my sample of 66 silent films show a mean ASL of 5.5 seconds for dialogue intertitles, whereas the mean for the dialogue shots in 351 sound films comes out to 14.9 seconds.[16] In sum, the dialogue shots run roughly three times the length of the dialogue intertitles, on average. As reported in the introduction, the mean ASL for action shots in silent films comes to 5.92 seconds, which is higher than the 5.5-second mean ASL for the intertitles. The difference suggests a rule of thumb for filmmakers of the period: whereas the editing pace in a silent film is increased by adding in dialogue, in a sound film it is increased by taking it out.

The aesthetic problem posed by dialogue shots in conversion-era films went beyond their excessive length. Also troubling was the speech-determined rhythm of the cutting, which seemed to inhibit the cinema's potential for visual action. A common pattern for both American and European sound films is that shots begin with the mute actor, who then speaks with her or his moving lips visible, and then, once the actor's line is finished, the cut to the next shot occurs.[17] Refinements discussed below, such as cutting on the last syllable rather than after it, or cutting away from the actor who is speaking to a listener, reduced the shot length. But they did not make the editing less determined by the actors' speech. Hence the complaint that in sound films "the editing [*découpage*] that previously had followed the visual action has become the prisoner of the word."[18]

Hollywood's Reaction

The shot-length increase associated with the talkies provoked a reaction in the American film community in the summer of 1930, when an industry-wide project quickly took form to reduce speech and song and increase the visual action. Carl Laemmle Jr. of Universal Pictures declared in July, "In the future we should develop as much of the drama as possible in pantomime and use dialogue and sound to give emphasis to the highlights of the film rather than make scenes one continuous barrage of talk or music." "It is with this thought in mind," interjected the interviewer, "that all forthcoming pictures from Universal will have an editorial writer to check scripts for superfluous dialogue as a newspaper editor corrects reportorial stories."[19] At Paramount, where, *Variety* reported, "the company has recognized the fault common to talkers—too much dialogue and too little action," the goal was to "increase the action."[20] At Columbia Pictures, too, the company's president announced "a policy of reducing dialogue to a minimum and building up the tempo that made silent pictures so popular."[21] Regarding musical films specifically, director Mervyn LeRoy announced that Warner Brothers would use "a new technique [involving] a faster tempo."[22] In a survey of current scripting practice, a journalist observed that "the tendency is to reduce the dialogue to a minimum while interpreting everything in terms of action as much as possible."[23]

One might assume that this collective effort would reduce the percentage of running time devoted to dialogue shots in American films. My analysis of 171 American films of 1927–34, however, does not show a decline in the amount of dialogue. In fact, it indicates that the running-time percentage for dialogue shots increases during 1929–34, rising from 64 percent in 1929–30 to 69.4 percent in 1933–34.[24] Nonetheless, a trend toward a lower ASL for dialogue shots is evident. After reaching around sixteen seconds in 1929–30, the dialogue-shot ASL then falls progressively for the next four years until hitting around twelve seconds in 1933–34.[25] So, while the running-time percentage for dialogue went up, the shots themselves became shorter.

The reduction in length can be explained by the refinements in dialogue editing that developed during the early 1930s, when, Barry Salt claims, it became common in dialogue scenes to cut earlier, "when the last syllable of the last word from the first speaker is still being spoken." The result is that "the cut usually falls [no longer] in the middle of the pause between the two speakers" but "on the last syllable of a sentence."[26] An additional change was the practice of cutting away to reaction shots and otherwise extending lines of speech over the shot changes, a trend noted by René Clair in his 1929 manifesto, "The Art of Sound": "Already in the films we are shown at present, we often feel that in a conversation it is more interesting to watch the listener's rather than the speaker's face."[27] The practice of inserting reaction shots into dialogue scenes likely increased in 1931, when the Hollywood studios adopted multitrack recording and mixing and began employing dubbing as their main means of preparing films for export.[28] The inclusion of reaction shots facilitated the making of a dubbed version by concealing the speaking actors' moving lips.[29] Reaction shots also served to increase the tempo during dialogue scenes. As Alfred Hitchcock had noted, the "overrunning of one person's image with another person's voice [allowed] the talkies to tell a story faster than a silent film could tell it, and faster than it could be told on stage."[30] Such techniques did not make the cutting less dialogue driven, but they did expand the options for controlling the pace.

Dialogue and the Export Market

The presence or absence of dialogue carried major implications for export distribution since films with abundant speech were costly to translate and, in any case, were believed to travel less well than films with minimal dialogue. The export market, observed a critic, necessitates a properly "cinematic" aesthetic in which the story is presented mainly through visual rather than verbal expression.[31] The imperative to "save the talkies from talk" by boosting the visual action counted as the period's principal trend in film aesthetics, a journalist in London proposed: "No one interested in the progress of picture making can ignore the development of the sound-film in which the dialogue is reduced to a minimum, and in which action once again takes the premier part in the telling of the story."[32] The musical comedies directed by René Clair, whose remarkable global success was attributed to their restricted dialogue, were a limit case.[33] In the world-famous *Sous les toits de Paris*, for instance, dialogue shots comprise a mere

18 percent of the film's running time, a fraction of the contemporaneous norm of 67.5 percent.[34]

Adding to concerns in sound-era Hollywood regarding the export market was the understanding that the opportunities for growth now lay outside the United States, whose film audience in 1930 was judged to have become as big as it could get. Seating in the United States, reported *Variety* in August, had met its "saturation point," so that "no marked increase in business can be expected here."[35] The perception that Hollywood's domestic market had peaked made the export market more important than ever. Unlike the United States, Europe, estimated in 1930 to contain some twenty-five thousand theaters, barely fifteen hundred of which were sound ready, offered great potential for growth.[36] As Europe's theaters began wiring for sound, the continent became the main export market for Hollywood talkies, providing 70 percent of the total foreign revenue for the American film industry in 1931.[37] Sound films that could draw audiences in Europe were considered essential to Hollywood's future.

American Speed

Weighing on Hollywood's ambitions for the world market were concerns regarding film editing. The notion that the popularity of American films rested on specific techniques of editing was established prior to sound's introduction into cinema. In 1926, D. W. Griffith observed that American films used editing technique to immerse the viewer in the flow of the film's story, whereas European films—and German films, specifically—place the viewer at a distance: "When the American school of pacing presents a film, it says to you: 'come and have a great experience!' Whereas the German school says: 'Come and see a great experience.'"[38] The idea that American films were cut in a more stimulating and even visceral fashion than German films carried over into the sound era, when American films were often said to move more quickly than German ones. Chris Wahl, citing German sources, reports that in the early 1930s "German films generally tended to be seen as somewhat drawn out."[39] An exception that proves the rule was Ufa's *Liebeswalzer* (dir. Wilhelm Thiele, 1930), praised by a critic in Berlin for its "American tempo."[40]

A national difference in pacing was noted by critics who compared the English and German versions of films from Ufa. For example, a reporter for

The New York Times who found "the English version of *Bomben auf Monte Carlo* (dir. Hanns Schwarz, 1932) much more skillfully cut" than the German goes on to single out the song sequences by restating Griffith's comparison of American to German style: "The action of the German [version] was often held up unmercifully by dragging musical and scenic sequences from which the director evidently could not bear to part because of their lyric or pictorial beauty. The English film has been mercifully cleared for action, running a half an hour shorter than its Teuton twin."[41] A similar point was made in the *Christian Science Monitor* by a critic who described the German-language edition of *Der Kongreß tanzt* (dir. Erik Charell, 1931) as "uncut to meet the requirements of American speed."[42]

As the European film industries converted to sound, producers in Germany and other European countries hired American editors to improve their success on the export market. A policy of engaging American-trained talent was undertaken at Ufa by Erich Pommer, the head of the company's international production unit. For *Der Blaue Engel*, Pommer hired Josef von Sternberg, an American director, who brought with him various collaborators, including the brothers Carl and Sam Winston, who edited both the English and German versions.[43] Starring Emil Jannings, winner of the inaugural Oscar for best actor, *The Blue Angel* was intended for distribution in the United States.[44] After *The Blue Angel*, Carl Winston continued to work for Pommer, supervising the editing of the English versions of Ufa's operettas, as well as assisting with the scripts, casting, shooting, selection of rushes, and other production tasks.[45] The huge American market, which comprised nearly one-third of the world's motion picture theaters, turned out to be largely inaccessible to European films. Nonetheless, European producers continued trying to make films for it. In 1931 British producer Basil Dean was reported to have hired "three cutters" from the United States "to ensure that the Dean pictures will be edited with the American audience in view."[46]

What Griffith had called "the American school of pacing" was not only favored by American audiences but was also crucial to the worldwide popularity of Hollywood films. One of the challenges that sound posed to Hollywood producers was that of maintaining the rapidity associated with American silent films. During 1928–30, when few theaters outside the United States were sound ready, virtually all Hollywood sound films were released also in silent versions with intertitles. Producers struggled to make these silent versions consonant in quality with the American films of the preceding decade. In this regard editing was crucial, enabling the "velocity of rhythm," as one critic put it, vital to the American cinema's transnational appeal.[47] A May 1929 memo from US trade commissioner George Canty advised American producers to refrain from releasing silent versions of sound movies in Europe on the grounds that such films were paced too slowly for Europeans accustomed to the rapid editing in American silent films.[48] A writer for *Variety* likewise singled out the "slow action" in the silent versions of talkies released in Europe as a cause for concern, warning that "a situation is created that will probably react in favor of European silent films."[49]

Editing-related problems surface as a focus of concern in a fascinating collection of correspondence from the Warner Brothers company.[50] The correspondence pertains to talkies released in Europe in silent versions. Made by replacing the spoken dialogue with foreign-language intertitles, these so-called X versions raised a variety of difficulties regarding editing. Indicative is the following passage in a letter from Anthony DeLeon, a Warner Brothers Foreign Department executive in Los Angeles, to Karl MacDonald, the New York agent responsible for "supplying prints to various foreign exchanges":

> We have been forced to cut in a great many titles into our 'X' versions which are not necessary to carry on the story and have only cut them in to fill up the long, gabby spots which still persist in our American production; and also, quite often, we have important dialogue lines to transcribe into the titles—the footage is so short and we have to carry these titles over three or four lines in different persons' dialogue—thus, not only making bad cuts and jumping people around rooms, but also robbing considerable entertainment value from our 'X' versions for the part of the foreign audience that is following the dialogue.[51]

The standard practice at Warner Brothers for dialogue in silent versions was to show the actor speaking, insert the title, and then return to the shot of the actor's moving lips.[52] We see this in *The Jazz Singer* (dir. Alan Crosland, 1927), for example, in scene after scene. As DeLeon's letter indicates, this practice was difficult to sustain in the X versions. Sometimes there was too much dialogue to fit onto a single title. Furthermore, to accommodate the titles, scenes had to be reedited in ways that involved "jumping people around rooms" and "bad cuts"—that is, continuity errors.

One way to make the pacing in these silent versions comparable to the norm for silent cinema was to interpolate extra shots. An intent to increase the pace by adding in further shots is suggested in a memo pertaining to *The Broadway Melody* (dir. Harry Beaumont, 1929), which includes the following recommendations from George Melford, the MGM director responsible for the film's silent version. Apropos of the first scene in the sisters' hotel room, Melford advised, "CUT in CLOSE-UPS to quicken action with the girls and Uncle Jed and Eddie," and regarding the appearance in the rehearsal scene of Zanfield and his entourage of yes-men, "Cut in several close-ups to quicken action during this episode."[53] A further way to "quicken the action" was to reduce the number of intertitles, as with the foreign version of Warner's *Public Enemy* (dir. William Wellman, 1931), which at one hundred titles had less than half the number of the typical silent version.[54] Such strategies point to the difficulties involved in maintaining an acceptable pace in talkies whose recorded speech has been extracted. Spoken dialogue did not simply substitute for dialogue conveyed via intertitles: it required additional editing choices, which brought with them new complications.

How Did Electric Sound Change Film Music?

Besides dialogue-determined editing, electric sound also brought about a transformation of film music. Indeed, "between 1929 and 1933," film-music scholar James Wierzbicki states, "the nature of film music changed more frequently, and more radically, than at any other time in the art form's history."[55] What did the transformation involve? A crucial element was the proliferation of songs with vocals, which in 1929–30 became, for the first time since the nickelodeon era, the main form of film music. This fundamental development registers in the running-time percentages displayed in figure 4.2.[56]

Drawing on a sample of 122 synch-sound films released over a seven-year period, figure 4.2 classifies shots according to the musical accompaniment, displaying, season by season, the mean running-time percentage for shots with no music, shots with source music, and shots with nondiegetic musical accompaniment (for further discussion of these categories, see appendix A).

A striking feature of the chart is the very high figure for the "no music" category for most of the years covered. The silent films of the 1920s were ordinarily accompanied by music from start to finish, the music virtually continuous from the film's opening title to the closing.[57] In contrast, in sound movies, the chart suggests, music-free passages dominate. The

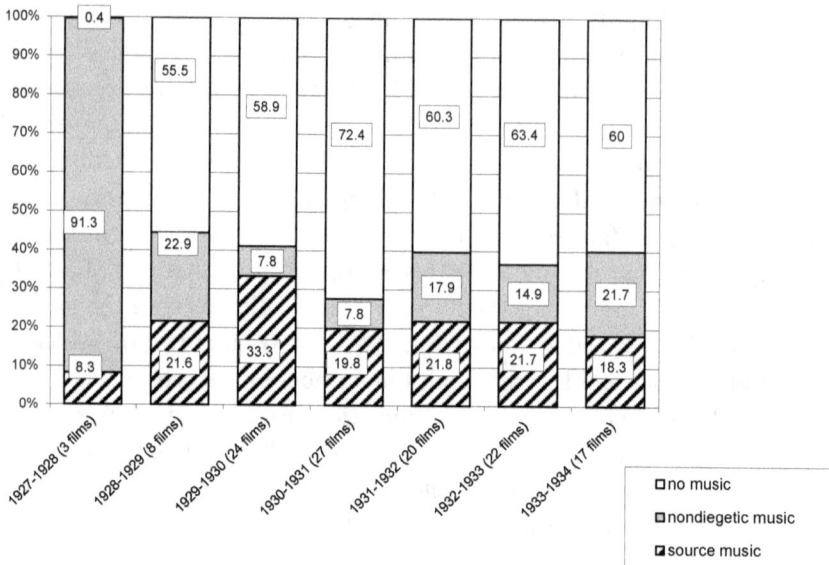

Figure 4.2. Mean running-time percentages for musical accompaniment in 121 sound films of 1928–34, by season

exception is the 1927–28 film season, whose "no music" number is miniscule. An explanation is that this season preceded the unexpected popularity of recorded dialogue. In 1927–28, talkies were largely nonexistent, sound films and sound-equipped theaters still rare, and soundtracks, in emulation of established film-music practice, ordinarily comprised almost wholly of music and very little if any recorded speech.[58] *Sunrise* (dir. F. W. Murnau, 1927), *The Jazz Singer* (dir. Alan Crosland, 1927), *Old San Francisco* (dir. A. Crosland, 1927), *The First Auto* (dir. Roy Del Ruth, 1928), *Lonesome* (dir. Paul Fejos, 1928), *Our Dancing Daughters* (dir. Jack Conway, 1928), and *The Pagan* (dir. Willard Van Dyke, 1929) differ from one another in important respects, but all have soundtracks that emulate the silent-cinema norm of more or less continual music from the start of the film to the finish.[59]

Over the next few years, however, as sound films increasingly included long stretches of spoken dialogue with no music at all, the music percentage falls dramatically. *Interference* (dir. Lothar Mendes, 1928), *Pointed Heels* (dir. Edward Sutherland, 1929), *Dangerous Curves* (dir. Lothar Mendes, 1929), *Morocco* (dir. Josef von Sternberg, 1930), *Ladies of Leisure* (dir. Frank Capra, 1930), *Hell's Harbor* (dir. Henry King, 1930), *Chasing Rainbows* (dir. Charles Reisner, 1930), and *Three Broadway Girls* (dir. Lowell Sherman,

1933) are among the Hollywood films of the period in which music comes in the form of song performances and title music only. The long dialogue-only stretches in films such as these presumably added to what critics at the time described as the "coldness" of the sound-cinema experience, as noted in chapter 2.

Sound film style continued to evolve over 1928–34, but as figure 4.2 suggests, music remained scarce. Sound films, in fact, sometimes included no music whatsoever except for the brief instrumental passages that played over the opening and closing credits, as in *Dracula* (dir. Tod Browning, 1931), *On purge bébé* (dir. Jean Renoir, 1931), *The Lost Squadron* (dir. George Archimbaud, 1932), and *Twentieth Century* (dir. Howard Hawks, 1934). For the hundreds of films examined for this book, the music total for individual films rarely rises above 40 percent of the overall running time. Even *King Kong* (dir. Merian Cooper and Ernest Schoedsack, 1933), a film famous for Max Steiner's lengthy musical score, is music-free for roughly 30 percent of its duration.[60] For the 1930–31 film season, the average for the "no music" percentage exceeds 70 percent. The numbers suggest that recorded sound's introduction into cinema had produced a paradoxical effect: the new sound films, unlike their "silent" predecessors, offered the audience much less music.

Songs versus Nondiegetic Orchestral Music

A further difference from silent-era practice concerns the nature of the accompaniment. Prior to electric sound, film music amounted mainly to so-called pit music, nondiegetic orchestral music that set a mood for the narrative action, helped establish identities for the main characters, and implied parallels across nonconsecutive story events. In sound films, however, this sort of background music often plays a minimal role. "Music—in the sense that it interpreted feeling, action or pictorial moods—has been relegated to a subordinate position in talking pictures," stated a critic in 1931.[61] This was especially true of American films, observed a critic in France: "Today the American sound film with synchronized music no longer exists."[62] In sound films, musical accompaniment—insofar as there is any—came mainly in the form of commercial pop songs sourced in the film's story world.

The impact on film style of Hollywood's reliance on songs is suggested by the source-music statistics in figure 4.2, which show that it peaked in 1929–30, the same season when nondiegetic orchestral accompaniment reached its minimum. In 1929–30, the running-time percentage for source music registers at over 33 percent of a sound film's total, on average—more than double what it had been the year before. In the next year, 1930–31, when American film producers began pulling songs out of films, the source-music figure drops to under 20 percent, roughly two-thirds of what it had been in 1929–30.

Also suggesting the exceptional nature of 1929–30 are the findings reported in the next chapter in figure 5.3, which tracks season by season the running-time percentage given to singing shots in American films. As with the percentage for source music, the singing-shot percentage reaches its maximum in 1929–30, when nearly 20 percent of an American film's running time, on average, was given over to singing shots.[63] The coincidence in 1929–30 of the high figures for both singing shots and source-music shots suggests that the abundant source music for that season involved singing performances specifically. Adding to the impression of correlation is the trend over the next two years, when, coincident with Hollywood's abandonment of the theme-song ploy, both the source-music percentage and the singing shot percentage fall drastically. It seems that the recorded-song accompaniment pervasive in sound cinema in late 1928 and early 1929 was on the wane less than two years later.

Also discernible in figure 4.2 is the radical divergence from silent-cinema practice mentioned earlier: the near disappearance in the talkies of the orchestral music that had become standard in the 1920s for the top exhibition venues. The difficulty of mixing music with speech in a manner that ensured the dialogue's intelligibility motivated a prohibition against combining dialogue with music, which became a film-aesthetic principle of the period. For example, composer Leonid Sabaneev declared that "music should cease or retire into the background when dialogue and noises are taking place. Except in rare instances it blends but poorly with them."[64] The choice between action and dialogue, noted earlier in this chapter, thus entailed musical consequences, with nondiegetic music ordinarily heard during the action scenes only, if heard at all. The consequence was that the typical film of 1929, an American critic proposed, comprised "spasmodic talking and silent sequences, leaving half the picture talking and half silent. Where the talking stopped the music was used for the pantomime."[65] Music-accompanied pantomime became reserved for special situations. Marking the limit once again is 1929–30, when the running-time percentage for nondiegetic music bottoms out at 7.8 percent, a tiny fraction of what it had been just two years before.

Hindering the blending of dialogue with music were the direct-sound practices at the time, according to which music was ordinarily recorded on the set, simultaneously with the actors' performances. While ensuring synchronization with the image, this "direct" capture of the sound, a technician explained, "hampers the editing of a picture," making it "impossible to rearrange sequences, and make additions or omissions wherever desired when cutting the picture."[66] Cutting a direct-recorded image meant chopping into the soundtrack too. The effects on sound-image continuity were potentially severe because the removal of even five frames from a film's image track was enough "to destroy definitively the ciné-musical synchronization," warned a film journalist in Paris.[67] Removing a shot, or a piece of a shot, caused a skip in the music. Better to refrain from using music altogether than to cut into the soundtrack. The result was that the orchestral music associated with the most ambitious feature films of the mid-1920s became rare in the talkies, many of which, as noted above, include no music beyond the opening credits and the song performances.

As with the song-accompaniment trend, the retreat in the use of nondiegetic music was temporary. The tide turned in the very next season, 1931–32, when, as figure 4.2 shows, the nondiegetic music percentage increases to around 18 percent, more than double what it had been during the preceding seasons.[68] Alluding to the change was a French critic who saw in the American films of 1932 "the return of musical accompaniment [*musique d'accompagnement*]": "The Americans no longer hesitate to create ambiance through the use for certain scenes in a film of a musical accompaniment mixed with words and other sounds."[69] Another signal of the change was the coining of the term *underscore* to refer to a new film-music phenomenon: music mixed with dialogue. The term, James Wierzbicki notes, was introduced into the lexicon of film production in Hollywood in 1931, the same year when, as figure 4.2 shows, the amount of nondiegetic music in films began, on average, to increase.[70] Arthur Franklin, the head of music at Warner Brothers and First National studios, promised in February of 1931 that "underscore [would] be increased to 60 to 70 percent in many forthcoming Vitaphones."[71]

A Case Study: The Marx Brothers at Paramount

The Marx Brothers cycle from Paramount illustrates the impact on musical films of underscoring, postsynchronized vocals and effects, and other

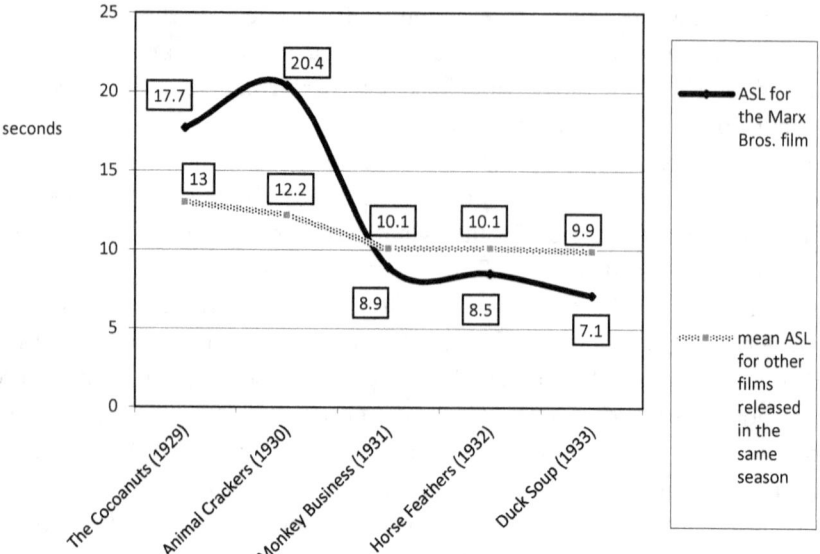

Figure 4.3. ASLs for the Marx Brothers' features, plus mean ASLs for 396 sound films

multitrack techniques. The five films comprising the cycle offer a useful case study for three reasons. First, the films' release dates invite evaluation relative to the seasonal norms presented in figures 4.1 and 4.2. Made over the five-year period emphasized in this book, beginning in 1929 with *The Cocoanuts* (dir. Robert Florey and Joseph Santley, 1929) and continuing through 1933 with *Duck Soup* (dir. Leo McCarey, 1933), the Marx Brothers films were produced at a rate of one per year, with each film released in the fall, at the start of the film season. Second, in featuring the same performers, the cycle provides the continuity that can allow the period's changes in technique and style to come to the fore: the Marx Brothers are the same, but the comedy has evolved in response to technical developments. Third, song performances in the Marx Brothers films are mostly farcical rather than sentimental or melodramatic in tone, and thus they exemplify the tendency toward comedy characteristic of the Hollywood musical film after 1930, as is discussed further in the next chapter.

How does the editing of the Marx Brothers films compare with the period norm? An indication is provided by figure 4.3, where the ASLs for Paramount's Marx Brothers cycle are juxtaposed with figure 4.1's statistics for the mean ASLs of hundreds of American and European sound films released during the same seasons.[72]

The Marx Brothers films, figure 4.3 shows, were cut more rapidly at the end of the period than at the beginning, which is in line with the shot-length trend for the early 1930s, when shots in all films were, on average, getting shorter, year by year. At the same time, the Marx Brothers films appear exceptional. ASLs for the first two Marx Brothers features run into the double digits, at a level well above the mean for those years, but then, beginning in 1931, the Marx Brothers' ASLs drop to single digits, with each film registering a lower average than its predecessor, and also lower than the yearly average. It seems that the films of the Marx Brothers were cut slower than the period norm until 1931, but then were cut faster, and increasingly so over the next few years. *Monkey Business* inaugurated the change. Twenty minutes shorter than *Animal Crackers* (dir. Victor Heerman, 1930), the previous film in the cycle, *Monkey Business* nonetheless contains nearly double the number of shots. The high shot count is in line with the general tendency for the 1931–32 film season, when, as noted earlier in this chapter, the head of Paramount, the studio behind the Marx Brothers' cycle, vowed to "increase the action" in the company's films. Also during this season, figure 4.1 suggests, the shot counts for American and European films—whether made by Paramount or other companies—went up, on average.

The sense that *Monkey Business* marked a style change for the Marx Brothers was evident in the critical writing, where the "wild" new film was contrasted to the slower *Animal Crackers*.[73] *Monkey Business*, according to *Variety*, "sets a fast pace from the start and seldom slows down to any noticeable extent."[74] A writer in France commended the "accelerated rhythm" of *Monkey Business*.[75] If the critics who described *Monkey Business* as faster than *Animal Crackers* had in mind the editing specifically, then they were right: *Monkey Business* is, in fact, cut more rapidly, on the whole, than the two previous films in the cycle. This is indicated by figure 4.4, which provides shot-type ASLs for both *Monkey Business* and its immediate predecessor.[76]

The visual impression of figure 4.4 is striking. Both films exhibit the stepwise contour characteristic of cinema generally in the early 1930s, with the ASLs for action shots lasting around half the length of the dialogue shots, which in turn run roughly half the length of the singing shots (see fig. 0.1). This similarity, however, brings to the fore a stark difference: the ASLs for all shot types, figure 4.4 reveals, are far lower for *Monkey Business* than for *Animal Crackers*.

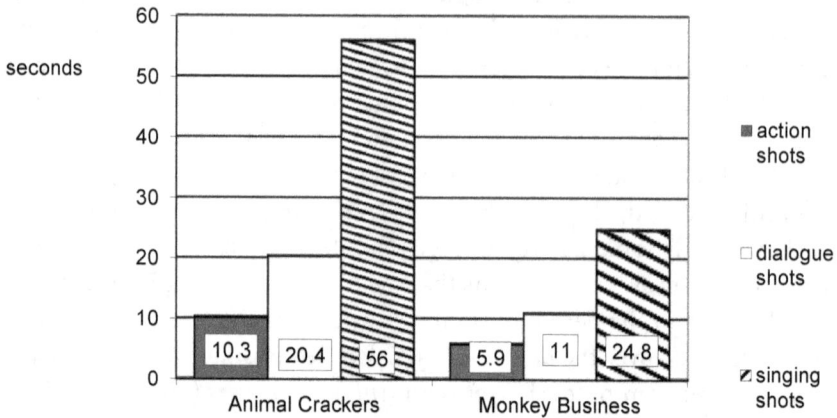

Figure 4.4. ASLs for three shot types for *Animal Crackers* and *Monkey Business*

Rhythm in the Marx Brothers Films

So remarkable are the numbers that an explanation of the perception that *Monkey Business* moves like "greased lightning," as one critic put it, may need go no further than the shot length: *Monkey Business* seemed fast because its shots, on the whole, were much shorter than audiences had come to expect from sound films and from the Marx Brothers specifically.[77] But as Lea Jacobs has shown in her important book *Film Rhythm after Sound* (2014), many other factors can come into play in shaping a film's rhythm.[78] Foremost is the rhythm of the actors' speech and physical movement and gestures, which tends to condition camera position, editing, and other style parameters. For sound-era comedy specifically, where the audience's laughter was the measure of success, the pacing of actors' performances confronted directors with special challenges. Among the "problems to be solved," declared Ernst Lubitsch in 1930, was "the timing of situations so that their full humor will not be lost, and how long to pause for a laugh."[79] Filmmakers had to anticipate how noise from a boisterous audience can impede the dialogue's intelligibility. "A successful comedy," observed cinematographer Bert Glennon, "is punctuated with laughs through which succeeding lines must penetrate."[80]

The need to factor in audience response became an explicit concern for the Marx Brothers, famous since their vaudeville beginnings for their rapid wordplay. As became clear with *The Cocoanuts*, what had worked on the stage, where the performers fed on the theater audience's laughter, was no longer effective in the sound-era movie studio, where the only audience was a mute film crew. Victor Heerman, the director of *Animal Crackers*, remarked that moviegoers had complained that Groucho's delivery in certain scenes in the previous film, *The Cocoanuts*, was so fast and relentless that one joke's laughter made the next inaudible.[81] In the verbal onslaught of the auction scene in *The Cocoanuts*, for example, Groucho's free associations spill out at a rate of three hundred words per minute: "Eight hundred wonderful residences will be built right here. They are as good as up. Better. You can have any kind of home you want to. You can even get stucco. Oh, how you can get stucco. . ." Heerman, to ensure that the wordplay in his film would not be occluded by a rowdy theater audience, scrutinized the stage version of *Animal Crackers*, timing the duration of the audience's laughter at specific jokes and then adding pauses into the film's dialogue scenes as appropriate.

The team behind *Monkey Business* went a step further by reducing the dialogue altogether. Verbal comedy remained essential to *Monkey Business*, but it came in smaller doses. The percentage of running time devoted to dialogue shots points to this reduction. While such shots make up 78.9 percent of the running time of *Animal Crackers*, they comprise only 65.1 percent of *Monkey Business*. Also, the dialogue shots in *Monkey Business* run, on average, less than half of the length of those in *Animal Crackers*, as reported in figure 4.4. In sum, in *Monkey Business*, the dialogue shots are not only shorter, on average, than in the preceding film but also take up less screen time overall.

Additional factors affecting a film's pace include the number of scenes. Around 1930, Hollywood scriptwriters, Jacobs reports, responded to the demand to accelerate a film's rhythm by writing shorter scenes and increasing the number of story locales.[82] The new preference for short scenes involving changes in locale is evident in *Monkey Business*, the first Marx Brothers film to be written directly for the screen rather than adapted from a stage show. Twenty minutes shorter than *Animal Crackers*, *Monkey Business* nonetheless includes far more scenes. With forty-four scenes in *Monkey Business* versus twenty-eight in *Animal Crackers*, the average scene length for *Monkey Business* works out to less than half of that for *Animal Crackers*, as is true also for *The Cocoanuts*, which contains twenty-one scenes by my count.

A related consideration is the number and variety of locations within a single scene. Scenes in *Monkey Business* are less confined spatially than those in *The Cocoanuts* and *Animal Crackers*. A common pattern, evident throughout the extended sequences on the ship and in the party in the Helton mansion, is for a character's entry into a room to be preceded by a brief cutaway showing the actor outside and approaching the door. Thus, what in *Animal Crackers* would have been one long take is in *Monkey Business* broken up into three shorter shots: (1) people interact in a room, (2) outside a new character approaches, and (3) the people in shot 1 are joined by the new character. The cutaways not only lower the ASL but also increase the variety of shot backgrounds. Compare the approach taken in *Monkey Business* to the fourteen-minute opening scene in *Animal Crackers*, which occurs wholly in the front room of the Rittenhouse mansion on an oversize art deco set, where developments in the action from one portion of the set to another are enacted mainly through camera movements rather than cuts.

Short Song Cues

Adding to the impression that *Monkey Business* moves more quickly than the preceding Marx Brothers films were changes in Hollywood's policies regarding music. The main change occurred in the 1930–31 season, between the releases of *Animal Crackers* and *Monkey Business*, when, as is discussed further in chapter 5, Hollywood pulled back drastically on its use of theme songs. Instead of adding songs into films, producers began taking them out. A critic at the time remarked that "*Monkey Business* has almost no music."[83] This assessment is inaccurate. *Monkey Business* is accompanied by music for roughly a quarter of its running time, which is less than for either *Animal Crackers* or *The Cocoanuts* but only slightly.[84] Further, the number of musical cues in *Monkey Business* is about the same as in the earlier Marx Brothers films. *Monkey Business* contains twenty-three cues whereas *The Cocoanuts* and *Animal Crackers* have twenty-six each. Nonetheless, the observation that *Monkey Business* contains almost no music points to an important aspect of the film, which is that its music is less noticeable.

For one, songs in *Monkey Business* are integrated into the comic action rather than presented separately as romantic or sentimental interludes. *Monkey Business* offers nothing equivalent to the six-minute block in *Animal Crackers* given over to two successive full-length performances of "Why Am I So Romantic?" or to the two sequences in *The Cocoanuts* devoted to Irving Berlin's "When My Dreams Come True," each of which runs around four minutes. In *Monkey Business*, numerous short extracts take the place of full-length performances. The one exception is the sequence devoted to

Harpo's harp solo, which is constructed around a shot that lasts nearly two minutes, making it the film's longest take. But even here a big reduction is evident, with the harp-solo shot in *Monkey Business* clocking in a full minute less than its counterpart in *Animal Crackers*, whose harp-solo shot runs longer than three minutes.

Also supporting the "almost no music" claim is the percentage of running time given to singing shots, which is much less for *Monkey Business* than for the preceding Marx Brothers films. Whereas shots of people singing make up 12.7 percent of the running time for *Animal Crackers* and 10.4 percent for *The Cocoanuts*, such shots comprise only 5.5 percent for *Monkey Business*.[85] The singing-shot percentage is low in *Monkey Business* because its songs are presented mainly in short extracts. Exemplary is the scene at the customs checkpoint, where each of the brothers performs the same lines from "You Brought a New Kind of Love to Me," Maurice Chevalier's hit from *The Big Pond* (dir. Hobart Henley, 1930), a Paramount production from the preceding season. Thus, instead of one long performance of the song, we get four short ones, ordered in the manner of a vaudeville act, with each rendition more manic than the one before, until the sequence tops out with Harpo scurrying across the table, scattering papers and repelling customs officers. A variation of the pattern plays out in *Horse Feathers* (dir. Norman McLeod, 1932), the next film in the cycle, with the four performances of "Everyone Says I Love You," the farce likewise escalating with each rendition.

Song repetitions occur in the earlier films too. In *The Cocoanuts*, "When My Dreams Come True" can be heard ten times, and in *Animal Crackers*, "Why Am I So Romantic?" surfaces six times. But the cues in *Monkey Business* are shorter, so that the screen time given to "You Brought a New Kind of Love to Me" (five cues total) works out to only two minutes and twenty-three seconds and that for "I'm Daffy over You" (six cues) adds up to three minutes and fifteen seconds. In contrast, "When My Dreams Come True" in *The Cocoanuts* involves cues that add up to twelve minutes and twenty-five seconds of screen time, and the total for "Why Am I So Romantic?" in *Animal Crackers* works out to eight minutes and fifty-three seconds. The amount of music-accompanied screen time is thus much higher in the earlier films than in *Monkey Business*.

In its recourse to numerous short cues, *Monkey Business* illustrates a trend in Hollywood film music in the early 1930s identified by Katherine Spring: instead of the full-length performances common in the Hollywood films of 1929–30, song cues increasingly came in the guise of "haphazard performances that crop up inconspicuously."[86] An indication of this is the spotting technique used for the novelty song "I'm Daffy over You." Credited to Chico Marx and songwriter Sol Violinsky, "I'm Daffy over You," also known as "Chico's Theme," became the theme song for the Marx Brothers' radio performances. The tune was first introduced in *Animal Crackers*, when Chico plays it at the party in the Rittenhouse mansion. It then resurfaces in *Monkey Business* in the film's only full-fledged song performance, when, roughly two-thirds of the way into the running time, in the film's final act, Harpo performs it on the harp at the party in the Helton mansion. Harpo's performance is typical of conversion-era song sequences in two respects. For one, the performance consists mainly of a single long take. Also—as always during the harp solos in the Marx Brothers films—once the playing starts, Harpo's demeanor changes, and along with it what might be called his ontological status. After the solo starts, Harpo's persona seems to exit the film's story, leaving us instead with Arthur Marx, a musician absorbed in the demands of his craft. When the song ends, the familiar Harpo character returns.

Like the song sequences in the earlier Marx Brothers films, Harpo's performance of "I'm Daffy over You" comes across as a self-contained interlude, a divergence from the film's narrative. Nonetheless, the performance is more integrated into *Monkey Business* than it might seem given the additional times the tune is heard on the film's soundtrack. Four cues occur prior to Harpo's solo performance: (1) at the end of the opening credits, when a ten-second extract plays; (2) in the captain's cabin when Chico whistles the melody during his interaction with Groucho ("Sure I can vessel"); (3) when Harpo, walking the ship's deck, whistles the tune again while approaching the chess game; and (4) at the party in the Helton mansion, when Chico sings the melody prior to introducing Harpo, who will perform the song on the harp. By preceding the harp solo, these four moments help naturalize the melody, preparing the viewer subliminally for the full performance.

After the solo, the melody for "I'm Daffy over You" is heard yet again, during the film's closing title, thus yielding a total of six cues. These cues, except for Harpo's harp performance, are perhaps too short and incidental to register in the viewer's consciousness. Nonetheless, they enhance the viewer's familiarity with the melody and thus naturalize the song's presence in the film. Moreover, since only a brief extract from a melody is needed to prompt the viewer's memory, the choice of multiple short song repetitions over one long performance does not impede the project of song advertising and promotion essential to commercial cinema at the time. Brief cues leave audiences no less likely to exit the theater humming the tune. Indeed, by repeatedly priming the viewer's recall of the melody, the use of numerous short cues instead of one long one may make the song *more* memorable rather than less.

Nondiegetic Music in the Marx Brothers Films

Also notable in *Monkey Business* is the innovative use of nondiegetic orchestral music during dialogue scenes. Two brief scenes stand out in their difference from comparable passages in the earlier films. The first happens during the meeting of Zeppo and ingénue Mary (Ruth Hall) in the ocean liner's hallway, which is covered in a single fifty-four-second shot. Romantic orchestral music swells up around six seconds into the shot, when Zeppo reenters the frame after eluding the ship's mate. The music continues through the remainder of the shot, which covers the following events: Zeppo, hiding from the authorities, crouches in front of a glass door; Mary enters through the adjacent door and walks toward the foreground of the shot; Zeppo follows and catches up with Mary; and Mary and Zeppo chat while continuing to walk, the camera tracking back with them. The second underscored moment likewise features Zeppo and Mary on the ship and facilitates one of the film's best gags: Zeppo, seated next to Mary, promises that he will never leave her to the accompaniment of romantic orchestral music very similar to that heard earlier during their encounter on the deck. But the mood deflates instantly when Zeppo, reacting to the approach of the ship's crew, leaps up from his seat, an action followed by the cut to the wide shot that shows him darting out of the frame to escape. The gag would work without the underscore, but it is far better with it.

The use of music differs from that in *Animal Crackers*, where the orchestral score surfaces mainly at moments without dialogue. Typical of this is the short scene near the film's end in which the mute Harpo squirts the flit-gun, whose sound, in the manner of an animated short, is simulated by the orchestra's violins. In scenes with speaking actors, however, overlap with music is avoided. Consider the moment when Chico and Harpo try to leave the mansion's library and are repelled by a rainstorm, causing them to rush to the room's opposite side, where the door, magically, opens out onto sunshine and chirping birds. At the end of the shot, just before the orchestral music comes in, Chico utters the scene's one word of dialogue: "California!" Music and dialogue occur during the same shot but not at the same time. The same rule plays out in the hallway when the butler Hives sneaks away with the painting while the guests remain oblivious. Hives's action plays out as pantomime accompanied by mystery-story music until Groucho fires off his wisecrack: "Mrs. Rittenhouse, how do you pay Hives, by the week or by the pound?" The music stops for Groucho's line and then resumes once he finishes talking. Again, dialogue and orchestral music occur in succession rather than concurrently.

Moreover, when music in *Animal Crackers* plays during dialogue, it is less responsive to how the characters are interacting than in *Monkey Business*. An example is the conversation near the beginning between Margaret Dumont and Lilian Roth, which is underscored by an orchestral rendition of "Why Am I So Romantic?," the film's theme. The music, with its constant volume and dynamic range, seems indifferent to the moment-by-moment flow of the conversation between Dumont and Roth. This use of underscore seems less modern, less like cinema today, than in *Monkey Business*, where the underscore functions within a layered soundtrack whose fluctuations amplify the nuances of the drama. In the first of the cues, for example, when Zeppo strides down the deck to catch up with Mary, the music's volume increases, as if emulating his energy. When he begins his banter ("It's mighty pretty country around here"), the volume tapers off slightly, thus bringing his voice into the perceptual foreground. When Mary speaks her first line of dialogue ("I beg your pardon?"), a brief pause in the music adds emphasis. Also, the multitrack technique allows the music to coincide not only with the dialogue but also with other sounds, as when Mary opens the door and the creak of the hinge can be heard. In *Monkey Business* a layered sound mix responds to split-second shifts in plot action.

Postsynch Sound

A further technical innovation essential to how *Monkey Business* sounds, and also to how it looks, is the liberal use of postsynchronized music and effects. In *The Cocoanuts* and *Animal Crackers*, the sound, by and large, had been recorded concurrently with the image. The honk of Harpo's horn, for instance, appears in most cases to have been produced on the set when the actors were filmed. The horn we hear likely was not the one that we see Harpo carrying but instead a different instrument operated off camera by a musician or stagehand who had timed the honks with Harpo's movements. Nonetheless, the sound was captured, in the typical manner, on the set at the same time as the actors' performances.

The production method affects the film's treatment of narrative space. In *Animal Crackers*, during the five moments in the film when Harpo operates the horn, we see Harpo squeezing the bulb, so that the sound and the visual action confirm one another. In *Monkey Business*, however, the horn is often first heard offscreen, in anticipation of Harpo's appearance. Examples include the opening scene in the ship's hold, where the first mate is distracted by an offscreen honk. Consider, too, the subsequent chase on the ship's deck, which includes a long shot in which the actors, led by Harpo, emerge from the depths of the set and then careen frantically into the shot's foreground. The postsynchronized honk gives the shot a telos and simplifies its impact: we hear Harpo's horn before we see him, causing us to scan the image until the instant he becomes visible.

The mute Harpo's performances, though often described as silent comedy, in fact rely on sound effects. The frog burp emitted from his top hat is one of many examples from *Monkey Business* that can be cited. The judicious use of postsynchronized sound shapes the comedy. When Chico, in the gangster's cabin, is punched by Harpo and a stunt double flies up in the air, his feet high off the ground, the sonic continuity provided by the crack of the fist and subsequent thump of the body hitting the floor helps conceal the substitution of the acrobat for Chico. Also notable is the hollow, artificial quality of the sound. In matching up to the image without fully belonging to it, the sound makes the moment funny rather than horrific.

Another action-oriented comic effect enhanced by postsynchronized sound is the fast-motion cinematography that occasionally surfaces in *Monkey Business*, as when Harpo arrives at the barber shop via skateboard and tumbles headfirst into the room. Such moments suggest an attempt to render cinematic the comedy of the Marx Brothers, to make it less verbal and more like the wild pantomime of the period's animated shorts. In any case, the increased use of postsynchronized sound correlates with an increase in the physical comedy, which is far more abundant in *Monkey Business* than its predecessors. Beginning with the extended chase on the ocean liner's deck, where the brothers and their pursuers, turning the corner at full speed, are foiled by the slick surface, and continuing through to the carnivalesque fight in the barn at the film's end, the physical stunts in *Monkey Business* exceed anything in *Animal Crackers* or *Cocoanuts*. The difference is reflected in the running-time percentages for action shots, which are not only shorter, on average, in *Monkey Business* than in *Animal Crackers* (see fig. 4.4) but occupy a much larger percentage of the overall running time. Whereas *Animal Crackers* gives 8.5 percent of its running time to action shots, *Monkey Business* accords 29.5 percent—nearly four times as much as the preceding film. In this regard, *Monkey Business* sets the pattern for the remaining films in the series, *Horse Feathers* and *Duck Soup*, each of which likewise devotes some one-third of its time to action shots.

As my analysis of the Marx Brothers suggests, editing practices evolved relative to changes in Hollywood's policy with regard to songs, and especially the decision in 1930–31 to cut back severely on the production of musical films, remove songs from films already in production, and retain songs mainly in farce comedies starring vaudevillians like the Marx Brothers. In Europe, where film songs remained continuously popular through the early 1930s, and direct-sound methods of song-sequence production were the norm, musical films developed in a somewhat different direction.

Notes

1. S. Eisenstein, V. Pudovkin, and G. Alexandrov, "A Statement," in E. Weis and J. Belton, *Film Sound*, 83–85. On sound's impact on the filmic avant-garde, see M. Hagener, *Moving Forward, Looking Back*, 22–24.

2. W. Koenig, "Studio Problems," 10.

3. A limit case was the release in Iran of *Cyrus the Great* (1928), a radically recut version of the "Fall of Babylon" sequence from Griffith's *Intolerance* (1915) in which the film's villain is redefined as its hero. See K. Askari, "An Afterlife for Junk Prints," 99–120.

4. H. Lewis, *The Motion Picture Industry*, 401–2.

5. Heinrich Fraenkel, "Can Industry Stay International?" 58, 64.

6. B. Brecht, *Bertolt Brecht on Film and Radio*, 194.

7. See "Jump of U.S. Film Exports First Six Months Explained," 59, which states, regarding Britain, that "American sound pictures and talkers have had to be printed in this country [the United States] whereas previously negatives were shipped."

8. A. Stevens, "Bad Sound Is Due to Bad Prints," v.

9. R. Vasey, *The World According to Hollywood*, 63. See also W. Hays, "Free Speech in Sound Pictures Endangered," 2.

10. W. Hays, "Motion Picture Industry Formulates New Code Made Necessary by Sound," April 1, 1930. Available on microfilm in D. Gomery, ed., *The Will Hays Papers*, reel 4, box 41.

11. The results of hypothesis tests performed on the samples used for fig. 4.1 are listed in table 4.1, appendix B.

12. B. Salt, *Film Style and Technology*, 2nd ed., 218.

13. The exact figures are as follows: For the action shots in silent films, $M = 86$ percent, $N = 67$, $SD = 13.4$, and $ME = 3.25$. For the sound films, $M = 30.1$, $N = 354$, $SD = 16.5$, and $ME = 1.72$.

14. J. O'Connell, "Talkers 'Producers' Rattles,' Says Pioneer," 117.
15. The differences between dialogue shots and dialogue intertitles are discussed further in appendix A.
16. The numbers for the intertitles are M = 5.5 seconds, N = 66, SD = 1.36, and ME = 0.32. The numbers for the dialogue shots are M = 14.9, N = 351, SD = 5.26, and ME = 0.55.
17. On the practice of cutting between lines of speech, see D. Fairservice, *Film Editing*, 235, 259, 261–62, 274.
18. A. Hoerée, "Essai d'esthéthique du sonore," 52.
19. Quoted in Douglas Hodges, "More Pantomime with Less Talk for Universal Films," 34.
20. See "Paramount Cuts Down Footage to Increase Action," 23.
21. J. Brandt, "Synchronized Films," 996.
22. "Filmusicals," 19.
23. G. Kingsley, "Action Usurps Film Dialogue," A7.
24. The exact figures for the running-time percentages for dialogue shots, along with the results of hypothesis tests on the samples, are listed in table 4.1a, appendix B.
25. The figures for the dialogue-shot ASLs are provided in table 4.1b, appendix B.
26. B. Salt, *Film Style and Technology*, 2nd ed., 217.
27. R. Clair, "The Art of Sound," in E. Weis and J. Belton, *Film Sound*, 94.
28. For further detail on dubbing's impact on film style, see C. O'Brien, "Dubbing in the Early 1930s: An Improbable Policy."
29. J. Morienval, "Film français synchronisés U. S. A," 224; P. Autré, "Attention au Dubbing!" 22; and M. Hall, "Clever Dubbing," X3.
30. A. Hitchcock, "Direction," 257.
31. W. Lipscomb, "Saving the 'Talkie' from Talk!" 95.
32. W. Lipscomb, "Saving the 'Talkie' from Talk!" 95.
33. See, for example, "René Clair's New Film," X6.
34. The figure for *Sous les toits de Paris* derives from my entry in the Cinemetrics database for film ID 727. The mean figure for the 1930–31 film season comes from table 4.1a in appendix B.
35. "Producers Optimistic Again that the 40 Percent Foreign Revenue Will Return to Former Status," 7, 58.
36. The statistics come from "Sound Rapidly Replacing Silents Abroad, Gov't Finds," 32.
37. C. J. North and N. D. Golden, "The European Film Market—Then and Now," 442–51.
38. D. W. Griffith, "Pace in the Movies," 19, 21.
39. C. Wahl, *Multiple Language Versions Made in Babelsberg*, 114, 131.
40. H. Pfeiffer, "Motif und Handlung im Tonfilm," 3.
41. "Notes of the Berlin Screen," X6.
42. M. L., "'Der Kongreß tanzt,'" 2.
43. Von Sternberg was born in Austria, but his entire film career prior to *Der Blaue Engel* was spent in Hollywood, so I refer to him as an American director.
44. The intent to break into the American market with a film featuring Emil Jannings was stated in Ufa's internal communications as early as 1928. See, for example, Hr. Hubert to Ludwig Klitsch, July 11, 1928, and Hr. Hubert to Dr. Donner, July 11, 1928, available in the Bundesarchiv in Berlin (Bestand R-109-1 Archivnummer 924).
45. An informative source on Carl Winston's work for Ufa is Erich Pommer's letter of reference for Winston, dated December 30, 1931, which can be found in the Carl Winston papers in the Deutsche Kinemathek in Berlin. See also "Ufa Casting Chief in London," 12.
46. "In Hollywood Now," 34.
47. The phrase "velocity of rhythm" appears in H. Matthews, "Post-haste from Paris," X4.

48. Quotations from the Canty memo appear in "Silent Film Versions of U.S. Talkers Apt to Aid Foreign Films Abroad," 2.

49. "Silent Film Versions of U.S. Talkers Apt to Aid Foreign Films Abroad," 2.

50. The correspondence, which dates from March 30, 1931, to August 23, 1931, is available at the University of Southern California's Cinematic Arts Library, where it can be found among the documents related to Henry Blanke, then head of the Warner Brothers Foreign Department.

51. Anthony DeLeon to Karl MacDonald, April 16, 1931.

52. The need to "start and finish a title on one person" comes from Anthony DeLeon to Henry Blanke, May 25, 1931, apropos of the release in Stockholm of the X version of *Sweethearts and Wives* (dir. Clarence Badger, 1930).

53. The quotations come from page two of an internal MGM document, "Notes on Possible Changes for Silent Version of *Broadway Melody*," March 12, 1929. The document can be found in a dossier of materials on *The Broadway Melody* available at the Margaret Herrick Library of the Motion Picture Academy in Los Angeles.

54. The number of titles used for the foreign version of *Public Enemy* is stated in Henry Blanke to Karl MacDonald, August 17, 1931.

55. J. Wierzbicki, *Film Music*, 114.

56. The results of hypothesis tests performed on the samples used for fig. 4.2 can be found in table 4.2, appendix B.

57. On the silent-era priority of continuous accompaniment, see K. Kalinak, *Settling the Score*, 49–56.

58. On the minimal use of orchestral music in conversion-era Hollywood films, see M. Slowik, "Diegetic Withdrawal and Other Worlds," esp. 4–10.

59. The similarity in musical accompaniment between early sound cinema and late silent is noted in M. Marks, *Music and the Silent Film*, 11–12.

60. This figure was derived from the entry to the Cinemetrics database for film ID 10062.

61. J. O'Sullivan, "Music as the Narrator," 14.

62. P. Autré, "Musique et disques de cinéma," 110.

63. The exact figures for the singing-shot percentages in American films are as follows: $M = 19.67$ percent, $N = 20$, $SD = 8.28$, and $ME = 3.81$. Further results are shown in fig. 5.3.

64. L. Sabaneev, *Music for the Films*, 20. See also the disparagement of "the musical accompaniment of dialogue" in N. Bell, "Those Cultural Arts and Flattery as a Bludgeon," A2.

65. B. Swigart, "Studio Music," 121.

66. G. Lewin, "Dubbing and Its Relation to Sound Picture Production," 43.

67. R. B., "L'exploitation du film sonore," 19.

68. In 1931–32, the percentage of a film's running time devoted to singing shots registers at 5.2 percent, whereas in 1930–31 it is 10.3. See fig. 5.3.

69. In "Bilan de fin d'année," 173. "Les américains n'hesitent plus, pour créer l'ambiance, à utiliser pour certaines scènes d'un film, une musique d'accompagnement qu'on 'mixte' avec les paroles et les autres bruits."

70. J. Wierzbicki, *Film Music*, 125–26.

71. Arthur Franklin is quoted in Philip Scheuer, "Musical Picture Quality Undergoes Renaissance," B20.

72. The hypothesis tests reported in appendix B for fig. 4.1 apply also to the sound film averages for this chart.

73. M. Hall, "Havens of Laughter," 111.

74. "'Monkey Business,'" 14.

75. F. Vinneuil, "'Monkey Business,'" 4. "Dans *Monkey Business* le dialogue est moins encombrant, la mise-en-scène moins lourd qu'auparavant. L'affabulation est aussi plus serrée, ce qui donne un relief nouveau aux cocasserie des épisodes se succédant d'ailleurs sur un rythme accéléré."

76. The figures for *Animal Crackers* and *Monkey Business* come from the entries to the Cinemetrics database for film IDs 9867 and 9838, which were derived using FACT, a time-accurate Cinemetrics tool that allows for the computation of shot length to an accuracy of one-tenth of a second. For more on FACT, see appendix A. All subsequent figures in this chapter for these two films derive from these entries, unless otherwise noted.

77. The quoted phrase is from S. Louvish, *Monkey Business*, 236.

78. See L. Jacobs, *Film Rhythm after Sound*.

79. The quotation from Lubitsch comes from P. Scheuer, "Theme Song Own Excuse," B13–14.

80. The quotation from Glennon appears in H. Lewis, "Getting Good Sound Is an Art," 65. The need for actors to pause to allow for the audience's laughter is stated also in P. Chaine, "A la poursuite du temps perdu," 6. See also the praise for the Wheeler and Woolsey comedy *Half Shot at Sunrise* (dir. Paul Sloane, 1930), which "moves rapidly, but the gags have been well-timed and therefore none of the dialogue is lost in the roars of the audience," in "New Product," 44.

81. The remarks from Victor Heerman come from an interview by Anthony Slide quoted in S. Louvish, *Monkey Business*, 214–15.

82. L. Jacobs, *Film Rhythm after Sound*, 180–86.

83. P. Scheuer, "A Town Called Hollywood," B11.

84. While *Monkey Business* gives 23.5 percent of its running time to music, *Animal Crackers* gives 24.6 and *The Cocoanuts* 31.7. These musical-accompaniment figures derive from the entries to the Cinemetrics database for the following film IDs: 3816, 18321, and 18317.

85. The figure for *The Cocoanuts* refers to the Cinemetrics database entry for film ID 9868.

86. K. Spring, *Saying It with Songs*, 9, 129.

5

AMERICAN FILM SONGS, INSIDE THE FILMS AND OUT

Conditioning sound cinema's engagement with popular song was a phenomenon unique to the film market in the United States: the rapid rise and fall in the popularity of film songs and the subsequent hiatus in the production of musical films. Initially, in 1929, American film producers, aiming to repeat the success of *The Singing Fool* (dir. Lloyd Bacon, 1928) and other song-loaded features, inserted songs into virtually all films, regardless of the ostensible genre. Westerns, slapstick comedies, action films, family melodramas—all were potential song vehicles. A year and a half later, however, a sudden reversal in policy occurred when the same producers began extracting songs from films and cutting back radically on the making of musical films. The songs that had become indispensable to sound cinema in the spring of 1929 were avoided in the fall of 1930. When songs returned to American cinema in 1932–33, they no longer permeated the entirety of Hollywood's output but instead featured in a distinct genre, "the musical."

The ups and downs of Hollywood theme songs can be explained with reference to two conditions specific to media distribution in the United States. One was Hollywood's attempt to integrate motion pictures into the country's large retail economy through the mass merchandising of film songs via sheet music, recorded discs, public performance, and radio play. Sound-era movie theaters, where discs and sheet music were sold in the lobbies, came to resemble other retail outlets, especially the chain stores essential to the consumer economy in the United States. In the summer of 1930, the aggressive marketing began to alienate moviegoers, who were said to avoid musical films particularly. A July report in *Variety* on audience tastes proclaimed, "Musical films of any kind are dead."[1] The second novel distribution condition was the centrality of commercial broadcast radio to the American mediascape, which differed from radio in other countries in two respects: the gargantuan audience in the United States, where half of the world's radios were said to be located; and the advertising-driven programming, which centered on popular songs that also circulated via additional media, including cinema. These circumstances made radio's impact on cinema far stronger in the United States than in other countries, and the repeated play of film songs on radio and via other media—the "overplay," as it was called—shaped the aesthetics of the musical film.

Film Songs in the United States versus Europe

Dramatic evidence for the effects of song distribution on the American film industry came in the 1930–31 film season, when the Hollywood studios quickly backed off from making musical films. Summing up the policy change was the editor of the London-based *Kinematograph Weekly*, who reported from Los Angeles that "the year 1931 saw the virtual disappearance . . . of the 'musicals.' No producer nowadays would attempt to build a picture around a theme-song; nor would he risk a heavy investment in an all-musical production."[2] It became clear that a moratorium had set in; in a piece announcing the genre's resurgence in 1933, the *New York Times* stated, "For a period of two years no studio dared touch a tune film."[3]

No such resurgence happened in Europe because film songs remained continuously popular there through the early 1930s, and producers thus felt no need to scale back on musical films. The foreign market's divergence from the domestic market became apparent in 1930, when (as noted in chap. 1) revue films such as *The Show of Shows* (dir. John Adolfi, 1929), *The Hollywood Revue of 1929* (dir. Charles Reisner et al., 1929), and *Paramount on Parade* (dir. Ernst Lubitsch et al., 1930) were reportedly more popular internationally than in the United States.[4] Some two-thirds of the income from *King of Jazz* (dir. John Murray Anderson, 1930), for example, came from overseas.[5]

Audiences in other countries, it seems, retained a fondness for musical films that American audiences had lost. The results of a poll in 1931 of some 1,250 German movie exhibitors were summarized in a headline in the trade daily *Film-Kurier*: "The votes are in: a film without music, without a 'hit song' [*Schlager*], will not succeed!"[6] The situation still held two years later, when in June 1933 a similar survey in the same publication concluded that from a financial standpoint, "a German film without an interpolated song [*Schlagereinlagen*] has no basis for existence."[7] An article in *La cinématographie française* in December 1931 pointed to comparable circumstances in France, noting that the popular songs now absent from American films remained prominent in their French counterparts: "One can no longer make a decent film in France, whether a comedy or a drama, without interpolating into it a song or two."[8] In sum, in Europe in the early 1930s, unlike in the United States, audiences still preferred films with songs, and film producers responded accordingly. While Hollywood was removing songs from films, the European companies continued to add them in.

Electric-Era Film Songs

The marketing of motion pictures in connection with songs can be traced back to the beginnings of the American motion picture industry. Songs, in fact, were the dominant form of film music during the nickelodeon boom late in the decade 1900–1910, when song slide performances, which involved film audiences singing along with a professional singer, became a regular component of film exhibition.[9] What was new in the late 1920s was the replacement of live performances by recordings circulating via the electric-sound media, which quickly and vastly expanded the market for both the songs and the films. The key factor behind the market increase was sound cinema's powerful simulation of human presence, which enabled a new, accelerated sort of song promotion, whereby a single singing star, via a movie performance, could "appear" in hundreds of theaters at once. The diffusion of recorded performances by star vocalists via sound films exponentially ratcheted up the speed with which songs were marketed. "Where before a theme song could be heard only in the larger cities where good orchestral accompaniment was available," observed a journalist, "now it belongs to the picture and can be heard in any theatre where there is sound reproducing equipment."[10]

Recorded songs became a hallmark of the 1928–29 film season, when the tunes featured in *Ramona* (dir. Edwin Carewe, 1928), *The Singing Fool*, *Our Dancing Daughters* (dir. Jack Conway, 1928), *The Pagan* (dir. Willard Van Dyke, 1929), *The Hollywood Revue of 1929*, and other soundtrack-accompanied movies topped the sales charts for sheet music and discs. Folio sales for the top film songs reached the dizzying rate of thirteen thousand to fourteen thousand copies per day, four times the figure for the most successful popular songs prior to sound movies.[11] Unprecedented numbers were logged also for film-related gramophone recordings, when, for the first time in the history of recorded music, individual recordings sold more than a million copies—and did so within months of a film's release. For both print music and discs, the numbers for film songs were unheard of.[12] The sales inspired a rhetoric of social uplift. Sound movies, film-industry promoters boasted, brought about an unprecedented democratization of elite culture, spreading artistic riches regardless of physical geography. As Martin Quigley, publisher of *Exhibitors Herald-World*, declared, "The studios are now enabled to send into the thousands of theatres . . . the voice of John McCormack, an original operetta, a great dramatic performance by John Barrymore, a Paul Whiteman musical revue, Lawrence Tibbett from the Metropolitan Opera Company in a great vocal and dramatic performance, and numerous other attractions of similar power and scope."[13]

Such attractions were sensational not only in the United States but internationally. A bellwether for its success on the foreign market was Al Jolson's "Sonny Boy" from *The Singing Fool*. The "Sonny Boy" sheet music sold 1 million copies in the first three months of the film's release, and 1.6 million copies by the end of 1929, including in Europe.[14] Also in that year, Al Jolson's Brunswick recording of "Sonny Boy" was declared the first million-selling disc.[15] As with *The Singing Fool* itself, up to one-third of the profits for the "Sonny Boy" recording came from European countries where languages other than English were spoken, such as France, Germany, the Netherlands, and Yugoslavia.[16] As reported by *Variety* ten months after *The Singing Fool*'s premiere in the United States, "More than 50 percent as many foreigners bought Jolson's 'Sonny Boy' record as did the native Americans."[17] The sky-high foreign income helped justify Hollywood's emphasis on musical films for its sound-era foreign-market strategy: such films exported well even when the lyrics went untranslated.

American Musical Films and the Retail Economy

Shaping Hollywood's theme-song trend was the American cinema's increased integration into the national retail economy, which had no parallel in other countries. Already in the early 1920s, prior to sound cinema, American movies were assumed to be stimulating the sale of American consumer goods, both at home and abroad. Everyone in the United States, declared secretary of the Motion Picture Producers and Distributors

Association Carl Milliken in 1930, has been inspired by a movie to make a consumer purchase: "The farm housewife sees a new labor-saving device and she purchases it. Her husband sees a new automobile. Their daughter gets an idea for a new dress. The son of the house discovers the type of overcoat he wants. In one picture a famous star used a special perfume, the name of which, as it happened, was easily identified, with the result that that brand of perfume had a tremendous vogue."[18]

A similar dynamic was believed to operate internationally, especially in Europe, where American consumer goods were currently making inroads.[19] Updating the colonialist slogan that "trade follows the flag," Hollywood's promoters in the 1920s declared that trade now followed the film, with each dollar earned from the exhibition of American motion pictures in Europe and other regions bringing in an additional dollar through the movie-stimulated sales of American consumer products.[20] "The film has become an 'animated catalogue' for American goods," declared the Motion Picture Producers and Distributors Association in 1928. "People the world over are turning to the screen for direction in their purchases of goods, with the result that millions of dollars are being poured into the pockets of [American] business men, whether they deal in soap, automobiles, ... dress goods, cosmetics, or whatnot."[21] Making the same point were Hollywood's European critics, such as French newspaper magnate and movie-studio owner Jean Sapène, who in 1929 had lobbied the French government on behalf of French film producers against the exhibition of Hollywood films in France. Echoing the MPPDA, Sapène proclaimed that "American's large growth in foreign trade was ... due largely to American films."[22] The films, suggests film historian Richard Maltby, were probably most popular in countries where the level of discretionary income was high enough to enable the consumer spending that Hollywood was promoting.[23]

Among the goods purchased were film songs, whose production and marketing had been stimulated in the late 1920s by a slew of media-industry mergers that gave film companies control over much of the song industry. By the fall of 1929, Douglas Gomery reports, "over ninety percent of the popular music in America was being generated by publishers owned by Warner Brothers, Paramount, RCA, or Loews."[24] Alliances between the major Hollywood studios and the country's top music publishers allowed the studios to cut the costs of the performance rights for the music used on soundtracks and to profit from the distribution of film songs via media besides cinema.[25] Essential was commercial radio, whose direct links to the motion picture industry included the creation in 1929 by the Radio Corporation of America (RCA) of RKO Pictures, which produced films starring celebrities from RCA's National Broadcasting Network (NBC), whose sixty-eight stations made it the nation's largest broadcaster. In a comparable move, Paramount purchased in 1929 a majority share of the Columbia Broadcasting System (CBS), the second-largest network at fifty-four stations.[26] By 1931, film historian Thomas Doherty reports, "the major studios not only spent huge sums on 'spot' advertising to plug current releases, but all were involved in elaborate programming tie-ins with radio. Paramount sponsored a weekly 'Paramount Hour' over the NBC network, Warner Brothers operated KFWB in LA as an adjunct publicity unit, and RKO's 'Theater of the Air' functioned as a thirty-minute commercial for studio releases."[27]

The promotion of the same songs and vocalists through radio, cinema, music publishing, and the recording industry rested on horizontal links between film and music industries that in the late 1920s proliferated to the point that, argues media historian David Suisman, the two industries effectively became one.[28] The convergence gave the film-song market an accelerated rhythm that confounded music-industry veterans. Prior to the talkies, "the life of a popular melody was long," reported the *New York Times*, with the sheet music for a single song selling for years on end; by 1930, however, a song's commercial existence ran a maximum of "about six weeks." The short time line made it extremely difficult to coordinate the distribution of songs with the distribution of movies: "Theme songs and other musical items of a synchronized nature cannot be plugged before the opening of a picture. The general run of a picture on Broadway is not long. So almost before the words and music are public property, the film has moved along and another one—with a new song—has taken its place."[29] The rapidity disrupted the retail music business. While some film songs were big hits, most were not. When a film failed to catch on with the moviegoing public, the discs and sheet music associated with it ordinarily went unsold, saddling music retailers with useless inventories.[30]

The Movie Theater as Chain Store

Adding to the store owners' plight was the direct competition from the many movie theaters now offering discs and sheet music for sale in the lobbies.[31] The merchandising stemmed from a conscious effort circa 1930 to model film exhibition on a definitive institution of American consumerism: retail chain stores. Offering standardized products at low prices at hundreds of outlets, "five-and-dime stores" such as Woolworths and Kresges, along with grocery outlets such as Safeway and A&P, were a distinctly American business phenomenon.[32] As the film industry converted to sound, the chain store concept served as an administrative model for the gathering together of movie theaters into vast networks.[33] Sound-era movie exhibition increasingly took on the characteristics of the nation's retail sector. Just as Woolworths, Safeway, and a few other massive retail chains competed against, and ultimately drove out of business, a vast number of small family-owned shops, a few movie-theater chains directly rivaled the nation's thousands of independent exhibitors. The economist Howard Lewis, in his 1933 book on the motion picture industry, described American film exhibition as a competition whereby the "chain store" was displacing the "independent retailer."[34]

Hollywood's efforts to imitate retail stores were direct and explicit. In late 1929 Paramount contracted executives from the Kresge and Gimbel Brothers companies to assist in the merchandising of music through Paramount's massive Publix chain, which comprised over one thousand theaters. The aim, *Variety* reported, was nothing less than to "turn this circuit's theatre chain into units in a nation-wide chain store system."[35] The main products sold were theme songs from films. Intended "to boost sales of the songs as well as gain added publicity for the picture," the system enlisted "1,400 managers and assistants [trained] in the art of song plugging for exploitation of all songs used in Paramount films."[36] By 1930, some sixty flagship Publix theaters were converted into "chain-store like emporiums," where one could see a movie and then, while exiting through the lobby, purchase film-related discs and sheet music.[37] Similarly, the Loews theater firm enlisted the J. J. Robbins Company to install booths in the company's theaters for selling film-related records and sheet music.[38] Brand identification was vital to the strategy. Regarding Paramount-Publix, architecture historian Maggie Valentine notes that "all advertising, promotions, prologues, design changes, architecture, and even the ushers' uniforms were determined by the central office and carried the Publix logo. Many newly acquired theatres were renamed Paramount to develop brand-name recognition and loyalty. They were selling more than movies; they were selling a corporate image."[39]

The administration of multiple movie theaters by a single owner can be traced back to the nickelodeon boom of the late aughts, when the American film market became the largest in the world. The practice took a leap forward in the early 1920s with the development of the national movie-theater circuits owned by Loews, Stanley, and Balaban and Katz.[40] Nonetheless, a new threshold was crossed with sound conversion in 1930, when theater chains became the dominant film-exhibition institution in the United States. Of the nine thousand sound-wired movie houses located in the country in May 1930, three thousand were said to be controlled by the four largest companies: Paramount-Publix, Fox, Warners, and RKO.[41] The chain theaters tended to be large and centrally located. They were among the first to convert to sound and the most likely to profit from it since they were exempt from the need to pay licensing fees for the performance rights to the soundtrack music.[42]

A similar conflict between chains and independents had shaped the emergent broadcasting industry, where the American radio networks, Steve Wurtzler explains, had likewise adopted the chain store as an administrative model: "A local NBC affiliate, like the downtown Woolworth's or Rexall, mediated between a national provider (of programs) and geographically dispersed consumers."[43] Also anticipating the film industry was the radio industry's strategy vis-à-vis its independent, nonchain competitors, which involved promoting standardized programming as an improvement in quality over what local providers could offer. Just as the radio networks had denigrated the local talent featured on independent radio stations, the sound-era theater chains promised to replace inferior local entertainers with sound film recordings of first-rate orchestras and acts from the metropolitan centers.[44] As with the independent broadcasters, the number of independent movie theaters declined in the face of competition from the chains.

The relevance of the chain store phenomenon to movie exhibition is an explicit theme in *Footlight Parade* (dir. Lloyd Bacon, 1933), where stage-show producer Chester Kent (James Cagney) faces devastating competition from "talking pictures." Chester revives his career after a chance visit to a retail outlet. Searching for aspirin to soothe his talkie-induced headache, he seizes on the chain store concept for a new business producing live-entertainment prologues for talkies. "The chain store idea solves everything!" declares Chester. In fact, however, a conception of film exhibition based on the retail chain contradicted the film industry's understanding of the movie theater as, to quote the 1927 handbook *Building Theatre Patronage*, a "land of romance" that provided "escape" from the "commercialized world."⁴⁵ As theaters were wired for sound and theater orchestras and other live entertainers vanished, the sense of respite associated with the motion picture experience dissipated. In the United States, "sound . . . killed off that sense of relaxation in a picture house," reported a journalist in January 1929.⁴⁶ In 1930, as the economic recession hit and the public began exploring entertainment alternatives such as miniature golf, weekly film attendance in the United States fell from ninety million to seventy-five million.⁴⁷ Low attendance combined with the high costs of sound conversion led a vast number of movie theaters in North America to close in 1930, when the total number plunged from 21,993 theaters at the beginning of the year to only 14,126 at the end.⁴⁸

Attempts by exhibitors to draw customers with door prizes, "giveaways" of dishes and other consumer goods, "blonde nights," and other such gimmicks only added to the sense that movie theaters had become indistinguishable from the retail economy at large. With theaters enlisting the sponsorship of local businesses for giveaways and other consumer-product promotions, "a list of the stuff handed out [made movie houses] sound more like general merchandising stores than theatres," protested *Variety* in April 1930.⁴⁹ The consumerist current in sound cinema was spiraling out of control, critics complained. In December 1930, as the economic recession deepened, the editor of *Motion Picture News*, a weekly for American film exhibitors, blamed consumerist incursions into the movie theater for affronting "the dignity of the motion picture's home."⁵⁰

Exemplifying the excessive commercialism were musical films, with their many product tie-ins via multiple media. As commodities, songs offered an advantage that was also a drawback: they were impossible to ignore. One can avert one's gaze from a billboard, but one can't refuse to hear a commercial song, thanks to singing ushers, incessant radio play, and "loud speakers that never stop bellowing."⁵¹ When ordinary promotional practice included the amplification of the songs from Universal's *Show Boat* (dir. Harry Pollard, 1929) in major cities across the country through "a super loud speaker on a truck," it became hard to draw the line between advertising and noise pollution.⁵² "Everywhere I go those terrible advertisements scream at me," complains Barbara (Claudette Colbert) in *The Big Pond* (dir. Hobart Henley, 1930), referring to the music used to promote Billings Chewing Gum. Compounding the aggravation is the news that her fiancé Pierre (Maurice Chevalier) has written a new jingle based on the melody of "You Brought a New Kind of Love for Me," the film's theme. Thus the commercialization that had been playing out in the culture at large is enacted in the film's story, where what begins as a romantic ballad ends up as an advertisement. The same phenomenon informs the beginning of *Say It with Songs* (dir. Lloyd Bacon, 1929), when Al Jolson sings "Crazy for You" and the representative of the Excelsior Automobile Company responds, "That was great, just great. I was wondering, though, if you could put something in the chorus about our new transmission." A backlash from audiences came in the summer of 1930, which led the Hollywood companies to try to change course. To cite merely one example, in December of that year, the Loews chain, in a bid to improve the ambience in its theaters, removed the sheet-music stands.[53]

Product Placements

Beyond the explicit story references, the American cinema's integration into the country's retail economy surfaced in the films' mise-en-scène via a wide variety of name-brand products, from automobiles, provided gratis to moviemakers by car manufacturers, to "national brands of food for kitchen scenes."[54] Warners/First National, for example, was reported in 1929 to have formal product placement and merchandising arrangements for Brunswick radios and discs, Jantzen bathing suits, LaFrance jewelry, Helbros watches, Leading Lady frocks, Max Factor cosmetics, Graybar electric appliances, Pharaoh draperies, Martin band instruments, Kellogg's All-Bran cereal, and other retail goods.[55]

Among the familiar commodities on display was Lux soap, boxes of which appear in various films of the period, whether produced by Warner Brothers or other companies. In MGM's *The Broadway Melody*, Hank (Bessie Love) not only pours from a box of Lux but also sings the radio jingle associated with the product: "It's the Lux 'bubble song,'" she announces to her sister. A box of Lux even finds its way into the mise-en-scène of the German-made *Der Blaue Engel* (dir. Josef von Sternberg, 1930). When the impressario Kiepert (Kurt Gerron) enters the dressing room to inform Lola (Marlene Dietrich) and Dr. Rath (Emil Jannings) that they must return to the Blue Angel nightclub, visible on a table, positioned in the middle of the frame, is a spotlighted box of Lux.

In *Bad Company* (dir. Tay Garnett, 1931), coproduced by RKO Pictures, an RCA-owned company, corporate connections are manifest in the mise-en-scène through the delivery of messages via "RCA Radiogram" and the large RCA radio set given by crime boss Goldie Gorio (Ricardo Cortez) to the young couple played by Helen Twelvetrees and John Garrick. They are also invoked via metacommentary through Goldie's ubiquitous logo, an ornate, plaque-like G, which turns up in numerous scenes, affixed on furniture, stationery, apartment buildings, cigarettes, a smoking jacket, a statue pedestal, and a wall ornament.

Priming viewers to come to the films ready to recognize the goods on display were the period's marketing campaigns, whose store-window displays, magazine advertisements, billboards, newspaper inserts, and radio programs singled out the products serving in films as props and costumes. Film-related advertising campaigns were a focus of coverage in *Motion Picture News*, a weekly intended for film exhibitors, which included in each issue a twelve-page survey in which theater managers across the country described a wide range of promotional practices linking consumer products to films. A report from Los Angeles regarding RKO's *Dixiana* (dir. Luther Reed, 1930) is typical, detailing how "effective and attention-arresting tie-ups were effected with a score of local merchants who plugged in their windows anything in the picture tied in with their product." Among the products were cigars, mint julep drinks, New Orleans pralines, Mission Dry drinks, toiletry items associated with costar Bebe Daniels, and, of course, the discs and sheet music for the film's theme songs, which featured in the windows of local music stores and also on radio programs for special "*Dixiana* Mardi Gras Festivals."[56]

Songs as Consumer Goods

Prominent among the commodities on display in films were the film-related discs and sheet music available for purchase in both theaters and various additional retail outlets, including department stores. Warner Brothers, for example, in the summer of 1930, began selling film music by concession in two hundred department stores in the United States.[57] In this context, the presence of the film's theme song in the mise-en-scène served an advertising function. Examples include the music visible on music stands in the nightclub scene in *Red-Headed Woman* (dir. Jack Conway, 1932), the scenes of the dress rehearsal and the opening night performance in *Pointed Heels* (dir. Edward Sutherland, 1929), and the orchestra performance during the prologue of *This Is the Night* (dir. Frank Tuttle, 1932). Moments when a character handles a disc whose label announces the film's theme are also prevalent. In *I'm No Angel* (dir. Wesley Ruggles, 1933), Tira (Mae West) chooses from her record collection "Nobody Loves Me Like that Dallas Man," a release from the Famous Recording Company, a Paramount subsidiary, which features as vocalist none other than West herself. In RKO's *Girl Crazy* (dir. William Seiter, 1932), when "the Arizona villain" (Stanley Fields) praises "the West" ("We love every cactus bush that blooms on the proud bosom of her sweeping plains"), comedian Robert Woolsey assumes that a film song is being promoted: "I got to buy that record!"

In some cases, song-related commodities instigate plot developments. In *Feet First* (dir. Clyde Bruckman, 1930), the romantic subplot begins when Harold (Harold Lloyd) helps pick up the armload of sheet music that Barbara (Barbara Kent) has spilled onto the sidewalk. While Harold retrieves the music, an insert reveals the Santley Brothers edition of Fats Waller and Harry Link's "I've Got a Feeling I'm Falling." In *Lonesome* (dir. Paul Fejos, 1928), the playing of Nick Lucas's Brunswick recording of Irving Berlin's "Always" (the label clearly visible in several inserts) instigates the plot's surprise conclusion by revealing to Mary (Barbara Kent, again) that Jim (Glenn Tyron), the lover she had feared was lost forever, has been in fact living next door all along. In *The Big Broadcast* (dir. Frank Tuttle, 1932), the final twenty minutes center on Stuart Erwin's surreal attempt to obtain from the "Erich Pohl Phonograph and Radio" store a disc featuring Bing Crosby's recording of "Please!," the film's theme. The disc, whose retrieval will allow the make-or-break broadcast to conclude with its grand finale, appears in cutaways that reveal the label of the Famous Recording Company.

Two common attributes of the period's song-related product displays are evident in *Say It with Songs* when Kitty (Marian Nixon) prepares to play for her boy (Davey Lee) a recording on the Victor label of "Little Pal" that features as vocalist her imprisoned husband, Joe Lane, played by Al Jolson (see fig. 5.1).

The first typical attribute is the depiction of the consumer of popular music as a young woman. In *Lonesome*, Mary, in her apartment following the climactic rainstorm, overhears "Always" while images of both the song's sheet music and a spinning disc player appear superimposed over her rapturous response. In *I'm No Angel*, Mae West chooses a disc from what appears to be a large personal collection. In *Feet First*, mentioned above, Barbara drops her armload of sheet music onto the sidewalk. In *Glorifying the American Girl* (dir. Millard Webb and John Harkrider, 1929), an insert showing the folio for Gene Buck and James Hanley's "No Foolin'" provides

Figure 5.1. A frame from the "Little Pal" performance (screen capture, *Say It with Songs*, 1929)

the establishing shot for the opening scene in the department store, where Gloria (Mary Eaton) plugs the tune to customers at the music counter. A simple but emblematic moment occurs in the cabaret scene near the beginning of *Millie* (dir. John Francis Dillon, 1931) when the film's heroine, responding to the band's performance of an instrumental version of the film's title song, interjects, "Oh, I love this tune they're playing!" In conversion-era cinema, the most appreciative listeners, it seems, are female.[58]

Also typical of product placements in conversion-era musical films is the shot composition for the insert of the disc that Kitty is about to play in *Say It with Songs* (see fig. 5.2).

The insert presents the label straight on, with no reminder of the scene's space.[59] The thumb of the actor supposedly handling the disc cannot be seen, nor can any portion of the bedroom where the scene is set. The product is presented in isolation from the film's story world. The same decontextualized presentation is characteristic of other song-related inserts in films of the period. Like the song sequences themselves, the discs and folios show up in the film's story world without fully belonging to it. The purpose is

Figure 5.2. A frame from the "Little Pal" performance (screen capture, *Say It with Songs*, 1929)

perhaps less to construct a convincing mise-en-scène than to remind the viewer of the recording's status as a separate commodity, available for purchase and consumption apart from the film.

The Singularity of American Radio

Beyond cinema's integration in the consumer economy of the United States, a further condition for the American cinema's theme-song fad was the unique role of commercial broadcasting in the American mediascape. In European countries, broadcast radio was typically administered as a state monopoly under the control of the ministries responsible for the postal service and the telegraph. Radio in Europe thus developed as a public service rather than in accordance with commercial imperatives, and often in deliberate avoidance of the commercialism of radio in the United States.[60] The public-welfare mandate carried aesthetic implications by favoring programming with no advertising and an emphasis on classical symphonic music over commercial songs. In contrast, radio in the United States featured, along with numerous advertisements, an "enormous amount of dance music," reported conductor Eugene Goossens in August 1930: "The average American radio enthusiast can tune in to fifty or sixty stations, [and] the great majority of the programs are comprised of jazz and light music."[61] The prominence of commercial songs made radio in the United States more relevant to cinema than radio in Europe.

Second, radio audiences in the United States were much larger per capita than in Europe, where administrative and financial barriers constrained radio's spread as a common household appliance. The radio sets that, by and large, were cheap in the United States were expensive in Europe. Also, radio owners in Britain, Germany, and other countries were required to register with the government and pay licensing fees. The extra fees, together with the high price of the radios themselves, restricted working-class access to the new technology.[62] In contrast, the American radio industry rested on a unique counterintuitive strategy whereby "free" advertising-driven programming stimulated the purchase of vast quantities of inexpensive radio sets and hence facilitated radio's widest possible dissemination throughout the populace. In 1930, 43 percent of all families in the United States were said to possess home radio sets. The prevalence allowed radio to evolve into a major competitor of cinema.[63] By 1932, reports film historian Peter Baxter, "Something like 75 percent of film tickets were sold after 7.30 in the evening, but for increasing numbers of Americans, the evening hours were given over to what the radio networks had to offer."[64]

The Overplay of Film Songs on Radio

The broadcasting of film songs had ambivalent effects on musical films. On the one hand, radio play served to promote film-related songs and hence the films themselves. With many films named after their theme songs, the mere mention on the air of the song's title was said to count as "free advertising" for the film.[65] On the other hand, radio, it was alleged, exhausted songs commercially, overexposing them to the point of sapping interest in the films with which they were associated. As reported by *Variety* in May 1930, "Constant repetition over the radio as many as eight and ten times from one station in a single day has the effect of killing songs.... Potential hits are actually 'old' in three weeks as a result of the air."[66] Endless song play was the norm in the radio-dense Northeast: "Any of the currently popular songs can be heard almost hour after hour and station after station right through from dinner-time until bed. Chances are even that more than one station will be performing the same [song] simultaneously."[67] In December 1929, a single tune was "clocked 24 times in one night."[68] The unwelcome consequence of the continual repetition was the exhaustion of the music's appeal.[69] "Popular tunes get on the wireless, on the gramophone, on the talkies—and on the nerves," went a joke at the time.[70]

Questions of timing became critical. Songs were usually released in advance of their films, so by the time the film came out, the songs might be already used up. Film producer Samuel Goldwyn claimed that he was reluctant to produce film versions of stage musicals because "the tunes [were] out of date by the time they reach[ed] the screen."[71] One solution, undertaken by Goldwyn for *Whoopee!* (dir. Thornton Freeland, 1930), his film adaptation of the Broadway hit starring Eddie Cantor, was to jettison most of the original music in favor of new compositions. Another option was to try to restrict the music's circulation through legal action. As early as 1929, the American Society of Composers, Authors and Publishers (ASCAP) had sought to block radio play of certain film themes, either by withholding the song altogether or by limiting the number of times per night or per week that a single station could broadcast it.[72] A playful allusion to the film audience's antagonism to overplayed songs comes up in the coda to *Big Boy* (dir. Alan Crosland, 1930), when Al Jolson, who appears out of character as himself, is asked to sing "Sonny Boy," which causes the audience to leap from their seats and dash for the exit. Jolson then quickly reassures, "Wait a minute, folks. I'm not going to sing 'Sonny Boy,'" and the audience, relieved, returns.

Adding to the problem of overplay was the alleged low quality of many of the songs. While a strong film had the "power to carry mediocre song material to hitdom," a weak song could sabotage a film's success.[73] In this regard, the formal simplicity of popular music was a mixed blessing. While making songs more memorable than "classical music," and thus enhancing their commercial potential, the predictable form could also make them seem cheap and ephemeral. Rather than a source of enchantment, a song could easily become an annoyance. There were not enough good songs to go around. Critics complained that the typical film song was too simple and clichéd to withstand the amount of play it would receive. "Repeated listening," observed a critic, "makes [popular music] recognizable for what it is and quickly turns liking into loathing."[74] A humorous reference to the period's formulaic songs occurs in *I'm No Angel* when Mae West, sorting through her record collection, settles on "Nobody Loves Me

Like that Dallas Man" after rejecting near copies whose titles refer to "that Memphis Man" and "that Frisco Man."

The Song Market's Aesthetic Effects

By the end of the summer of 1930, the bottom had fallen out of the film-song market, and the Hollywood companies responded by suddenly curtailing the making of musical films and extracting songs out of films already in production.[75] In September, at the beginning of the 1930–31 film season, "only the most daring of the producers [were] risking films with interpolated songs," reported the *New York Times*.[76] The "theme song," declared *Time* magazine in December, was "now obsolete in Hollywood."[77] "Musical shows just could not get a hearing at theatres throughout the country," reported MGM's head of music apropos of *The Prodigal* (dir. Harry Pollard, 1931), an MGM vehicle for opera tenor Lawrence Tibbett. "We were forced to cut out all but a few numbers due to the exhibitor's attitude in the matter."[78] Even songs composed by top-flight writers such as Irving Berlin, Cole Porter, and the Gershwins were scrapped.[79] *Reaching for the Moon* (dir. Edmund Goulding, 1930), for example, whose music and scenario were written by Berlin, was released in December 1930 with only one of the songs still included. The song in question, "When the Folks High-Up Do the Mean Low-Down," was likely retained because it features Bing Crosby, whose celebrity status at that point, thanks to radio, was on the rise. Reflecting the policy change was a reduction in the workforce. By the end of 1930, the number of composers and lyricists under contract to Hollywood companies dropped from 143 down to 20, and the music divisions of the large studios were reduced to a small fraction of their size a year before.[80] The same songwriters who flooded into Hollywood in 1929 were now returning to New York.[81]

The aesthetic impact of the new film-music policy is reflected in the statistical research conducted for this book. Figure 5.3 provides a stark illustration, tracking season by season the percentage of a film's running time devoted to singing shots in a sample of 121 American films of 1928–34.[82]

The sample includes musical films along with films belonging to other genres that nonetheless contain song performances. The criteria for inclusion in the sample were that the film be made in the United States and that it contain at least one shot depicting someone singing or whistling a commercial pop song.

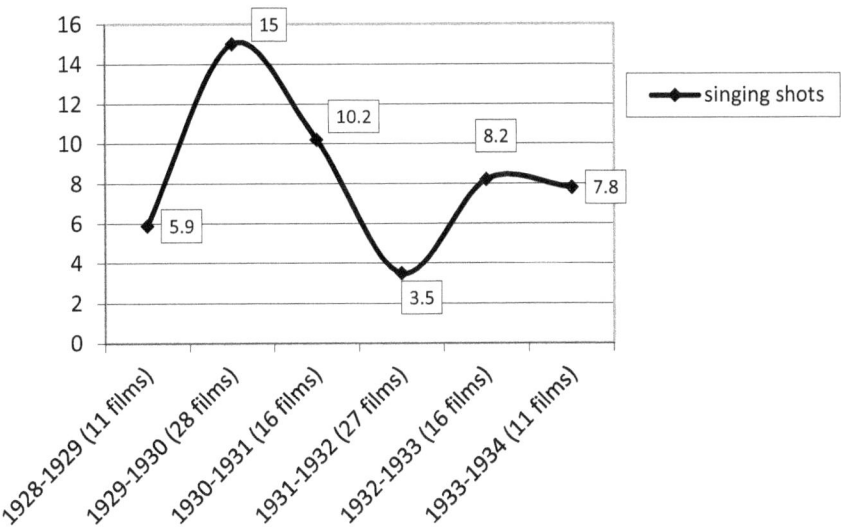

Figure 5.3. Running-time percentages for singing shots in 121 American films of 1928–34, by season

The 1929–30 season stands out in figure 5.3 as the peak for singing shots, topping out at 15 percent, a level three times higher than for the previous season. In the next season, however, 1930–31, when producers began removing songs from films and ceased making musical films, the singing-shot numbers start falling. The decline continues until 1931–32, when singing shots make up a mere 3.5 percent of a film's total running time, on average—a tiny fraction of what they were two years before. A change becomes evident in the next season, 1932–33, when the singing-shot percentage once again starts to rise. Facilitating the increase was the release in that season of a wave of musical films, including *Forty Second Street* (dir. Lloyd Bacon, 1933), the first film in Warner Brothers' Busby Berkeley cycle, and *Flying Down to Rio* (dir. Thornton Freeland, 1933), the forerunner to RKO's Astaire and Rogers series. These films, whose success led critics to proclaim the musical film's rejuvenation, borrow elements from the musical films of 1929–30, but they can also be seen to comprise a unique genre with a characteristic syntax where song performances function to advance romantic-comedy plots.[83] This emergence of "the musical" as a distinct genre is perhaps reflected in figure 5.3's singing-shot percentage for 1932–33, which, though higher than for the preceding seasons, is lower than for 1929–30, as if the singing shots that return in 1932–33 no longer permeate Hollywood cinema in its entirety but surface mainly in a specific genre.

The Shift Away from Melodrama and toward Comedy

A movement toward comedy was evident already in 1930–31, when "musical pictures with comedy predominating" surfaced as one of the season's trends.[84] During the next two years, the musical films that drew audiences in the United States typically featured vaudevillians rather than professional singers. Trained vocalists such as Lawrence Tibbett, John McCormack, and Dennis King—the new film stars of 1929–30—were out, while comedians like the Marxes, Cantor, and Wheeler and Woolsey were in.[85] Labeled by Cantor "comedies with music" as distinct from "musical comedies," the new films included *Animal Crackers* (dir. Victor Heerman, 1930), the second Marx Brothers film from Paramount; Cantor's own *Whoopee!*, the first in Sam Goldwyn's cycle of films starring Cantor; and no less than three features from RKO starring humorists Wheeler and Woolsey: *Dixiana*, which premiered in August; *Half Shot at Sunrise* (dir. Paul Sloane, 1930), which came out in October; and *Hook, Line and Sinker* (dir. Edward Cline, 1930), released in December.[86] Farce, it seems, made songs palatable for an American public weary of the song-loaded melodramas of the preceding two years. Symptomatic of the new policy was Warner Brothers' editing of *Fifty Million Frenchmen* (dir. Lloyd Bacon, 1931), which involved the replacement of Cole Porter's songs with scenes featuring the comedy duo Olsen and Johnson, whose "ability for crazy comics," a critic noted, had become "the whole show."[87]

Song Repetitions and Parody

The move toward comedy, and specifically farcical comedy, was perhaps inevitable in light of the alleged overplay of film songs via radio and other media. Song repetitions in films invite an ironic or parodic treatment. The pattern is clear for sentimental ballads, for example, which—inevitably, it seems—become less sentimental through repetition. In *Tanned Legs* (1929), Bill sings the romantic ballad "With You, With Me" when he asks Peggy to marry him. Several scenes later, vaudevillian Allen Kearns performs a comic version of the same tune. In *Girl Crazy*, the Gershwins' "But Not for Me" is first performed "straight" by Eddie Quilian and Arline Judge and then in multiple comic styles by Mitzi Green, who impersonates Bing

Crosby, vaudevillian Roscoe Ates (famous for his stutter), dramatic actor George Arliss, and stage spinster Edna May Oliver. In melodramas, late performances of a film's theme often deflate the emotional heft they carried earlier, as in RKO's *Millie* (dir. John Francis Dillon, 1931), in which Nacio Herb Brown's title song is repeated in a scene "eight years later" but with Millie's charm now referred to in the past tense. In *Party Girl* (dir. Victor Halperin, 1929), the film's theme "Oh, How I Adore You" is heard first when Helen (Clara Bow), alone in her apartment, fervently sings it. The tune is then heard again, a few scenes later, when Diane, the cynical roommate, questions the sincerity of Helen's boyfriend, Jake, by mockingly quoting the song's lyrics. In comedies, songs that start out as comic devolve into buffoonery, as in *Whoopee!* when Eddie Cantor alters the lyrics of his signature hit "Makin' Whoopee" to produce the mock version "Makin' Waffles."

Parodic song repetition is an explicit theme in *The Big Pond* (dir. Hobart Henley, 1930), in which Pierre (Maurice Chevalier) struggles to win over his boss and the father of his fiancée, Barbara (Claudette Colbert). The crisis comes when Pierre, after hearing a street musician perform "You Brought a New Kind of Love to Me," is inspired to rewrite the lyrics so that the song advertises "Billings Chewing Gum" with lines like "I've brought a new kind of gum to you." The crass new lyrics please Barbara's father but antagonize Barbara, who abruptly calls off the marriage. Parodic renditions of "You Brought a New Kind of Love to Me" resurface in *Monkey Business* (dir. Norman McLeod, 1931), where the Marx Brothers, one after the other, imitate Chevalier's performance in *The Big Pond*, the level of absurdity rising with each rendition. The same pattern plays out in an extended form in *Horse Feathers* (dir. Norman Z. McLeod, 1932), where Zeppo's sentimental treatment of "Everyone Says I Love You" is followed in later scenes by comic renditions by Harpo, Chico, and Groucho. The rule of thumb is that the parody will increase in intensity with each repetition, so that the more a song is repeated, the more farcical the tone becomes.

Parody is the norm, too, for the numerous cases involving the repetition in one film of a song from another, as with the performances of "Sonny Boy" by Frank Richardson in Fox's *Sunny Side Up* (dir. David Butler, 1929) and by Marie Dressler and Polly Moran in two separate sequences in MGM's *The Hollywood Revue of 1929*. The same holds in *Palmy Days* (dir. A. Edward Sutherland, 1931) when Charlotte Greenwood parodies Marlene Dietrich's performance of "Falling in Love Again" from *The Blue Angel* (dir. Joseph von Sternberg, 1930) and in Warner Brothers' *The Show of Shows* (dir. John Adolfi, 1930) in the parody of MGM's "Singin' in the Rain." The parodic inclination is pushed to the limit in the many short films of the period intended to exploit songs associated with a studio's feature films, as with Warner Brothers' Looney Tunes and Merrie Melodies cartoon series, where virtually all performances are parodies.

Song repetitions animated by an ironic or parodic intent have it both ways, so to speak. In deriding the commercialism of the song industry, they encourage a conspiratorial bond with the audience. The Marx Brothers win our respect because they know what we know: that the sentiment behind songs like "Everyone Says I Love You" is contrived. At the same time, the mockery does nothing to impede the commercial goal of inscribing the song into the viewer-consumer's memory. From a marketing standpoint, a parody is no less effective than a straight rendition. Either way, the viewer ends up more likely to recall the tune.

The American musical film's shift in genre, away from melodrama and toward comedy, did not simply coincide with the excessive repetition of songs in films and in the culture at large. Instead, the two were causally connected, with the move toward comedy enabled by the period's practices of song repetition. To repeat a song is to open the way for comedy, especially the broad comedy associated with the vaudeville comedians who became prominent in American musical films during 1930–32. Another way to make the point is to propose that the initial prevalence in American musical films of melodramatic stories and serious vocalists was not sustainable given the extent of the song repetition in films and in the culture at large. Parody appears less prominent in musical films made in Europe, where radio play was not a major factor, and musical films often exhibited a different, more unified aesthetic, so that the songs, instead of coming forward as distinct interludes, condition the film's entire form, the dialogue scenes included.

Notes

1. "Ducking Musicals," 35. See also M. Quigley, "Musical Pictures," 24.
2. "The Year in America," in S. Rayment, ed., *The Kinematograph Year Book, 1931*, 17.
3. D. Churchill, "Hollywood Arranges for a Moment Musicale," X3.
4. K. Thompson, *Exporting Entertainment*, 159; and C. Trask, "Audible Films Inspire German Producers," 114.
5. The exact figures are $1,198,172 for the foreign market and $548,683 for the domestic. J. Layton and D. Pierce. *King of Jazz*, 197.

6. "1,250 Kinos haben abgestimmt," 1.
7. W. Meisel, "Der Tonfilmschlager," 3.
8. P. Autré, "Musique et disques de cinéma," 110. Regarding the size of the market, see the extensive documentation for recordings of film songs in France in G. Basile and C. Gavouyère, *La chanson française dans le cinéma des années trente*.
9. On song-slide performances in the nickelodeon era, see R. Altman, *Silent Film Sound*, 182–93.
10. M. Babcock, "Tin Pan Alley Invades Town," C13.
11. "The Dealers and Theme Song Sales," 57; and "Tonfilmschlager mit 1.8 Millionen," 3.
12. J. Hoffman, "Westward the Course of Tin Pan Alley," 38–39, 94, 98–100.
13. M. Quigley, "The Truth about Hollywood: 'No Silent Pictures,'" 27.
14. A. Green, "The Theme Song," 28.
15. "Jolson-Brunswick Renewal," 56; and "Jolson's Talker Royalties," 56.
16. "'Fool' Tops Holland as Disk Sales Soar," 5; "'Fool' Big in Belgrade; Talkers Help Music Sales," 7; G. Clarriere, "'Singing Fool' Receipts," 19; and "Prague Hails 'Fool,'" 4.
17. "Jolson Leads All International Disc Sellers with 'Sonny Boy,'" 227.
18. Quoted in an untitled press release from Will Hays, dated January 28, 1930. D. Gomery, ed., *The Will Hays Papers*, part II, reel 3.
19. V. de Grazia, *Irresistible Empire*.
20. See, for example, "Pictures on Way to Third Place in World's Industrial Importance," 5.
21. "Motion Pictures and Trade," 8.
22. The quotation from Sapène comes from "Sapène Center Entire French Situation," 6. An overview of French complaints regarding the presence of American films in France can be found in G. Clarrière, "The Western Peril," 153–56.
23. On the link between Hollywood's overseas popularity and a country's level of discretionary income, see R. Maltby, "On the Prospect of Writing Cinema History from Below," 89–90.
24. D. Gomery, *The Coming of Sound*, 152–53.
25. R. Sanjek and D. Sanjek, *The American Popular Music Business in the Twentieth Century*, 40. See also "Witmarks Line Up with Warners for Music Publishing Combo," 57.
26. "Paramount-Publix and CBS Like Radio-Keith with N.B.C.," 65.
27. T. Doherty, *Pre-Code Hollywood*, 32.
28. D. Suisman, *Selling Sounds*, 259–70.
29. L. Nichols, "Tin Pan Alley Is Weaving Its Lyrics in New Ways," 81.
30. "Radio, Over-Production, High Prices, Mechanicals—All Blamed for Slump," 81; and "Jobbers Can't Wait, Send Back Film Songs," 74.
31. "The Dealers and Theme Song Sales," 57; and "Publix Music Counters Have Edge on Stores," 56.
32. On the chain store as an American phenomenon and its limited adoption in Europe during the interwar decades, see V. de Grazia, *Irresistible Empire*, 130–83.
33. On theater chains in the United States in the 1920s and 1930s, see M. Valentine, *The Show Starts on the Sidewalk*, 72–75, 88, 90–92.
34. H. Lewis, *The Motion Picture Industry*, 333–34.
35. "Lobby Chain Stores—Publix," 9. See also "Publix Music Counters Have Edge on Stores," 56.
36. "All Publix Managers to Learn Song Plug," 65.
37. "Publix Convinced on Music Sales Enlarging," 55.

38. "Special Metro Song Discs in Loew's Lobbies," 227.
39. M. Valentine, *The Show Starts on the Sidewalk*, 73.
40. On theater chains in the 1920s, see Crafton, *The Talkies*, 68.
41. "Circuits 1/3 of Wired," 13. See also D. Crafton, *The Talkies*, 256; and H. Lewis, *The Motion Picture Industry*, 345.
42. On the advantages of the chains relative to the independent theaters, see D. Gomery, *The Coming of Sound*, 3–4.
43. S. Wurtzler, *Electric Sounds*, 181–83.
44. S. Wurtzler, *Electric Sounds*, 175.
45. J. Barry and E. Sargent, *Building Theatre Patronage*, 12, quoted in L. Fischer, *Designing Women*, 185–86.
46. S. Silverman, "The Smothering Talker," 17.
47. The attendance statistics, which were taken from *Film Daily Yearbook* and other sources, are reported in "Appendix A: Movie Theatre Statistics, 1922–1992," in M. Valentine, *The Show Starts on the Sidewalk*, 195.
48. The theater numbers are listed in M. Valentine, *The Show Starts on the Sidewalk*, 195.
49. "Giveaways in Lobbies," 3.
50. "From Cinema Palaces to Country Stores," 12.
51. "From Cinema Palaces to Country Stores," 12.
52. "Loud Ballyhoo," 5.
53. D. Crafton, *The Talkies*, 261–62.
54. "Manufacturers Want that Screen Plug," 1; and "Big Biz Uses Showdom Aid," 3, 10.
55. H. Crooker, "Tie-Ups, Tie-ins, Advertising and Exploiting F. N. Pictures," 32, 98.
56. "Here's Dope on 'Dixiana' Campaign," 98.
57. "Warners Plan Music Counter Chain," 72.
58. The depiction of song listeners as young females is characteristic of European films too. Exemplary is the song-loving devotee of radio, recorded music, and cinema played by Käthe von Nagy in *Ich bei Tag und du bei Nacht* (dir. Ludwig Berger, 1932).
59. Strangely, this label differs from the Victor label visible in the preceding shot. It may refer to a fictional company since I have been unable to find any information on Metropolitan Recordings, let alone a release on that label of "Little Pal."
60. On the intent of radio administrators in Europe to avoid the commercialism of American radio, see A. Briggs and P. Burke, *A Social History of the Media*, 219–23.
61. Eugene Goossens, "The Gramophone in America," 119.
62. On radio in Germany specifically, see P. Jelavich, *Berlin Alexanderplatz*, 38–42.
63. "The American Listener: A British Impression," 131.
64. P. Baxter, *Just Watch!*, 31.
65. "Picture Title Plugs Dropped," 69.
66. "Air Killing Off Music Quickly," 73.
67. "Faint Hearted Publishers," 253.
68. "Along the Coast," 55. The tune in question was Shapiro and Bernstein's "What Do I Care?," which had been featured in a short film from Paramount.
69. "Music Sales and Radio," 73; and L. Goldstein, "Recording Companies Finding Things Improving despite the Slump and Radio Competition," 226.
70. "They Say . . ." 70.
71. E. Schallert, "Laugh Feature Brightens Sky," 9.

72. "Restricted Radio Use Continued of Show and Talker Musical Hits," 58.
73. A. Green, "Words about Music," 96.
74. A. Schmuck, "The Case for Mere Listening," 108.
75. See, for example, "Warners Curtailing Theme Songs in Pcts.," 57; and "Paramount Next to Ban Musicals as 'Sales Poison,'" 51.
76. "Doings in Hollywood," X6.
77. "Cinema: The New Pictures."
78. M. Merrick, "It's In, So It Can't Be Out," B11.
79. "Jobbers Can't Wait, Send Back Film Songs," 74.
80. The employment figures are taken from R. Sanjek and D. Sanjek, *The American Popular Music Business*, 43. Statistics for music-related jobs in Hollywood are cited in B. Swigart, "Studio Music," 121.
81. Regarding the exodus of songwriters, see "West Coast No More a Gold Coast," 97, 100; and "Music Men Again on Top," 73, 75.
82. Further details on the singing-shot percentages, including margins of error, are provided in table 6.1, appendix B.
83. On the emergence in 1933 of "the musical" as a distinct genre with a characteristic romantic-comedy syntax, see R. Altman, "The Musical."
84. "Operettas Out at First National," 1.
85. C. Stone, "Film Notes," 418; and "Come-Back for 'Musicals'? A 'Whoopee' Experience," 40.
86. The quotation from Cantor comes from P. Scheurer, "Eddie Cantor's Chief Asset: Eddie Cantor," B9.
87. "'Fifty Million Frenchmen,' without Music!" 74.

6

MUSICAL FILMS MADE IN GERMANY

SHAPING SOUND CINEMA'S EMERGENCE AS A GLOBAL PHENOMENON was Hollywood's rivalry with the German film industry. In the early 1930s, film producers in countries around the world made native-language sound films that competed with Hollywood films in their home markets. The German industry, however, rivaled Hollywood internationally.[1] In Germany, as in the United States, large production companies that were linked to powerful electric-sound conglomerates produced sound films that played to audiences worldwide.[2] Also in Germany, musical films were essential to the export strategy, especially with regard to Europe, where up to twenty-five thousand movie theaters—some 43 percent of the world's total—were located.[3] Particularly significant for the German musical film was France, where local production was too weak to supply a market comprising some three thousand theaters.[4] As these theaters began wiring for sound, film producers in Germany and Hollywood invested heavily in achieving success in France, which promised to open up access to other European countries.[5]

German films with French stars were highly competitive in this regard, ranking among the top films shown in France and in other countries where French-language films were popular, to the point of edging out the American films. In 1931, "French dialogue films made in Germany," warned the US Commerce Department, were more popular at the French box office than American films, ranking second only to native French productions.[6] The competition facilitated stylistic similarities between American and German musical films. Exemplary were the operettas directed by Ernst Lubitsch, whose musical pantomime and verse-like dialogue drew comparisons to the top German productions of the day.[7] With respect to the American cinema's mainstream, however, the Lubitsch films were unusual, as is suggested in a review in the *Los Angeles Times* of Ufa's breakthrough operetta *Die Drei von der Tankstelle* (dir. Wilhelm von Thiele, 1930), in which Lubitsch is identified as "the only director to fully realize musical comedy on American screens," in contrast to the many filmmakers in Germany working successfully in the genre.[8]

This chapter attributes the main style characteristics of German musical films to film-industrial conditions in Europe. The primary factor was the German film industry's strategy for exports, which came to differ from the American strategy in ways that carried aesthetic implications. The key difference became evident in 1931, when the Hollywood producers, keen to exploit their publicity investment in the films' stars, changed their method for the principal foreign markets: instead of producing films with foreign actors, they began taking American films with the original American stars and dubbing the voices. In contrast, the German producers continued making separate versions with actors who spoke the language of the film's target market. These actors can also be considered stars, but (as also discussed in chap. 3) motion picture stardom in Europe differed from that in the United States in ways that made acceptable a music-based style in which actors' performances merged into a film's formal patterning.

Music-Dominant Form in German Cinema

Films featuring singing performances were ubiquitous in the early 1930s, when all sound-equipped film industries produced them. They were essential to the output of Ufa, Tobis, and other German companies, where the project of incorporating recorded music into feature films was explored with unusual sophistication. Music-based filmmaking had a substantial history in Germany prior to electric sound. By 1907, the so-called *Tonbilder*, which matched up the image of a singer's performance to music from a recorded disc, became essential to the German film industry.[9] In the 1910s and 1920s, German inventors developed sound-image synchronization systems intended to help the musicians in theaters align their music with the moving image.[10] These included the Rhythmograph, which ultimately was adopted in Germany and other countries for tasks of sound film production and postproduction, including the dubbing of American films.[11]

The sound-era musical film, by some accounts, was uniquely suited to the film industry in Germany, where musical talent was abundant.[12] An anecdote attributed to Ufa executive Ludwig Klitsch concerns the visit of the company's management team to New York in 1928 to assess how Ufa might respond to American advances in sound cinema. As the story goes, the company's senior officers, though initially apprehensive at the prospect of competing with Hollywood, took solace from the music heard in the lobby of their New York hotel, which had been composed mainly by Germans and Austrians: "Suddenly a picture of the future emerged in which German music in consort with sound film would conquer the world."[13]

Justification for the optimism came with the *Operettenfilmen* released in 1930, the first year of industrial-level sound filmmaking in Europe, when *Die Drei von der Tankstelle, Zwei Herzen im Dreivierteltakt* (dir. Géza von Bolváry, 1930) and *Liebeswalzer* (dir. Wilhelm Thiele, 1930) proved popular not only in Germany and Austria but also in other European countries, where they circulated in the original German editions as well as various foreign-language versions. By the end of 1930, German musical films were said to dominate the film trade in Poland, Czechoslovakia, Austria, Hungary, Yugoslavia, Romania, and Bulgaria.[14] They also did well in France, where the successful premiere in November of *Le chemin du paradis* (dir. Wilhelm Thiele and Max de Vaucorbeil, 1930), the French edition of *Die Drei von der Tankstelle*, opened the way for further French-language versions of German musical films, which drew audiences not only in France but also in Romania, Switzerland, and other countries receptive to French-language films.[15] French versions soon comprised the majority of the German-made foreign productions.

In the early 1930s, during the last years of the Weimar Republic, the international popularity of the *Operettenfilmen* helped establish the German cinema, led by Ufa, as Hollywood's only rival in the sound-cinema field.[16] Musical films, and the hit songs linked to them, were bringing about a "musicalization of the world," proclaimed art historian Oscar Bie in 1931.[17] The main limit to the German cinema's international reach was the American film market, which turned out to be closed, by and large, to films made outside the United States. Nonetheless, among the relatively few foreign films that played in the United States, German films were unusually prominent. Of the 141 films imported into the United States in 1932, 67 came from Germany.[18] These films played mainly in New York and other cities with large German immigrant populations, where they drew devoted audiences. The *Kinematograph Year Book, 1931* (London), reported that "the foreign talkers which have been most successful in America are 'musicals,' mostly of German origin, shown here in their original language in the 'little theatres,' for engagements that lasted, in some instances, for months."[19] A celebrated case was *Zwei Herzen im Dreivierteltakt*, which ran in New York's Europa Theatre for nearly a year with no translation of the film's German speech.[20]

The German Musical Film as Exemplar

The significance of the German musical films is suggested by their exemplary status for filmmakers in other countries. In the United States, admirers included comedian Eddie Cantor, the star of a cycle of successful musical comedies beginning in 1930 with *Whoopee!* (dir. Thornton Freeland, 1930). A devoted viewer of German musical films in theaters in New York City, Cantor, in an interview in the fall of 1931, regretted that the aesthetic innovations of *Zwei Herzen im Dreivierteltakt* and other German productions of the day had failed to inspire emulation in Hollywood.[21] These films offered a potential model for the genre that Hollywood had seemed to overlook.

German musical films are distinct in some ways, but it should be noted that they also exhibit important similarities with their American counterparts. My analysis of shot types shows that musical films, regardless of the country of production, give less running time to dialogue and more to singing than do films belonging to other genres. Indeed, in this regard, almost no difference between German and American musical films is evident: in both cases, singing shots make up, on average, just over one-fourth of a film's running time, while dialogue shots clock in at around 57 percent and action shots at 27 percent.[22] In sum, regarding the parameters used for my analysis, the profile for the German musical films is virtually identical to that for the American. There *are* important differences in style between the German and American films, as Cantor's remarks suggest, but to see them we need to look beyond the statistics.

The main consideration taken up in this chapter is the extent to which the music-dominant form of the song sequences tends to surface also in the film's narrative passages. Wilhelm von Thiele, who directed *Die Drei von der Tankstelle, Liebeswalzer* (1930), *Die Privatsekretärin* (dir. Wilhelm von Thiele, 1931), and other operettas, emphasized that music in German films worked in tandem with the actors' movements to amplify the meaning of the dialogue.[23] A similar point was made by composer Kurt London, who found in *Einbrecher* (dir. Hanns Schwarz, 1930) a "musical development of the film's plot" through a rhythm "expressed in gestures, noises, or accented words."[24] *Die verkaufte Braut* (dir. Max Ophuls, 1932), for example, offered what a critic described as "a complete fusion of the musical form with the rhythm of the succession of images."[25] Replete with cartoonlike moments when the actors' speech and physical movements synch up with the music's pulse and meter, the German musical films combine, as composer Heymann put it, "music and image [into] a unified artwork."[26] An impression of music-image unity also defines Hollywood song sequences, but in the German films such unity obtains during not only the songs but other scenes too.

Musical Pantomime

With respect to the German films' music-driven form, two specific practices merit emphasis. One is music-accompanied pantomime during passages without dialogue; when the actors' movements match up to the rhythm of the nondiegetic musical accompaniment, a "construction in dumb show," as London put it, is achieved.[27] The "absolute coincidence of rhythm and form in music and picture" departed from the norm for the period's talkies, where, as discussed in chapter 4, scenes often played with no musical accompaniment at all. One might say that in the Hollywood films speech takes the place of music, whereas in the German films the opposite was the case: music supplants speech. The oddity of the German practice of music-driven action was noted in the *New York Times* apropos of Ufa's *Melody of the Heart*, the English version of *Melodie des Herzens* (dir. Hanns Schwarz, 1929), which includes "long periods when no lines are spoken and none of the characters has a chance to be lonely, for no matter where they go they seem to be followed by an unseen orchestra."[28]

The matching of visual action with musical movement in the German operettas was said to restore the visual action of silent cinema but in a manner unique to the sound-on-film techniques of the present day, with the exact synchronization of the image to the music in certain German films comparable to the musicalized visuals in Disney's animated shorts.[29] Examples include the slapstick interlude in *Ein Lied, ein Kuss, ein Mädel* (dir. Géza von Bolváry, 1932), when the drunken employee careens through the record shop, his pratfalls punctuated by cymbal hits, whoops on a slide whistle, and other musical effects; the concert-of-typewriters sequence in *Die Privatsekretärin*, where dozens of female typists tap keys, shift carriages, and toss their hair in unison to the music's tempo; the scene in the theater in *Viktor und Viktoria*, where the stage hands, via a montage sequence, react in mock surprise to the revelation from "Viktor" (Renate Müller) that "he" is, in reality, a woman; and the "silent cure" scene in *Quick* (dir. Robert Siodmak, 1932), when Lilian Harvey, accompanied by an orchestral rendition of the film's title song, reacts in pantomime to the nurses who monitor her.

Comparable moments can be found in certain Hollywood films, such as *The Smiling Lieutenant* (1931), perhaps the most music-determined of the films directed by Lubitsch. Recall the opening scene, when the bill collector trudges up and down the staircase to Maurice Chevalier's apartment, his footsteps dotted by quarter notes played on the horns; and then a moment later, when the young woman dashes up the same steps, her movement emulated by an up-tempo flurry on the strings. A further example is the cartoonlike opening of *The Big Broadcast* (dir. Frank Tuttle, 1932), when the ticking of the clock matches up to the mail boy's action of shuffling through letters and the cat's slow-motion footsteps; or the later scene in the same film, when Stuart Erwin's fast-motion search for the Bing Crosby disc synchs up with the music of the Vincent Lopez Orchestra, whose trumpet player simulates the voice of the irate neighbor.

For the most part, however, moments of musical pantomime are less prominent in Hollywood films, where they are normally reserved for conventional transitions like the film's opening scene. Paramount's *This Is the Night* (dir. Frank Tuttle, 1932) may open with a homage to René Clair's Paris, with rhyming dialogue and a musicalized rendition of actors' movements, but once the prologue-like opening concludes and Cary Grant and Charlie Ruggles appear, a conventional narration kicks in, and the film reverts to the dialogue-based scenography typical of Hollywood cinema.

In German films, however, passages of musical pantomime occur not only during the opening scene but also periodically through the whole film, and they are sometimes extended in screen duration, running for three minutes or more. Extralong passages include the scene in the Supraphon record shop in *Ein Lied, ein Kuss, ein Mädel*, where the station manager mistakenly assumes that the female employee's gestures are intended as flirtation; the barbershop scene in *Viktor und Viktoria*, where Susanne (Renate Müller) and Robert (Adolf Wohlbrück), sitting side by side, receive haircuts and shaves while nondiegetic orchestral music plays in tight cartoonlike synchronization with the comic action; or the five-minute dressing-room scene in the same film where Susanne, disguised in drag for the first time, awkwardly shares the room with the clown and strongman, their speechless activity of costume changing interspersed with orchestral music. This sort of sustained pantomime is common in German cinema and rare in American.

Verse-Like Dialogue

The German films are also distinguished by dialogue passages in which speech acquires songlike characteristics, so that the actors do not speak their lines so much as sing them. Examples include the songwriting sequence near the beginning of *Die verliebte Firma* (dir. Max Ophüls, 1932), where the collaborators propose lyrics against intermittent piano accompaniment; the three-minute scene in *Leise flehen meine Lieder* (dir. Willy Forst, 1933) where the young Franz Schubert's taming of the unruly schoolboys is signaled through the boys' rote repetition of the mathematical formula, which begins in unison speech and ends in choral singing; and numerous scenes in *Viktor und Viktoria*, such as—to cite merely one example—the two-and-a-half-minute scene in the automated restaurant, where Susanne and Viktor discuss the ups and downs of their stage careers in verse-like speech. Moments of musicalized speech are not absent from American films. In *The Big Broadcast of 1932*, Crosby is fired from his job at the radio station and the news spreads among his coworkers via songlike dialogue. But such scenes very rarely comprise a majority of the scenes as they do in German films. An indication is the advertising for the Al Jolson vehicle *Hallelujah, I'm a Bum* (dir. Lewis Milestone, 1933), touted as the "first ever picture done in rhythmic dialogue."[30] This claim is defensible regarding American cinema, where such films were an anomaly, but it does not apply to German cinema, where "rhythmic dialogue" was mainstream practice.

German Musical Film Technique

The aesthetic distinctiveness of the German films derives not only from the music-driven form but also from a film-technical peculiarity: the enduring commitment in German filmmaking to the concurrent recording of sound and image. The use of direct sound was common in Hollywood filmmaking too, especially for song sequences. But in Hollywood the production technique for songs began to change in 1931 when the use of "noiseless" multitrack systems became standard in the Los Angeles studios and dubbing became the principal means of preparing Hollywood films for export. At that point, American producers began recording the music for song sequences separately from the visuals, and did so increasingly over the next few years, to the point that postsynchronized vocals came to define the American film musical.[31] In Germany, in contrast, the default practice through the early 1930s was to record the music for song sequences, vocals included, while the actors' performances were filmed. Effects that in American films involved techniques like playback were in German films achieved instead via the concurrent recording of sound and image.

Note that the point made here regarding postsynchronized voices concerns a specific sort of film: musical films made for export. If the analysis were to extend beyond musical films, the use in German filmmaking of postsynchronized sound, including for vocals, might appear more prevalent. Indeed, German films sometimes made extensive use of postproduced sound, as film historian Corinna Müller shows in her analysis of *Der Sohn der weißen Berge* (dir. Mario Bonnard, 1930), virtually all of whose sound, the dialogue included, was postsynch.[32] *Der Sohn der weißen Berge*, however, was not a musical but a "mountain film," a genre that today would fall under the action-adventure heading; and it was produced in a single German version, unlike the musical films, which were often made with at least one full-length foreign version, normally in French.

The policy at Ufa, Tobis, and other German companies of preparing films in separate versions with foreign-language casts was motivated by the assessment of the German producers that only films with French-speaking actors passed muster with French audiences.[33] Until 1931, Hollywood also relied on foreign versions on the conviction that films for the major foreign-language markets must be produced in the target market's language, with actors who were native speakers. "Nowadays," observed a journalist of American filmmaking in 1930, "if a producer wishes to cater to another big market, he has to produce in that market's language. He has to hire a director, a writer, a cast, a whole national unit of the other market, and he has to invest in a production which he can use there and there only."[34] In Hollywood, however, this sort of foreign-version production, with a few exceptions, lasted only until 1931, when the studios, led by MGM and Paramount, took up a new policy and began grafting dubbed voices onto American films.[35] By the end of 1931, dubbing had replaced multiple-version production as Hollywood's main export-film technique.

The same switch in export policy did not occur in the German film industry, where foreign-version production endured as the default method into the mid-1930s. Dubbing technologies were used in Germany for American films, including those destined for the French market, and, in some cases, for the dubbing of German films. For the most part, however, the German companies relied on foreign-language versions for the export market. Foreign versions, reports film historian Joseph Garncarz, account for fully one-third of the 251 feature films made in Germany during 1929–31.[36] The number for Ufa is estimated by Chris Wahl to have been higher, with foreign versions—most of which fall into the category of what Wahl calls "the musical romantic comedy of errors"—comprising more than 50 percent of the company's output during 1931–35.[37] That these films, unlike the Hollywood films, had not been dubbed was emphasized in the publicity. An advertisement from

Ufa on the cover of *La cinématographie française* in April 1932 proclaimed that "a talking film from Ufa is never a dubbed film!"[38]

The Stylistic Consequences of Foreign-Version Production

The German film industry's reliance on foreign versions affected the style of the German musical films, certain of whose peculiarities can be attributed to multiple-version production methods. The essential method was the making of the foreign versions simultaneously with the German prototype. Different teams of actors rotated through the sets, one shot setup at a time, with up to four takes produced for each version. This method of making the versions "next to one another [*nebeneinander*]," observed a journalist for the film trade daily *Film-Kurier*, differed from the American practice at the Paramount studio in Paris of making them in succession ("*hintereinander*"), with, in some cases, the foreign versions produced up to a year or more after the Hollywood original.[39] Documenting the German approach are photographs of activity on the set during the shooting of *Der Kongreß tanzt* (dir. Eric Charell, 1931), *Die Dreigroschenoper* (dir. G. W. Pabst, 1931), *Quick*, and other German films, which show actors in costume waiting for their foreign-speaking counterparts to finish a scene.

Suggesting the technical challenges of the German method is a photo taken during the filming of a scene in *Die Dreigroschenoper*, a production of the Tobis company in collaboration with Warner Brothers (see fig. 6.1).[40]

The photo documents the production of *Die Dreigroschenoper* in two versions, German and French. (An English version had been planned but not undertaken.) Facing the camera toward the rear of the set is actor Albert Préjean, the star of the French version, presumably waiting to take his turn in front of the camera. The presence of the film's French and German actors on the set at the same time, all in costume, is evident in numerous additional photos of the film's production.[41] Director G. W. Pabst, wearing a white shirt, is visible in the center of the image, looking away from the camera. To Pabst's left, behind the music stands, can be seen members of the "Lewis Ruth Band," also known as the Ludwig Roth Band. (Like many European "jazz" bands at the time, they had adopted an anglicized name.) The musicians were present during the shooting because, as was typical in German film production at the time, the film's sound, music included, was recorded simultaneously with the image. An intriguing document in this regard is the film *Die verliebte Firma*, which includes two scenes that

Figure 6.1. A photo taken on the set of *Die Dreigroschenoper* (Stiftung Deutsche Kinemathek)

depict the filming of song performances during which an assistant director coaches the offscreen musicians on how to accompany the scene.

The rigors of German multiple-version production are discussed in correspondence pertaining to the shooting of *Ein blonder Traum* (dir. Paul Martin, 1932) and its French and English versions at the Ufa studios in Berlin.[42] Robert Stevenson, who supervised *Happily Ever After*, the English version, complained to Michael Balcon, chief producer at British Gaumont and the film's coproducer, about "the boring, dangerous and laborious business of trilingual shooting."[43] The English version, Stevenson's account confirms, was shot together with the German and French, with different teams of actors rotating through the same sets. Each song sequence, the contract for *Ein blonder Traum* specified, was to be recorded often enough to produce four acceptable takes for each of the versions. With three such versions of the film planned, at least twelve takes total for each song were required. For the rooftop performance of "Irgendwo auf der Welt gibt's ein kleines bißchen Glück," the repeated performances came from an offscreen orchestra, with the microphone capturing not only the music and the actors' voices but also noises from the automobile traffic on the streets below, as can be heard on the DVD edition of the film.

The declaration by Ludwig Klitsch, Ufa's head of production, that "sound-film cannot be altered, it must be screened the way it was shot," is an exaggeration, but it gets to an important fact regarding direct-sound technique, which is that there is no way to fix the sound in postproduction: one instead must get it right while on the set.[44] Regarding *Ich und die Kaiserin* (dir. Friedrich Hollaender, 1933), another musical film produced by Ufa in three languages, John Heygate, the dialogue editor on the English version of the film, commented on the difficulties involved in recording Lilian Harvey's performance of "Mir ist so milliomär zu Mut," which required that Harvey sing while "perched on the back of a farm cart full of pigs and sheep."[45] The sequence involved Harvey engaging in a call-and-response with the animals, whose "grunts and bleatings" were produced on the set by a technician and recorded simultaneously with a live orchestra and Harvey's image and voice. Heygate praises Harvey's skill in anticipating the animal noises, which came at slightly different moments for each take and thus added to the danger that errant sounds might mask the lyric and thereby ruin the shot.

The making of *Der Kongreß tanzt* (dir. Erik Charell, 1931), which included German, French, and English versions, likewise required the presence of musicians on the set, as is documented in various production photos, including the one reproduced in figure 6.2.

In the photo, dozens of actors, musicians, and other production personnel can be seen gathered outside, waiting, one assumes, to shoot and record one of the film's shots. Whatever the shot, its production required coordinating the visual action and dialogue with music performed simultaneously by the dozen or so musicians appearing in the photo. Also, the action would have to be repeated multiple times with different actors for the French and English versions.[46]

Under this system, even apparently simple scenes entailed difficult technical challenges. Consider the short scene when Christel (Lilian Harvey) and Pepi (Carl-Heinz Schroth) argue over whether Czar Alexander will visit their town. The scene, which appears to employ the set depicted in

Figure 6.2. A photo taken on the set of *Der Kongreß tanzt* (Wisconsin Center for Film and Theater Research)

the photograph in figure 6.2, runs just over two minutes and includes only two shots. Shot 1 is a medium long shot in which the two actors exchange verbal jabs in a call-and-response pattern: "Yes, he [the czar] will come!" and "No, he won't!" (*"Er kriegt sie doch!" "Er kriegt sie nicht!"*). The back-and-forth exchange begins as straight dialogue but becomes songlike when matched at the end of the shot by the march-time rhythm of an offscreen snare drum. Judging from the quality of the recorded dialogue, which stays constant even with the addition of the music, shot 1's drum sound was not added to the film later but produced on-site by a musician positioned outside the camera's visual field.

The drum's rat-a-tat motivates the cut to shot 2, whose more distant camera position shows the approach of the full marching band. The new shot continues for over a minute, during which the camera tracks to follow the procession of musicians. The precise match of the marchers' batons with the musical rhythm suggests that the music was captured by an on-set microphone simultaneously with the image of the marchers. The band ultimately passes in front of Christel's shop, where she and Pepi are seen still arguing. After the camera stops its lateral movement, allowing the band to pass out of the visual field, it pushes in straight toward Christel and Pepi to frame them in a medium long shot. The dialogue then picks up where it had left off in shot 1: "Yes, he will!" "No, he won't!" The scene's entire action, music and dialogue included, appears to have been recorded in a single take, using two cameras. The filming of the action and dialogue in shot 1 thus had to anticipate the cut to shot 2's musical performance, which was timed to begin just prior to shot 1's conclusion.

Similar challenges related to the reliance on direct sound in German musical film production are examined in film editor Don Fairservice's detailed analysis of *Der Blaue Engel* (dir. Josef von Sternberg, 1930), which shows how the recording of the music required an elaborate and precise coordination of actors, musicians, and film crew.[47] In the scenes in the nightclub dressing room, for example, the Weintraub Syncopators, located offscreen, had to start and stop playing exactly when the room's doors opened and closed. Hinting at the split-second timing needed for such scenes are moments in German films when actors deliberately match their voices and movements to a metronomic pulse. In *Leise flehen meine Lieder*, for instance, Franz Schubert (Hans Jaray) instructs the Countess (Martha Eggerth) in how to sing to the click of a metronome. A timekeeping gag provides the armature for the opening scene in *Walzerkrieg* (dir. Ludwig Berger, 1933), which involves an elaborate choreography in which timpanist Gustl (Willy Fritsch) leaves the bandstand to dance with girlfriend Kati (Renate Müller) and then ultimately returns to strike the kettledrum exactly as the song concludes. The comedy comes during the dancing, when Gustl's attention is split between Kati and his need to prepare for the drum cue. During pauses in their interaction, Gustl resumes the count ("fier und zwanzig, fünf und zwanzig."). Eventually, after seventy measures, he races back onto the stage, hits his mark, and stumbles into the drum set, thereby motivating the cut to the next scene.

Long Takes in Song Sequences

Symptomatic of the German film industry's direct-sound methods were the long takes in song sequences. Variation in musical performance from one direct-recorded shot to the next gave filmmakers an incentive to shoot songs in single takes and thus avoid altogether the challenge of joining separate direct-recorded shots.[48] Nonetheless, long takes, while helping ensure continuity, raised additional technical problems.[49] Exemplifying the possibilities and perils of the long take was *Arm wie eine Kirchenmaus* (dir. Richard Oswald, 1931), which includes performances of the film's title song in which lengthy moving camera shots show multiple actors who sing while traversing large sets.

Imagine the ordeal involved in filming the complex shot that occurs roughly seventy minutes into the film in one of the scenes set in the luxurious Parisian hotel. The shot begins with the camera tracking laterally to follow actors Paul Morgan and Fritz Grünbaum, who enter singing in extreme long shot while crossing the lobby on the upper floor. They sing while walking from the right side of the screen to the left, visible in silhouette from behind a translucent wall. After emerging from behind the wall, the two actors, while continuing to sing, reverse direction to descend the stairs. The camera continues tracking until they enter a nightclub located in the shot's deep space, where, in extreme long shot, they sing along with a band and its female vocalist.[50] The two actors then emerge from the bar back into the lobby, where, prior to exiting the hotel on the right side of the frame, they encounter a maid who sings to them from the staircase, a line of singing bellboys, and finally, outside the hotel, a singing doorman. All voices heard during this complex ninety-seven-second tracking shot—Morgan's, Grünbaum's, the lounge singer's, the maid's, the bellboys', and the doorman's—appear to have been captured simultaneously with the image and with the music. Such a complex choreography, involving not only the actors but also an orchestra and a film crew, was not unusual in German filmmaking. A 1931 report on practices at Ufa describes the use of up to nine microphones to record multiple actors for a scene involving both dialogue and music.[51]

Postsynchronized Shots in Song Sequences

The technical complications linked to direct sound might seem likely to hasten a move in German filmmaking toward the separation of music recording from image recording, perhaps with the same music track being used for all a film's versions. But this rarely happened in song-sequence production in Germany in the early 1930s, when the final edit of the scene would ordinarily include the sound recorded on the movie set. This held even when certain shots had been replaced, as with inserts involving extreme camera distance, which are often accompanied by vocals taken from other shots. Examples occur in *Quick* during the stage performances when the title character (Hans Albers) slides down the giant banjo neck, and at the beginning of *Die verliebte Firma*, when the couple performs the duet on a distant mountaintop.

A more complex example of a direct-sound sequence with a repurposed vocal track occurs in *Viktor und Viktoria* in the Berlin nightclub where Renate Müller sings "Komm doch ein bißchen mit nach Madrid," the film's main song. Judging from the demeanor of the musicians, who, in certain shots, appear to be playing the music that we are hearing, the music was recorded during the shooting. Inspection of the sequence's first shot, however, reveals a change midshot from direct to postsynchronized sound. The shot, which runs around twenty seconds, begins with Müller, framed in medium shot, waiting in the wings and ends with her strutting onto the stage, where she paces back and forth while singing. At the beginning of the shot, Müller, in close-up, can be heard and seen coughing, which points to the presence of a microphone on the set. During the latter portion of the shot, however, Müller's singing voice does not match her lip movement, which suggests that the sound has been postsynchronized. In sum, a direct-recorded shot appears to have had a postsynch voice grafted onto to it at the end. The voice is presumably Müller's, and the continuous quality of the recording suggests that it was recorded on the set with the other vocals, but for a take whose visuals were discarded.

Another direct-sound sequence in which a vocal take was repurposed to create a postsynch moment is the climactic song performance in *Ich und die Kaiserin* (1933), when Friedel Schuster, pushed onto the stage to sing, holds a high note for twenty seconds. The long-note voice, the poor lip synchronization reveals, was added to the shot in postproduction. Relative to the entire sequence, however, this out-of-synch shot is exceptional. Subsequent shots of Schuster singing suggest a more straightforward situation whereby Schuster's voice and image were recorded together. Moreover, the difference in technique is acknowledged in the visual style. The postsynch shot of Schuster entering the stage involves an unusual high angle. But for the subsequent direct-recorded shots, the camera is at eye level and the staging frontal, as if to emphasize the immediacy of the event of performance. Such an emphasis was appropriate given Schuster's reputation primarily as a singer rather than an actor.

Playback in German Cinema

Full-length postsynchronized song sequences are rare in German cinema and easily identified by the weak synchronization.[52] A famous example occurs in *Der Kongress tanzt* (1931) when Lilian Harvey sings "Das gibt's nur einmal" in an open carriage while riding from the city out to the country and then ultimately to the palace. For this seven-minute sequence, Harvey's voice was recorded separately, in a recording studio, and then added to the image track in postproduction, as can be seen from the obvious mismatch of Harvey's lip movement to the recorded vocals. The nonexistent lip synchronization, together with the exterior location and physical distance covered by the carriage, suggests that "Das gibt's nur einmal" was probably not made with playback. Moreover, in 1931, when *Der Kongress tanzt* was filmed, the playback method may not have been in use yet at the Ufa studios. Records of the meetings of the company's board of directors indicate the purchase of a playback system in the summer of 1933, years after such systems became standard in the United States.[53]

The new system appears to have been employed for a sequence in *Walzerkrieg* (dir. Ludwig Berger, 1933), an Ufa production filmed in midsummer and released in October, in which Renate Müller sings "Wenn der Lanner spielt einen Walzer" while dashing through the castle in search of Johann Strauss's orchestra. For roughly two minutes and twenty seconds, Müller sings while racing down stairs, through a hallway, and down more stairs, where, after dodging a guard, she charges down yet another hallway and up a further flight of stairs, finally locating the orchestra. A journalist who witnessed the shoot observed that the use of "playback" (*Rückspiel*) had involved playing a single recording of the music for all the takes, which made it easier for the actor, no longer required to cope with variations in the music, to calibrate her performance.[54]

A further benefit of playback is that it saved money. In a memo dated December 13, 1933, and addressed to Wilhelm Meydam, Ufa's chief of distribution, production chief Hugo Ernst Correll comments on the costs of various film-music techniques, including an arrangement that produces "a combination of music and visual material" (*eine Verbindung von Musik und Stoff*). The latter appears to refer to the direct-sound technique common in multiple-version filmmaking, which, Correll complains, is too expensive.[55] A better approach, he proposes, is to produce the music separately from the image. "Musical accompaniment for the most part, including for the operettas," Correll writes, "must be reduced to music that we subsequently provide the film." He then adds a reference to two recent films made mainly with direct-sound: "With respect to sound, I will in no case complete further operettas in the manner of *Viktor und Viktoria* or *Walzerkrieg*."[56] Here Correll seems to announce the change that the Hollywood studios had already undertaken two years earlier, with the standardization of playback, dubbing, and other voice-replacement practices.

An Incongruous Realism

The simultaneous recording of sound and image became associated with an aesthetic of realism early in sound film history. When critics in the late 1920s characterized sound-era acting performances as realistic (see chap. 3), they were responding to effects that stemmed from the talkies' direct-sound methods. The realism was at odds with the aesthetic requirements of the film operetta, a genre known for its artifice.[57] Film historian Colin Crisp, in an unpublished paper on film music in France, cites various sources suggesting that the musicalized style characteristic of the operetta conflicts with the sound cinema's realism.[58] According to Chartier and Desplanques, for example, in their handbook of film technique, "We need to believe in the reality of the characters; if the music systematically underlines their acts . . . we no longer find the story credible . . . ; it seems to follow the music, like a well-regulated dance."[59] The notion that actors in German musical films function like dancers surfaces in the critical writing on the genre. Kurt London proposed that in *Die Drei von der Tankstelle* and other German operettas, music dominates the visual design to the point that "the dance, as the highest conception of rhythmic action, is reached."[60] Critic and film translator Herman Weinberg observed that in *Zwei Herzen im Dreivierteltakt* (dir. Géza von Bolváry 1930), *Walzerkrieg* (Ludwig Berger, 1933), and other *Operettenfilmen*, the dance-like musical patterning left "no time for acting." In *Walzerkrieg*, for example, "the players were part of a general pattern comprised of dialogue, music, and acting. . . . The actors were used as in a ballet. Their entire persons were thrown into the percussive shocks of the Strauss waltz rhythms."[61] This subordination to the film's overall form was noted also by a critic in Berlin, who in 1930 proposed that German musical films exhibit a *Puppenspiel-Stil*, or puppet-theater style.[62]

Actors in German films of the early 1930s, in fact, often appear as dolls or puppets. In *Melodie des Herzens*, the fairground scene concludes with the circle of automated figurines dissolving into a circle of dancing soldiers and women. A metaphorical dissolve also intervenes in the final shot of *Stolz der dritten Kompanie* (dir. Fred Sauer, 1932), when the image of the three soldiers gives way to a graphically identical composition showing three soldier dolls in the puppet theater. In *Die Drei von der Tankstelle*, the three young men who flirt with Harvey show up in facsimile as dolls in her collection.

In *Ein Lied, ein Kuss, ein Mädel*, Gustav Frölich flirts with Martha Eggerth at the record-shop counter by modeling their relationship with a pair of hand puppets. In *Liebe muss verstanden sein*, the scientist and inventor (Georg Alexander) creates a life-size radio-controlled replica of stenographer Margit (Rosa Barsony) who sings and dances at the turn of a dial. Among the titles considered for the English version of *Ein blonder Traum* was "Dolly Daydream," an allusion to Harvey's "doll-like appearance" in the film's Hollywood dream sequence.[63] The doll metaphor is integral to the narrative of *Einbrecher* (dir. Hanns Schwarz, 1930), in which Lilian Harvey's character, the wife of a master doll maker, appears both as herself and as a mechanical double.

The actor-as-puppet references in German musical films suggest the genre's affinities with traditions in theater that can be traced back to the 1800s, when, Donald Crafton notes, puppets became associated with a conception of dramatic art that privileged the playwright's vision over the actor's virtuosity.[64] Unlike ordinary actors, puppets brought into the play's story world few elements from life outside, which made them ideal dramatic vehicles for playwrights who sought to create a fantastic, self-contained diegetic world, one divorced from everyday social experience. An impression of story-world autonomy was what the film operettas of the early 1930s were aiming for. Protesting the notion that song performances in films ought to be "realistic," Ernst Lubitsch declared, "An operetta is not real; it is a fairy tale peopled by romantic creatures of the imagination."[65] A critic in Germany made the same point: "The characters in operettas are not real. They are only an amusing diversion from reality."[66]

Establishing a fantastic world was made more difficult by the direct-sound methods of multiple-version production. As K. J. Donnelly proposes, direct sound is especially suitable for reproducing "a performance that appears to be real."[67] Examples include the simulated theater-orchestra performances in films like *The Hollywood Revue of 1929* (dir. Charles Reisner, 1929) discussed in chapter 2. More appropriate for the operetta, however, is what Donnelly calls the "lip synch mode" associated with playback, which "tends to signify a hyperbolic move to 'fantasy.'" Such a move suggests the "injection of the ideal into the real" that film historian Rick Altman associates with the use of playback in American musical films.[68] It is also what composer Heymann seems to have had in mind when he described music in the operetta as effecting "a transition from stylized reality to over-reality."[69]

In German musical films, the operetta's inclination toward theatrical exaggeration, its *"Groteskstil,"* as one critic put it, existed in tension with the film industry's direct-sound methods.[70] Song-and-dance sequences in which singing is combined with strenuous physical action provide examples, such as the cabaret scene in *Viktor und Viktoria* described earlier in this chapter, which includes a shot of Müller singing that ends with her taking a pratfall; the song-and-dance performance by Lilian Harvey in *Ich und die Kaiserin*, in which a shot begins with Harvey singing and concludes with her kicking her leg high during a vigorous cancan; and the sequence in *Liebe muss verstanden sein* (dir. Hans Steinhof, 1933) in which Rosa Barsony, playing the role of a robotic doll, likewise sings and dances while an offscreen orchestra provides accompaniment. These direct-sound scenes belong to films that were released in the 1933–34 film season, which, from the standpoint of Hollywood practice, is a late date for the direct recording of song-and-dance sequences, especially ones involving adventurous dance moves and physical stunts. Such sequences, unlike their playback-produced counterparts in American films, offer less a flight of fancy than a documentation of an athletic performance.

German Musical Film after 1933

The German film industry's status as a producer of musical films ended shortly after the Nazi takeover of the country in 1933. The political crisis was catastrophic for the musical film, causing the rapid exodus from Germany of producers, composers, and other film personnel whose talent had been crucial to the genre's centrality to German cinema during the previous three years. Key artists ended up pursuing their careers in other countries, including the United States, as was the case with the composers R. W. Heymann, Friedrich Hollaender, Hanns Eisler, and Kurt Weill. Besides the loss of essential personnel, changes in German film policy in the months after the Nazi takeover hastened the collapse of the foreign market for German films. In 1933, the German film industry took in only 3.4 million marks from foreign sales, a small fraction of the 30 million marks earned in 1931.[71] By 1934–35, only 8 percent of the German film industry's income came from exports.

The effects were devastating for the German musical film, a genre shaped by creative responses to the challenges and opportunities of export distribution. Foreign-version production declined steeply in 1933, when Ufa and Tobis immediately cut back on foreign-language versions.[72] At this point, the *Operettenfilmen* were denounced by Nazi Party activists as "products of shallow entertainment" characteristic of the supposed decadence of the Weimar Republic.[73] Though foreign-version production continued in Europe on a cottage-industry scale, Germany's industrial-scale production of musical films for the foreign market was finished. In the fall of 1935, Wahl reports, Ufa's directors decided to fund the making of original French films rather than make French versions of German films.[74] With Ufa's abandonment of the French-version strategy, the sound operetta, so prominent early in the decade, virtually disappeared from German film production.

The musical films of the early 1930s, regardless of where they were made, tend to exhibit important similarities in style that are linked to the genre's preference for singing over dialogue. Certain aesthetic consequences tend to follow from the inclusion of songs in films, such as the alignment of a film's cutting and staging with the song's tempo and meter. Songs alter a film's style, at least during the time the song is heard. The German musical films of the early 1930s are unusual in how much the music-driven style extends beyond the songs and into other scenes. But the tendency toward a musicalized treatment of a film's visuals is common in American films, too, although ordinarily for the song sequences only. Moreover, a music-based style for song performances may count as a universal, defining not only the transatlantic cinema of the early 1930s but also the cinema of other times and places.

Notes

1. T. Saunders, *Hollywood in Berlin*, 4–6, 8, 13–14.
2. "World War of Talking Pictures Seen Raging," 25.
3. See the overview of the European exhibition market in Europe in D. Miller, "The Influence of the Talkies on the Film Industry," 5.
4. On the French market during the early sound years, see C. North and N. Golden, "The European Film Market—Then and Now," 442, 446.
5. See, for example, the remarks on MGM's investment in French-language films in Cedric Belfrage, "Money for Foreign Market Talkers," 26.
6. *The Motion Picture Industry in Continental Europe in 1931*, 30.
7. On similarities between Lubitsch's films and the German operettas of the period, see, for example, "Same Scene in Two Films, Lubitsch's-Schwartz'; German's Made First," 2.
8. "Engaging Musical Screened," A9.
9. M. Loiperdinger, "German Tonbilder of the 1900s," 187–200; and C. O'Brien, "Sound-on-Disc Cinema," 42–51.
10. M. Wedel, *Der deutsche Musikfilm*; and C. Beinroth, "Between Practice and Theory."
11. M. Wedel, "Vom Synchronismus zur Synchronisation: Carl Robert Blum und der frühe Tonfilm," in Polzer, *Aufstieg und Untergang des Tonfilms*, 97–112.
12. On Germany's film-music advantage, see the remark from attorney Nathan Burkan, cofounder of the American Society of Composers, Authors and Publishers (ASCAP), in W. Mühl-Benninghaus, *Das Ringen um den Tonfilm*, 242.
13. The anecdote is attributed to a 1943 book on Ufa by Hans Traub, the company's publicist, in K. Kreimeier, *The Ufa Story*, 180.

14. D. Brown, "The Film Situation in Central Europe," 27.
15. J. Garncarz, "Made in Germany."
16. On the competitiveness of musical films relative to Hollywood, see H. Claus and A. Jäckel, "'Der Kongress tanzt,'" 89.
17. The quotation from Bie comes from B. Currid, *A National Acoustics*, 71.
18. H. Lewis, *The Motion Picture Industry*, 428.
19. "The Year in America," *Kinematograph Year Book, 1931*, 17.
20. "'Zwei Herzen im Dreivierteltakt,'" 2; M. Hall, "A German Film Operetta," 33; and "'Zwei Herzen' Ends Long Run Soon," 15.
21. "Eddie Cantor Discourses of Music Films," X7.
22. The exact percentages, along the results of t-tests performed on the samples, can be found in appendix B in table 6.1.
23. W. Thiele, "Des lois que régissent l'opérette filmée," 6.
24. K. London, *Film Music*, 156.
25. H. Angel, "'Die verkaufte Braut,'" 2.
26. W. Heymann, "Musik und Bild als einheitliches Kunstwerk," 13.
27. K. London, *Film Music*, 129. London refers specifically to *Die Drei von der Tankstelle*.
28. M. Hall, "Ufa's English Dialogue Film," 16.
29. E. Vuillermoz, "Le film musical."
30. The quotation is from the press book cited in "Hallelujah I'm a Bum," AFI Catalog of Feature Films: The First Hundred Years, 1893–1993, accessed September 9, 2018, https://catalog.afi.com/Catalog/moviedetails/6133.
31. See the remarks on playback and postsynchronization in R. Altman, *The American Film Musical*, 64.
32. C. Müller, *Vom Stummfilm zum Tonfilm*, 339–50.
33. "Das Sprachproblem des Tonfilms: Deutsche Filme in Paris," 2.
34. J. D. Williams, "Americans in a Quandary," 38. See also H. Fraenkel, "Can Industry Stay International?," 58, 64.
35. On Hollywood's methods of multiple-version production, see N. Ďurovičová, "Local Ghosts: Dubbing Bodies in Early Sound Cinema"; M. Barnier, *Des films français made in Hollywood*, 13–118; C. Wahl, *Multiple Language Versions Made in Babelsberg*, 49–64; M. Danan, "A la recherché d'une stratégie internationale," 109–30; and H. Waldman, *Paramount in Paris*, vii–xiii.
36. J. Garncarz, "Made in Germany," 254.
37. C. Wahl, *Multiple Language Versions Made in Babelsberg*, 132.
38. J.-F. Cornu, *Le Doublage et le sous-titrage*, 75. "Un parlant français Ufa n'est jamais un film double!" The reference is to an advertisement appearing in *La cinématographie française* 14, no. 703 (April 23, 1932).
39. "Eindrücke aus Film-Frankreich," 3.
40. For more on the two versions, see C. O'Brien, "A Multimedia Presentation on the Differences between the German and French Versions."
41. This photo is among over one thousand taken during the shooting of *Die Dreigroschenoper* by photographer Hans Casparius. A large selection of these images can be found in H.-M. Boch and J. Berger, eds., *Photo: Casparius*.
42. The correspondence can be found at the British Film Institute in London in the Michael Balcon collection, box B-57.
43. The quotation from Stevenson comes from his undated letter to Michael Balcon, chief producer at British Gaumont, drafted, it seems, in late May or early June 1932.

44. The quotation from Klitsch can be found in Chris Wahl, *Multiple Language Versions Made in Babelsberg*, 95.
45. C. Wahl, *Multiple Language Versions Made in Babelsberg*, 140–41.
46. The exception was the trilingual Lilian Harvey, who played the female lead in all three versions.
47. D. Fairservice, *Film Editing*, 236–39.
48. On variation in musical performance from one direct-recorded take to the next, see C. Courant, "Aus der Tonfilmpraxis des Kameramanner," 7; and "Bei der Ufa," 2.
49. On the advantages of long takes, see C. Courant, "Aus der Tonfilmpraxis des Kameramanner," 7.
50. A telltale indication of the direct-sound technique is the match of the up-and-down arm movement of the banjo player with the music's pulse, including when the tempo slows.
51. "Neuf microphones dans chaque studio," 6.
52. See the criticism of the poor postsynchronization of the duel scene in *Die Verkaufte Braut* (dir. Max Ophuls, 1932), in H. Angel, "'Die verkaufte Braut,'" 2.
53. In June 1933, Ufa's board of directors approved the purchase of a "Play Back" apparatus at a cost of 8,100 reichsmarks. See Niederschrift no. 920 (June 2, 1933), available on microfiche in the Bundesarchiv in Berlin (Bestand R 109-1, Archivnummer 1027a).
54. "Bei der Ufa," 2.
55. The Correll memo is quoted in R. Rother, "Zwischen Parodie und poetischem Wachtraum," 275.
56. The entire quotation is as follows: "Die musikalische Austattung muß sich zum größten Teil darauf beschränken, daß wir einschließlich der Operetten den Film nachträglich mit Musik versehen. Ich werde auf keinen Fall mehr Operetten tonlich so auflösen können, wie das bei *Viktor und Viktoria* oder bei *Walzerkrieg* geschehen ist."
57. On the operetta's artificiality, see R. von Hessert, "Wie soll man in Tonfilm singen?," 3.
58. C. Crisp, "Film Music in the Classic French Cinema, 1930–1960," 5.
59. J. Chartier and R. Desplanques, *Derrière l'écran*, 164.
60. K. London, *Film Music*, 131.
61. H. Weinberg, "Old Wine in New Bottles," 21.
62. "'Einbrecher,'" 2.
63. C. Wahl, *Multiple Language Versions Made in Babelsberg*, 152–53. The information source is correspondence from British Gaumont available at the British Film Institute in London.
64. D. Crafton, *Shadow of a Mouse*, 64.
65. Lubitsch is quoted in P. Scheuer, "Theme Song Own Excuse," B13, 3.
66. Elisabeth O., "Dreht 'menschliche Filme'!" 1285–86, 1288.
67. K. Donnelly, *Occult Aesthetics*, 160, 164.
68. R. Altman, *The American Film Musical*, 64, 151.
69. The quotation from Heymann comes from H. W., "Musikalische Charakterisierung als Element der Film-Komödie," 5: "Musik als Überleitung von der stilisierten Realität zur Ueberwirklichkeit."
70. "'Die Privatsekretärin,'" 2.
71. K. Kreimeier, *The Ufa Story*, 196.
72. D. Welch and R. Vande Winkel, "Europe's New Hollywood?," 18.
73. H. Claus and A. Jackel, "'Der Kongress tanzt,'" 95.
74. C. Wahl, *Multiple Language Versions Made in Babelsberg*, 193, 210.

CONCLUSION

Songs in Cinema, from Electric to Digital

THE MUSICAL FILMS EXAMINED IN THIS BOOK EXEMPLIFY a period in the history of cinema's engagement with popular song that seems, in retrospect, foundational. Recorded songs circulating via multiple media became ubiquitous in cinema in the early 1930s, and they have become prominent again in recent decades. How can examination of conversion-era musical films illuminate cinema's links with popular music, both in the past and the present?

The Comparative Project

Musical films are approached in this book through an investigation into differences and similarities in style between Hollywood and German films. The comparative analysis is unusual. The two bodies of films are ordinarily studied separately, according to different if not divergent priorities. In the study of the German cinema of the late Weimar years, dramas have been privileged over musical comedies, while critical writing on the musical films of the period often concerns American films exclusively. In juxtaposing Hollywood musical films with German, this book has attempted two innovations: it delineates a new transnational context for understanding the Hollywood musical, and it examines in detail an important and neglected corpus of films, the German operettas of the early 1930s.

Analysis of the export market for sound films in the early 1930s, when German and American companies competed against one another for control over the world film trade, facilitates this comparison. Musical films were the main vehicle for the rivalry. Offering an appeal beyond differences in language and nationhood, musical films produced by American and German firms ranked among the most popular films in the world in the early sound years. These films, as has been detailed in the preceding chapters, differ in style from other sorts of films in important respects. The running-time percentages devoted to the book's principal shot types, for example, reveal a distinctive profile for musical films, which give, on average, less time to dialogue shots and more to singing shots than do films belonging to other genres. This reliance on songs in place of speech carries major style implications because singing performances are ordinarily staged, filmed, and cut in distinctive ways. Films with song performances look and sound different from other sorts of films, at least during scenes in which the songs are heard.

Musical Films and the Export Market

The pressures of foreign distribution led to style differences between American and European films. Initially, in the late 1920s, big-budget films intended for export, whether made in the United States or in Europe, were produced in separate versions, with actors who spoke the languages of the target markets. These films were ordinarily made with the sound and image recorded concurrently. The dubbing of actors' voices was avoided. Then, in 1931, the Hollywood companies changed their policy. Instead of relying on separate full-length foreign versions, they began dubbing the American originals with foreign voices, or they contracted this work out to producers in other countries. Thus, while German producers continued to record sound and image together, the Americans began producing the music separately. The use of playback for song performances, whereby the singer lip-synched to prerecorded vocals, exemplified this practice. Playback, voice dubbing, and other such methods were used also in Germany, but they were developed first in Hollywood and practiced most extensively there.

Hollywood's reliance on postsynchronized voices helped differentiated German and American musical films by affecting what might be called a film's syntax, the ordering of scenes and sequences within an overall structure. The most ambitious of the German producers had tried, in effect, to render musical the form of the entire film, extending the music-based design of the song performances out to the film's dramatic scenes. Aiming for a unified aesthetic, they sought to efface the difference between dramatic scene and musical number, to blend the two into a single form. Essential to this project were music-based pantomime and verse-like dialogue, two techniques common in German musical films and rare in American.

The Hollywood filmmakers—besides Lubitsch and a few others—did not, by and large, try to musicalize the narrative. While constructing the song sequences in a music-determined manner, they were content to organize the dramatic scenes around the actors' dialogue. On rare occasions when the Hollywood companies emulated the European film operetta, they did so selectively, exploring the genre's potential for a music-driven style only during the song performances or conventional transitions like the film's opening scene. As a result, song sequences in Hollywood films tend to come up as distinct interludes, stylistically distinct from the dialogue scenes. This tendency was so pronounced that formal differences between song-and-dance number and dramatic scene are regarded today as the defining attribute of the American film musical (as noted in chap. 1).

Why in Hollywood was a music-based form acceptable in a three-minute song sequence but not when extended out to an entire feature film? Two answers have been offered. The first cites the commercial forces operative at this transitional moment in media history, when film songs were marketed via not only cinema but multiple additional media, including the robust new medium of commercial broadcast radio. Film songs not only could enhance a film's appeal but also were consumer goods available for purchase and consumption apart from the films in which they featured. The song sequence's tendency to come across as a separate unit, different from the film's other scenes, thus reflected the film song's commodity status, as Eisler and Adorno had contended.

This intermedial dynamic was not unique to the United States but operated in Germany, too, where hit songs, called *Schlager*, likewise circulated through multiple media, including cinema.[1] In the United States, however, the consumer economy was more advanced, and the culture of film-song promotion more pervasive, with film songs playing incessantly on commercial radio.[2] The rapid and intensive circulation of songs in the United States directly affected the Hollywood musical film, most notably during the 1930–31 season, when the Hollywood companies, facing the "overplay" of songs through radio and other media, decided to remove songs from films and to cease making musicals. A more subtle consequence was the prevalence in Hollywood films of song performances informed by an intent to parody, which enabled the farcical comedy prominent in American musical films after 1930, just as it undermined the tearful melodrama common in the years immediately before.

Hollywood's Reliance on Stars

A further reason for the American cinema's resistance to the ideal of formal integration was the star cult essential to Hollywood cinema, described by a journalist in 1931 as "one of the greatest factors" behind Hollywood's global success.[3] Major developments in Hollywood filmmaking invite explanation with reference to the practice of selling films through their stars. The decision in 1931 to adopt dubbing as the main means of preparing films for export, for example, appears to have been motivated by the perception that European audiences preferred American films with the original stars over foreign-language versions with actors who spoke the language of the target market but who lacked a star profile. Germany had film stars, too, and as Wahl explains, "the implementation of Hollywood-style policies concerning stars was ordered by Ufa's management shortly before the switch to sound film."[4] Nonetheless, stars functioned differently in German cinema, whose publicity, Joseph Garncarz argues, emphasized their professional accomplishments over their personal lives.[5] In any case, in European film culture, the music-drama ideal of formal unity, in which actors' movements become subordinate to the film's overall design, encountered fewer obstacles than in Hollywood, where stardom implied a sense of agency unavailable to actors whose movements are musically determined and who thus come across as effects of the film's form rather than causes.

Relevance to Cinema Today

How can the book's findings regarding cinema in the 1930s help illuminate cinema in the present? The pertinence of the musical films of the early 1930s to contemporary cinema has been implied in the preceding chapters. However, there are also explicit parallels between the electric-sound past and the digital present. Historical comparisons are a familiar topic for film historians, who investigate an art whose history is relatively short and recent. Film history remains under perpetual revision, with the cinema's past continually reinterpreted in light of the latest developments in film technology.[6] As the technology evolves, so does our understanding of not only the cinema's present but also its past. Sound conversion, for example, prompted critics and theorists to rethink the whole of cinema history relative to the sound cinema of the current moment. A similar situation obtains today regarding digital conversion, which is inspiring further reinterpretations of the entirety of cinema history.[7]

This book has been concerned to relate the conversion-era musical film to contemporaneous film-industrial forces and conditions through extensive historical documentation. But the task of explaining the style of the conversion-era musical films often entailed recourse not only to the facts of history but also to traits of human psychology that would seem effectively transhistorical and cross-cultural. At issue is a corpus of films intended to appeal to viewers beyond differences in language and culture. Signaling this attempt at universality is the extent to which the formal attributes of recorded song accompaniment discussed in this book can be found in the cinema of other times, including the present. Music-image alignment may be a universal feature of song accompaniment in narrative cinema, evident not only in song performances in conversion-era musical films but also in virtually any song-accompanied moment in any film. Song sequences tend to exhibit—necessarily, it seems, regardless of when and where the film was made—a music-driven style, where the image adapts to the song's form. When a song is performed in a film, the visuals tend to line up with the music's tempo and meter to condition how the action is blocked, when the cuts occur, and when the camera moves and comes to rest. Even when the song is relegated to sonic background during a dialogue scene, it tends to "musicalize" the image. Understanding how songs function in films requires investigating how psychological forces intersect with historical conditions.

A Media-Technological Sea Change

The second parallel between past and present concerns the scale of the technological and media-industrial transformation. As with the transition to electric sound, digitalization has involved an overhaul of the technology of film production and exhibition, the effects of which have extended to various entertainments other than cinema, to the point of creating the impression that the new technologies are instigating a convergence of all media. Furthermore, songs are at the nexus, the common element shared by the media in question.[8] The main difference is that the impact of the "digital revolution" on cinema aesthetics appears mild in comparison to what happened in the late 1920s and early 1930s, when electric sound seemed instantly to reduce the range of options for how films were edited, sets constructed and lit, actors' movements blocked, and lenses and camera positions deployed seemed instantly reduced. Dissolves and superimpositions, extreme close-ups, slow- and fast-motion images, and other cinematographic hallmarks of the mid-1920s quickly became rare in sound movies.[9] Sound cinema seemed inherently less expressive than silent, suited more to recording actors' performances than creating novel artistic effects. Indicative of the trauma was the sudden turnover in the ranks of film actors, as established stars lost their following and new stars arose.

The same impact has not been evident for digital cinema. The artists popular in photochemical films haven't been made less so because of digitalization, and filmmakers often use digital technologies to emulate photochemical methods. "Everything we do in HD [high-definition digital video] is an effort to recreate the look of film," stated director Martin Scorsese in 2014.[10] A similar impulse was evident during sound conversion, when filmmakers likewise tried to adhere to established aesthetic norms. Various historians, myself included, have explained developments in sound film style as a collective, transnational attempt to reaffirm silent-era editing norms. But the trauma today seems less severe than in 1930—and the successful emulation of past practice easier to achieve.

Technology's Effects on the Theater Experience

A related issue concerns technology's effects on the ontology of cinema. Digital movies involve processes that differ from the cinema's traditional photochemical methods, to the point that film and media theorists have argued that digitalization has effectively brought cinema history to an end.[11] Motion pictures continue to be made, of course. But digital representations, the argument goes, lack the authority of the celluloid films of the past. The claim that digital images are less credible as representations than photochemical images seems at odds with the vast numbers of filmgoers who appear unable to distinguish one from the other. Digital technologies, to be sure, have wrought powerful changes with far-reaching implications for cinema's identity. Most significant perhaps are the changes in distribution. The viewing of films on cell phones, laptops, and other small-screen devices has eroded the centrality of theatrical exhibition to movie culture, fostering new ways of viewing and otherwise interacting with films that may transform the future of cinema as art and entertainment.

Nevertheless, cinema traditionally is defined by the theatrical experience: seeing a movie means paying to sit with other people to watch a film projected on a screen. In this context, the changes wrought by digital technologies—it seems fair to say—have been less profound and distressing than those associated with electric sound.[12] John Belton, referring in 2002 to digital cinema as a "false revolution," proposed that digital exhibition offers minimal "novelty value" to the filmgoer, for whom the digital film experience remains basically the same as the photochemical.[13] Subsequent developments seem to confirm this assessment. The recent push toward digital 3-D notwithstanding, "so much in our movie-going experience" over the past thirty years, Thomas Elsaesser observed in 2013, "has remained the same: the two-hour feature film, the narrative format, the genres-and-stars formula, the racked seating, the projector position, the social habit of going to the movies, and the popcorn and the soft drinks."[14] In short, seeing a digital movie today is largely the same as seeing a photochemical movie thirty years ago.

Electric sound's impact on the theatrical experience cut more deeply. Viewing a sound film meant partaking in an experience transformed through the replacement of live music with recorded. Moreover, the change often disappointed, as when moviegoers rebelled against the "colder," less empathetic accompaniment provided by recorded music. In 1930, hundreds of the theaters that had wired for sound reverted to exhibition programs with live music (as noted in chap. 2). It's hard to think of an analogous reversal with respect to digital exhibition. No digital theater, as far as I am aware, has gone back to photochemical, assuming such a move were possible. Even the Pordenone Silent Film Festival, with its unparalleled access to film-archival holdings in thirty-five millimeter, now shows mainly DCP films instead, and we cinephiles, as far as I can tell, are not complaining. If digital technologies are affecting the theatrical experience, they are doing so quietly, in a mainly subliminal manner.

An investigation into the conversion-era musical film highlights a familiar dynamic, whereby exaggeration of the novelty of today's media facilitates amnesia over the power once assigned to the media innovations of earlier times. The challenge posed to the historian by the sound movies of eighty-eight years ago thus looks like the inverse of the challenge facing a critic of digital media today. Whereas the critic, wary of journalistic hype, must anticipate how the new medium, before we know it, will come to seem old, the historian reconstructs how an old medium had once appeared new.

Such a dynamic informs the examination of musical films in *Movies, Songs, and Electric Sound*, which aims to facilitate balanced appraisal of media change in the present as well as the past.

Notes

1. On *Schlager* culture in Germany in the early 1930s, see B. Currid, *A National Acoustics*, 65–118.
2. Regarding the advanced state of the consumer economy in the United States circa 1930 relative to that in Germany, see V. de Grazia, *Irresistible Empire*, 75–183.
3. J. Carstairs, "Looking at Hollywood," 30.
4. C. Wahl, *Multiple Language Versions Made in Babelsberg*, 139.
5. J. Garncarz, "The Star System in Weimar Cinema."
6. D. Bordwell, *On the History of Film Style*, 9–10.
7. An explicit parallel between the sound cinema of 1930 and the digital cinema of the present day is drawn in J. Polzer, ed. *Aufstieg und Untergang des Tonfilms*.
8. On the effect of song distribution on film reception, see, for example, A. Kassabian, *Hearing Film*, 50–52, 72–73, 84–85, 87–89.
9. See, for example, A. Bakshy, "The Shrinking of Personality," 590.
10. The quotation is from M. Scorsese's open letter in support of Kodak's decision to continue making film stock, quoted in Dave McNary, "Martin Scorsese Backs Kodak on Film Stock Production."
11. Arguments for digitalization as a break from cinema's ontology are advanced in D. Rodowick, *The Virtual Life of Film*, 28–31; and L. Manovich, *Language of New Media*, 244–59.
12. On aesthetic continuity between digital and photochemical cinema, see S. McClean, *Digital Storytelling*. The digital emulation of photochemical aesthetics is taken up in interviews with numerous prominent filmmakers in the documentary *Side By Side* (dir. Chris Kenneally, 2012).
13. J. Belton, "Digital Cinema," 114.
14. T. Elsaesser, "The 'Return' of 3-D," 226.

APPENDIX A

Methods of Measurement

This appendix presents a short survey of issues specific to the book's use of quantitative methods of film analysis. Building on remarks on statistical methods in the introduction, the appendix weighs the benefits and drawbacks of specific choices in how the shot categories were decided, evaluates the ease and accuracy of different methods of counting shots, and discusses the hypothesis tests used to measure the extent to which the film samples can be taken to represent their populations. The appendix ends with a defense of the book's attempt to cover transnational trends in film style, which required expanding the scope of statistical analysis beyond a single film to samples made up of hundreds of films. The overall aim is to provide information that will make it easier for the reader to evaluate the quantitative findings presented in the preceding chapters.

Statistical Research in *Movies, Songs, and Electric Sound*

First, a disclaimer: I have no formal training in statistics. As with most film historians, my background is in the humanities, where, in contrast to the social sciences, research projects rarely involve recourse to quantitative methods. Motivating my adoption of such methods was a commitment to examine the conversion-era musical film on a transnational scale. Statistical methods, when supplemented by other sources of information, seemed likely to help illuminate the stylistic trends among the period's films. What I know of the technicalities of quantitative research has been acquired while conducting the research for this book.

The research began with a traditional film-statistical task: measuring shot lengths. The history of shot-length analysis is nearly as long as cinema history itself. For over one hundred years at least, critics have timed the length of shots and produced averages pertaining to single films and to bodies of films.[1] In the 1980s, the pioneering work of Barry Salt helped bring the statistical analysis of film style into the emergent field of academic film study.[2] Nonetheless, quantitative methods, with a few notable exceptions, were rarely taken up by film scholars.[3] The situation has changed over the past decade, when a wave of quantitative research in film aesthetics was occasioned by a crucial new resource: the Cinemetrics website, created in 2006 by Yuri Tsivian and Gunars Civjans. The website provides shot-counting tools that produce visual displays showing the ebb and flow of shot-length patterns across the body of a film. It also offers a film database, articles on statistical film analysis, and a venue for discussion and debate.

The statistical work for this book began prior to the appearance of Cinemetrics, but the website quickly affected how that work evolved.[4] My approach to cinemetrics derived from the specifics of my research project, which entailed questions pertaining less to an individual film's overall structure than to the aesthetic effects of developments in film-sound technology and technique. The remarks in this appendix refer only to my own, selective adoption of cinemetrics. Readers interested in the full variety of research possibilities can consult www.cinemetrics.lv.

Why These Shot Categories?

My use of quantitative methods involved, in most cases, labeling a film's shots according to a set of predetermined categories and then comparing averages for each category. The charts in figures 0.1, 4.3, 4.4, and 5.3 report on what I call "action shots," "dialogue shots," and "singing shots," while figure 4.2 provides breakdowns for an alternative triad, which refers to the nature of musical accompaniment or lack thereof: "shots with source music," "shots with nondiegetic music," and "shots with no music." These shot categories were first mentioned in the introduction and chapter 4. What follows is an overview of some of the problems and puzzles that arose in deciding on criteria for certain of the categories. Explicit criteria were needed to ensure consistency in application and hence meaningful comparisons from film to film. What exactly distinguishes one sort of shot from another? Any attempt to settle on an answer yields advantages as well as limitations, depending on the priorities of one's research.

My shot categories, as noted in the introduction, referred not only to the surface characteristics of the films but also to underlying film-industrial conditions. An example concerns the dialogue shots, which in my scheme include any shots that show someone talking. The amount of speech is irrelevant. A single word is enough for a shot to count as a dialogue shot. So, unlike dialogue intertitles, which are entirely verbal, dialogue shots do not necessarily contain speech from beginning to end. A film that gives a lot of running time to dialogue shots is thus not always a film with a lot of talking. But it *is* likely a film with an ample use of direct sound, given production conditions at the time, when dialogue was ordinarily recorded simultaneously with the image. The figures for dialogue shots, as with all other shot categories, therefore exhibit a forensic aspect, revealing a shot's surface features (e.g., that the shot contains an actor who can be seen speaking) as well as the circumstances behind how the film was made.

What happens when a shot fits into more than one category? For example, it is common for shots to include both dialogue and singing, as when a shot begins with the actor speaking and then ends with her or him singing a song lyric. My decision was to label as a singing shot any shot in which an actor sings or whistles a song lyric, even when the shot also includes dialogue. The justification for this choice was twofold. First, I wanted to track song performances in films, and since even a short extract from a melody is enough to spark a listener's memory of the tune, it seemed proper to slot hybrid cases into the singing-shot category. The second justification has to do with one of the period's production techniques. In the early 1930s, to include singing in a shot required special conditions during shooting, such as the presence on the set of an orchestra or the playing back of a recording for the actor to lip-synch to. Thus the singing shot category, like the one for dialogue shots, acknowledges not only the shot's surface attributes but also its conditions of manufacture.

Further complications stem from the arbitrary nature of the dialogue/singing distinction. Dialogue in cinema, including naturalistic dialogue, is an artistic construction and hence can be said to exhibit quasimusical characteristics such as tempo, rhythm, and melody. In certain of the musical films that were the focus of my research, the dialogue's musicality is, in fact, overt. In German films particularly, actors often sing their lines, or come close to doing so, as is discussed in chapter 6. Such films invite the question, when in cinema does speech leave off and singing begin? Or, put in my project's terms, how exactly is a singing shot to be distinguished from a dialogue shot?

My answer was to restrict the singing-shot category to shots whose vocalizations involve song lyrics. With lyrics easy to recognize, the song-lyric constraint gave me a criterion that was simple to apply in most cases. It also helped me gauge a film's level of commercial-song content, a further priority of my analysis, with, for example, a high running-time percentage for singing shots suggesting a high incidence of song promotion. The drawback of the song-lyric criterion is that insofar as musicalized dialogue is present, it goes unmarked, since shots containing songlike speech are counted as dialogue shots. In *Viktor und Viktoria* (dir. Reinhold Schünzel, 1933), for example, musicalized speech runs through virtually the entire film, from beginning to end, but because the vocals ordinarily do not involve song lyrics, their musicality goes unacknowledged in my statistics. This insensitivity to aspects of style that are difficult to quantify points to a limitation of quantitative methods in film analysis. Hence the position taken in the introduction: quantitative methods can supplement but not replace conventional film-analytical methods.

Categories for Music Accompaniment

Troublesome questions likewise arose for the categories referring to musical accompaniment: shots with no music, shots with source music, and shots with nondiegetic music. The main complications concern the distinction between source music and nondiegetic music. Film soundtracks, as film-music scholars can attest, are typically constructed in ways that blur the distinction between diegetic and nondiegetic music, to the point that ambiguities in diegetic status have become integral to how film music functions. Countless sound films feature instances of what composer Leonid Sabaneev described as a change from "invisible" music to "visible," which happens when music that begins offscreen, and thus might be taken to be nondiegetic, is attributed ultimately to an on-screen source.[5] Should all the scene's music-accompanied shots be labeled as source-music shots, or only the shots that begin with or follow the revelation of the music's on-screen source? I decided to count as source music the shot depicting the music's source and all subsequent shots in the sequence but not the preceding shots that become diegetic only in retrospect. In other words, from my standpoint, once the music becomes visible, it counts as source music, but not until then.

The virtue of the criterion of explicit representation is that it helped in the assessment of the policy at RKO, MGM, and other studios in Hollywood around 1930 of visualizing music's ostensible source, as discussed in chapter 3. The drawback, however, is that the visualization requirement may misrepresent films whose diegetic music is implied rather than explicit.

In *Grand Hotel* (dir. Edmund Goulding, 1932), for example, much of the music might be taken to originate in the hotel, where "music plays all the time," states the Lionel Barrymore character in the film's opening scene.[6] The orchestra, presumably located in the hotel lobby, is not actually visualized, so, to remain consistent in the application of my categories, I counted these music-accompanied shots as nondiegetic music shots. This seemed like the right choice given the contours of my project. But the ambiguities of the distinction between source music and nondiegetic music also point to the limitation noted above, which is that quantitative methods appropriate for questions of shot length may be unsuited for other aspects of film style, for which different, nonquantitative methods may be needed.

A further complication with this distinction is that visualization of the music's source may be only partial. Incomplete visualization became common as early as 1929. Recall the scene in *The Broadway Melody* (dir. Harry Beaumont, 1929), analyzed in chapter 1, in which Charlie King performs the film's title song for the sisters played by Anita Page and Bessie Love. I counted the sequence's shots as source-music shots. But the case is complicated by the accompanying instrumental music, which comes from an unseen orchestra that cannot be located in the small hotel room where the scene is set. The scene thus exhibits a familiar equivocation: the singer's voice originates in the film's story world, but the orchestral backing, it seems, cannot. This peculiarity was noted by critics at the time.[7]

Two considerations informed my decision to label such shots as source-music shots. First, King's voice is anchored in the on-screen visualization of his body, a powerful cue whose impact likely obviates any hesitation that the offscreen orchestra might raise. We are too busy scrutinizing King, Page, and Love—at least one of whom appears in every shot—to become aware of the orchestra's impossibility. The second consideration concerns what is known about how such shots were produced. At the time of *The Broadway Melody*, singing shots usually required the presence of musicians on the set, whether visible in the shot or not. For the scene in *The Broadway Melody*, for example, my examination of the film suggests that the orchestral accompaniment had been recorded together with the shots of Eddie singing. Shots featuring nondiegetic music were ordinarily made differently, with the music recorded separately from the image and with no dialogue coinciding with the music, as is discussed in chapter 4. So the source-music designation refers not only to the visualization of the music's source but also to the production practice enabling such visualization.

The Challenge of Accuracy

My procedure for this book was to view and count all the films myself rather than delegate the task to research assistants. Counting the films myself, I had reasoned, would ensure that I came to know the films intimately and hence would better discern what was happening stylistically during the period. To ensure that other scholars could retrace my steps and reach the same results, I hired assistants on several occasions to tabulate shots for certain films using the same categories.[8] Their results were close enough to mine to make me think that others using my shot criteria would reach essentially the same conclusions. Nevertheless, the results produced by research assistants also often diverged from mine to some extent. Furthermore, I recounted dozens of films myself, multiple times, and the recounts also ordinarily yielded slightly different results. The variations were small enough to make me think that they probably would not affect the outcome of the research to a meaningful degree. If, for example, I were to recount the hundreds of films used for figure 0.1 using a frame- or time-accurate tool (see below), I find it hard to imagine that the basic ASL proportions for the shot types would change. Still, the slight inconsistencies from one count to the next were troubling.

The variations can be attributed to the manual fashion in which the calculations were performed. Most of the films examined for this book were counted using the Cinemetrics "standard tool," which involved clicking the mouse while watching the film, with each click marking not only the shot change but also the length of the preceding shot. The virtue of this procedure is that it is simple and fast. One clicks while the video plays, in real time. If there is no interruption in the work process, then no more time is needed to count a film than to watch it. With this method, I was able to count over five hundred films. The problem is that counting by hand inevitably yields errors. As careful as one tries to be, mistakes happen. One may click too late or too soon. A further danger is choosing the wrong category—mislabeling a dialogue shot as an action shot, say. Sometimes, when I knew I had made an error, I scrapped the file and started the count over. But starting over anytime a mistake occurred was not a feasible policy, and in any case, it would eliminate only mistakes that one had noticed while counting.

The solution to the problem of inaccuracy is to use a frame- or time-accurate computing tool such as FACT (Frame Accurate Counting Tool), designed by Gunars Civjans and available on the Cinemetrics website. Capturing shot duration to within a tenth of a second, FACT allows for even hyperfast sequences to be counted with near-perfect accuracy. FACT became available relatively late in my research, after I had already counted several hundred films using the standard tool. I then used FACT to recount roughly forty films. The drawback is that the procedure entails an intermittent process whereby the viewing of the film is momentarily interrupted with each shot change. So the process is relatively slow. To count a film using FACT, in my experience, takes triple the time needed to count it by hand. Nonetheless, if I were to do things over, knowing what I know now, I would use a time-accurate tool to count all the films. If FACT becomes unavailable, then other time-accurate methods can be employed, such as those devised by Barry Salt and Lea Jacobs using nonlinear film-editing software.[9] In any case, the future of statistical film analysis, as I see it, lies in the use of time- or frame-accurate procedures.

Studying Trends in Style

Two basic objects of statistical film analysis can be distinguished: an individual film and a body of films. From a methodological standpoint, the individual film offers a relatively straightforward case. Examining shot categories for a single film involves drawing samples from a finite and knowable data population, which ensures the reliability of the statistical findings. If I say that there are 435 shots in *Die Drei von der Tankstelle*, my statement can be readily proven or disproven by anyone who takes the trouble to count the same DVD.[10] If I say that 84 of these shots are singing shots, then someone can challenge or confirm my assertion by asking if I correctly applied my criteria for the shot category. But if I say that the singing shot figures for this film are typical or atypical of cinema in 1930, then I am making a bigger, more complex kind of claim. Backing it up requires taking the measurements for multiple films and then generating an average for those results.

Such an approach is evident in most of the book's charts, which report on what I call the "mean average" for a body of films. The mean averages refer either to the ASL for a body of films, a shot type's ASL, or a shot type's running-time percentage. These averages come from computing figures for dozens or hundreds of individual films, adding the figures for the shot type, and then dividing the result by the total number of films to produce a mean figure for the sample. This mean average, refers, in effect, to the mean for a sample of means.

To what extent can figures drawn from these samples be said to represent the populations to which they refer? Postulating the norms operative during a specific period in film history involves making claims regarding a population whose exact size and contours are unknown and effectively unknowable. Who can say exactly how many films were made during 1928–34? In researching this book, I examined roughly five hundred films, sound and silent. This is a lot of films for a single scholar to cover. Nevertheless, the Internet Movie Database (www.imdb.com) lists some seven thousand American and European films for the period.[11] If these figures are an indication, my corpus represents barely 14 percent of the period total. Also, my analysis often refers to smaller subsamples, as it were, as when silent films are distinguished from sound, American films from German, musical films from films belonging to other genres, and films of one film season from those of another.

How is the reliability of the various samples to be evaluated? One of the wonders of statistical science is its panoply of tests for measuring a sample's reliability as an indicator of a population, even when the population size is unknown.[12] Using software for statistical calculations, I ran what is known as a single-sample t-test for all the samples used for the findings reported in this book.[13] The test results for the book's charts are reported in the tables in appendix B, while those for various ad hoc findings are listed in the endnotes. The reports include basic information regarding the samples: the mean (M), the number of films (N), and the standard deviation (SD). They also report a figure from the tests: the margin of error (ME), performed at a confidence level of 95 percent. The ME provides a standard statistical estimate of the likelihood that the results reported for my samples will conform to the results for the actual population of films of the period, if the latter were available for measurement.

The ME tends to vary in inverse proportion to the size of the sample and the sample's standard deviation, so that as the sample size and standard deviation increase, the ME gets smaller. The rule of thumb is that the lower the ME, the better—that is, the more likely it is that the findings are indicative of the population to which the sample refers. For instance, figure 0.1.'s mean ASL for action shots in 354 sound films comes out to 6.11 seconds, whereas the ME for the same sample, as reported in table 1.1, is 0.2 seconds.

The implication is that if we were to measure the action shots for an additional, 355th film, it is 95 percent likely that the action-shot ASL for that film will be either 0.2 seconds less than 6.11 seconds or 0.2 seconds greater. In other words, the new result is 95 percent likely to fall between 5.91 and 6.31 seconds. The short range reflects the large sample size (N = 354) and also the relatively small standard deviation (SD = 1.92). Smaller samples with high standard deviations will yield higher MEs, as in figure 5.3's running-time percentages in American films devoted to singing shots. Consider the sample for 1928–29, which includes only eleven films and features a relatively high standard deviation (SD = 5.73 percent; M = 5.95), along with a relatively high ME of 3.85 percent. The high ME for the singing-shot running-time percentage indicates a lower reliability as a representation of the population than for the preceding example of the action-shot ASL. For readers who wish to assess the reliability of specific samples, the ME is provided in appendix B and in various endnotes for all statistical findings in the book.

Generalization in Style Analysis

Large samples were needed to meet the film-historiographical challenge of positing aesthetic norms for the period. The introduction ended with the proposal that shot-length computations are best seen as an extra tool to be used in conjunction with other critical methods, including old-school practices of mindful film viewing and the examination of an array of nonfilmic documents, so that statistical methods supplement rather than replace conventional film-analytical research practices. Nevertheless, I also identified two distinct benefits that quantitative methods offer to the study of film history. One is the insight that can come from seeing important aspects of a film, or body of films, that might otherwise go unnoticed, which was illustrated in the introduction by a specific finding, the extreme length for the singing shots in conversion-era films.

The other benefit is increased precision in making claims concerning film style. The precision, it's fair to say, diminishes when the analysis extends beyond a single film to involve averages pertaining to hundreds of films. But the decline in information quality is not unique to statistical research. It occurs with any sort of analysis, statistical or not. Generalizations regarding a large corpus are inevitably less precise than findings for a single film. More to the point, generalizations in style analysis are hard to avoid, since they supply the frame of reference for what is unusual (or normal) about a particular film. Even when the focus is on a single film, the analysis tends to appeal, if only tacitly, to an understanding of the period's artistic norms. An unusual feature of this book is the attempt to make period norms an explicit focus of analysis. In this context, quantitative methods, which provide an unusually precise way of accounting for period norms, have been essential. The challenge for the study of film style is that methods that can be extremely useful for measuring changes in film editing and film music may be less helpful in accounting for other dimensions of film style. To examine style, a mix of research methods is needed, as is an attempt—like the one in this appendix—to be explicit about the criteria employed in the analysis.

Notes

1. E. Sargent, "The Photoplaywright," 542.
2. B. Salt, *Film Style and Technology*, 1st ed.
3. The main example is D. Bordwell, J. Staiger, and K. Thompson, *The Classical Hollywood Cinema*, whose analysis of classical film style rests on an analysis of a random sample of several hundred Hollywood films.
4. C. O'Brien, "Multiple Language Versions and National Cinema, 1930–1933; Statistical Analysis."
5. L. Sabaneev, *Music for the Films*, 115.
6. The music-accompaniment percentage of 46 percent is based on data from my entry for *Grand Hotel* in the Cinemetrics database for film ID 16266. The music-accompaniment norm for 1931–32 of 34.6 percent comes from an analysis of a sample of six Hollywood films released during that season, which involved taking the percentage of a film's running time devoted to shots without musical accompaniment and subtracting it from one hundred. The precise figures for the shots without accompaniment are $M = 65.4$ percent, $N = 6$, $SD = 12.14$, and $ME = 11.89$.
7. S. Silverman, "'The Broadway Melody,'" 13. "[The] instance of [actor Charles] King singing the love song to Miss [Anita] Page in an apartment is marked by the theatrical license of bringing in an unseen orchestra for accompaniment."
8. Research assistants who submitted shot counts to the Cinemetrics database as part of their work for me include Kira Vorobiyova and Mohsen Nasrin.
9. An additional option is to develop one's own technique, as Barry Salt and Lea Jacobs did. See L. Jacobs, *Film Rhythm after Sound*, 36–37; and B. Salt, "Statistical Film Analysis."
10. See my entry for *Die Drei von der Tankstelle* in the Cinemetrics database for film ID 18395.
11. "Advanced Title Search," Internet Movie Database, https://www.imdb.com/search/title, accessed September 15, 2018. The exact total for feature films from the United States, the United Kingdom, France, and Germany released during 1928–34 is 7,059. This figure was derived by adding up the totals for each country.

12. The tests used for the ME require samples that conform to a lognormal distribution. For a debate regarding whether shot lengths exhibit the characteristics of lognormality, see the submissions by Nick Redfern, Barry Salt, and Mike Baxter on the Cinemetrics website (http://www.cinemetrics.lv/articles.php) under "Question 1: Mean or Median," beginning with Y. Tsivian, "Film Statistics: Give and Take," Cinemetrics, accessed February 18, 2018, http://www.cinemetrics.lv/dev/fsgt_q1a.php.

13. I used SamplePower 3 for some of the one-sample t-tests and SPSS 24 for others.

APPENDIX B

Samples and Tests

The tables below report the results of hypothesis tests performed on the samples used for the book's charts. For all samples, one-sample t-tests were performed at a confidence level of 95 percent using the software for either SamplePower 3 or SPSS Statistics version 24. The key figures are indicated via the following code: M = mean, SD = standard deviation, N = number of films in the sample, and ME = margin of error. Further discussion of the tests can be found in appendix A.

Table 0.1: Mean ASLs for Action, Dialogue, and Singing Shots in 354 Sound Films of 1928–34

	Action	Dialogue	Singing
M	6.11	14.88	20.77
N	354	351	276
SD	1.92	5.26	15.20
ME	0.20	0.55	1.80

Table 4.1. Mean ASLs for 73 Silent Films and 396 Sound Films of 1927–34, by Season

Silent films			
	1927–28	1928–29	1929–30
M	6.13	6.44	5.53
N	29	29	15
SD	1.36	2.29	1.47
ME	0.51	0.86	0.79

Sound films						
	1928–29	1929–30	1930–31	1931–32	1932–33	1933–34
M	9.57	12.80	12.08	10.09	10.09	9.90
N	19	56	90	78	89	64
SD	3.01	3.94	4.04	4.05	3.05	3.70
ME	1.42	1.05	0.84	0.91	0.64	0.92

Table 4.1a. Mean Running-Time Percentages for Dialogue Shots in 170 American Films of 1928–34, by Season

	1928–29	1929–30	1930–31	1931–32	1932–33	1933–34
M	60.56	64.15	67.53	72.39	64.52	69.38
N	17	35	39	22	35	22
SD	21.20	17.61	17.07	10.87	12.8	9.30
ME	11.29	6.05	5.53	4.82	4.40	4.12

Table 4.1b. Mean ASLs for Dialogue Shots in 170 American Films of 1928–34, by Season

	1928–29	1929–30	1930–31	1931–32	1932–33	1933–34
M	14.42	16.05	14.74	14.78	13.13	11.86
N	17	35	39	22	35	22
SD	4.13	4.21	3.71	4.45	4.62	4.61
ME	2.12	1.45	1.72	1.97	1.59	2.04

Table 4.2. Mean Running-Time Percentages for Musical Accompaniment in 121 Sound Films of 1928–34, by Season

Shots with No Music

	1927–28	1928–29	1929–30	1930–31	1931–32	1932–33	1933–34
M	0.42	55.49	58.86	72.37	60.27	63.45	59.98
N	3	8	24	27	20	22	17
SD	0.59	35.88	21.36	18.66	19.18	17.50	24.89
ME	0.38	28.56	8.89	7.29	8.82	7.64	12.53

Shots with Source Music

	1927–28	1928–29	1929–30	1930–31	1931–32	1932–33	1933–34
M	8.29	21.64	33.26	19.77	21.80	21.67	18.32
N	3	8	24	27	20	21	17
SD	13.11	16.03	15.43	11.50	11.76	11.36	19.17
ME	27.11	12.76	6.42	4.49	5.41	5.08	9.67

Shots with Nondiegetic Music

	1927–28	1928–29	1929–30	1930–31	1931–32	1932–33	1933–34
M	91.31	22.90	7.77	7.84	17.94	14.87	21.66
N	3	8	23	27	20	22	17
SD	13.76	31.27	15.95	11.20	17.43	14.04	19.64
ME	28.46	24.89	6.79	4.37	8.01	6.13	9.89

Table 5.3. Running-Time Percentages for Singing Shots in 121 American Films of 1928–34, by Season

	1928–29	1929–30	1930–31	1931–32	1932–33	1933–34
M	5.95	14.97	10.37	3.52	8.22	7.79
N	11	25	26	16	27	16
SD	5.73	10.32	10.20	4.74	7.85	5.40
ME	3.85	4.00	4.12	2.53	3.10	2.88

Table 6.1. Running-Time Percentages for Action, Dialogue, and Singing Shots of German and American Sound Films of 1928–34, with Musical Films Distinguished from Other Films

German Musical Films

	Action	Dialogue	Singing
M	29.93	56.05	14.01
N	35	35	35
SD	9.89	11.43	8.03
ME	3.36	3.89	2.73

American Musical Films

	Action	Dialogue	Singing
M	25.88	57.00	16.52
N	63	63	60
SD	11.11	15.00	7.83
ME	2.78	3.76	2.00

German Films Belonging to Other Genres

	Action	Dialogue	Singing
M	42.95	57.23	3.48
N	49	47	34
SD	24.04	20.24	2.99
ME	6.86	5.90	1.03

American Films Belonging to Other Genres

	Action	Dialogue	Singing
M	25.31	71.97	2.82
N	106	106	65
SD	11.63	13.05	2.59
ME	2.24	2.51	0.64

BIBLIOGRAPHY

Archives

Bibliothèque nationale de France, Paris
Bibliothèque du film (BiFi), Paris
British Film Institute, London
British Library, London
Bundesarchiv-Filmarchiv, Berlin
Deutsche Kinemathek, Berlin
Library of Congress, Washington, DC
Margaret Herrick Library, Academy of Motion Picture Arts and Sciences, Los Angeles
UCLA Film and Television Archive, Los Angeles
Warner Bros. Archive, University of Southern California, School of Cinematic Arts, Los Angeles

Periodicals

American Cinematographer, Los Angeles
Bioscope, The, London
Le cinéopse, Paris
La cinématographie française, Paris
Ciné-miroir, Paris
Close Up, London
Comoedia, Paris
Exhibitors Herald World, Chicago
Film-Kurier, Berlin
Die Filmwoche, Berlin
Gramophone, The, London
Los Angeles Times, Los Angeles
Motion Picture Herald, Chicago
Motion Picture News, New York
Journal of the Society of Motion Picture Engineers, New York
Kinematograph Yearbook, London
Licht-Bild-Bühne, Berlin
New York Times, New York
Photoplay, Chicago
Pour vous, Paris
Radio Times, London
La technique cinématographique, Paris
Variety, New York

Other Sources

Adorno, Theodor. "The Curves of the Needle." In *The Weimar Republic Sourcebook*, edited by Anton Kaes, Martin Jay, and Edward Dimendberg, 605–7. Berkeley: University of California Press, 1994. First published 1927.
"Air Killing Off Music Quickly." *Variety* 99, no. 5, May 14, 1930.
Albright, Daniel. *Untwisting the Serpent: Modernism in Music*. Chicago: University of Chicago Press, 1999.
"All Publix Managers to Learn Song Plug." *Variety* 98, no. 5, February 12, 1930.
"Along the Coast." *Variety* 97, no. 11, December 25, 1929.
Altman, Rick. *The American Film Musical*. Bloomington: Indiana University Press, 1989.
———. "Cinema and Popular Song: The Lost Tradition." In *Soundtrack Available: Essays on Film and Popular Music*, edited by Pamela R. Wojcik and Arthur Knight, 19–30. Durham: Duke University Press, 2001.
———. "Moving Lips: Cinema as Ventriloquism." *Yale French Studies* 60 (1980): 67–79.
———. "The Musical." In *The Oxford History of World Cinema*, edited by Geoffrey Nowell-Smith, 294–303. Oxford: Oxford University Press, 1996.
———. *Silent Film Sound*. New York: Columbia University Press, 2004.
American Film Institute. "AFI's 100 years . . . 100 Songs." Accessed August 31, 2017. http://www.afi.com/100years/songs.aspx.
———. "Hallelujah I'm a Bum." AFI Catalog of Feature Films: The First Hundred Years, 1893–1993. Accessed September 9, 2018. https://catalog.afi.com/Catalog/moviedetails/6133.
Angel, Hanne. "'Die verkaufte Braut.'" *Licht-Bild-Bühne* 25, no. 207, September 3, 1932.
Antoine, André. "Inquiétudes des musiciens." In *Musique d'écran: L'accompagnement musical du cinéma muet en France, 1918–1995*, edited by Emmanuelle Toulet and Christian Belaygue, 101. Paris: Réunion des Musées Nationaux, 1994. First published 1930.
Askari, Kaveh. "An Afterlife for Junk Prints: Serials and Other 'Classics' in Late 1920s Tehran." In *Silent Cinema and the Politics of Space*, edited by Jennifer M. Bean, Anupama Kapse, and Laura Horak, 99–120. Bloomington: Indiana University Press, 2014.
Auslander, Philip. *Liveness: Performance in a Mediatized Culture*. London: Routledge, 1999.
"Au studio: Les maîtres du son." *Ciné-miroir*, January 1, 1932.
Autré, Pierre. "Attention au dubbing!" *La cinématographie française* 14, no. 691, January 31, 1932.
———. "La musique dans les films." *La cinématographie française* 14, no. 734, November 26, 1932.
———. "Musique et disques de cinéma." *La cinématographie française* 13, no. 686, December 26, 1931.
B., R. "Disappointing International Congress: Avant Garde Dead?" *Bioscope* 85, no. 1261, December 3, 1930.
———. "L'exploitation du film sonore." *La cinématographie française* 11, no. 552, March 31, 1929.
Babcock, Muriel. "Song Doubling Now in Discard." *Los Angeles Times*, July 14, 1929.
———. "Tin Pan Alley Invades Town." *Los Angeles Times*, December 9, 1928.
"Back to Orchestras? Gaumont Revert to 'Flesh and Blood.'" *Bioscope* 85, no. 1254, October 15, 1930.
Bakshy, Alexander. "The Shrinking of Personality." *Nation* 27, no. 32, May 27, 1931.
Balázs, Béla. *Early Film Theory*. Translated by R. Livingstone. Edited by Erica Carter. New York: Oxford University Press, 2010.

Barnier, Martin. *Des films français made in Hollywood: Les versions multiples, 1929–1935.* Paris: L'Harmattan, 2004.

———. *En route vers le parlant: Histoire d'une évolution technologique, économique et esthétique du cinema, 1926–1934.* Liège: Editions du Céfal, 2002.

Barry, John F., and Epes W. Sargent. *Building Theatre Patronage: Management and Merchandising.* New York: Chalmers, 1927.

Basile, Guisy, and Chantal Gavouyère. *La chanson française dans le cinema des années trente: Discographie.* Paris: Bibliothèque nationale de France, 1996.

Bauër, Gérard. "Maintenant que le cinéma a parlé." *L'echo de Paris*, August 21, 1930.

Baxter, Peter. *Just Watch! Sternberg, Paramount and America.* London: British Film Institute, 1993.

Bazin, André. "The Evolution of Film Language." In *What Is Cinema?*, edited and translated by Timothy Barnard, 87–106. Montreal: Caboose, 2009.

"Bei der Ufa." *Licht-Bild-Bühne* 26, no. 163, July 13, 1933.

Beinroth, Carolin. "Between Practice and Theory: Silent Film Sound and the Music Archive." In *Today's Sounds for Yesterday's Films: Making Music for Silent Cinema*, edited by K. J. Donnelly and Ann-Kristin Wallengren, 29–44. Basingstoke: Palgrave Macmillan, 2016.

Belfrage, Cedric. "Hollywood's Multi-Lingual Quandary: Different Dialects Present Difficulty." *Bioscope* 82, no. 1218, February 5, 1930.

———. "Money for Foreign Market Talkers." *Bioscope* 82, no. 1223, March 12, 1930.

Bell, Nelson. "Those Cultural Arts and Flattery as a Bludgeon." *Washington Post*, November 11, 1928.

Bellis, Richard. *The Emerging Film Composer.* San Bernardino: R. Bellis, 2006.

Belton, John. "Digital Cinema: A False Revolution." *October* 100 (Spring 2002): 98–114.

"Big Biz Uses Showdom Aid." *Variety* 99, no. 13, July 9, 1930.

"Bilan de fin d'année." *La cinématographie française* 14, no. 738, December 24, 1932.

"Bildmontage nach einer primären Musik." *Film-Kurier* 12, no. 269, November 13, 1930.

Boch, Hans-Michael, and Jürgen Berger, eds. *Photo: Casparius: Filmgeschichte in Bildern, Berlin um 1930.* Berlin: Deutsche Kinemathek, 1978.

Bolter, Jay David, and Richard Grusin. *Remediation: Understanding New Media.* Cambridge: MIT Press, 1999.

Bordwell, David. *On the History of Film Style.* Cambridge: Harvard University Press, 1997.

Bordwell, David, Janet Staiger, and Kristin Thompson. *The Classical Hollywood Cinema: Film Style and Mode of Production, 1917 to 1960.* New York: Columbia University Press, 1985.

Boswell, Albert. "Trials of the Talkies." *Photoplay* 36, no. 2, July 1929.

Bradley, Edwin. *The First Hollywood Musicals: A Critical Filmography of 171 Features, 1927 through 1932.* Jefferson, NC: McFarland, 1996.

Brandt, Joe. "Synchronized Films." In *The 1931 Film Daily Year Book*, edited by John Alicoate, 996. New York: John D. Alicoate, 1931.

Brecht, Bertolt. *Bertolt Brecht on Film and Radio.* Edited and translated by Marc Silberman. London: Methuen, 2000.

Briggs, Asa, and Peter Burke. *A Social History of the Media.* Cambridge: Polity, 2002.

British Broadcasting Association. "The American Listener: A British Impression." In *The B. B. C. Year Book 1930*, 131–36. London: British Broadcasting Corporation, 1931.

"British Cinema Back to Music." *Variety* 96, no. 12, October 2, 1929.

Brown, D. L. "The Film Situation in Central Europe." *Bioscope* 85, no. 1262, December 10, 1930.

Brown, Geoff. "The Euro-British Flagship That Sank: The Short Life and Lingering Death of Associated Sound Film Industries, 1929–1936." *Historical Journal of Film, Radio and Television* 33, no. 2 (July 2013): 187–213.
Buhler, James, Caryl Flinn, and David Neumeyer, eds. *Music and Cinema*. Hanover: University Press of New England, 2000.
Buhler, James, David Neumeyer, and Rob Deemer. *Hearing the Movies: Music and Sound in Film History*. Oxford: Oxford University Press, 2010.
"Canadian Conference on Film Canned Music." *Variety* 100, no. 5, August 13, 1930.
Cardona, Arturo. "Spain." *Variety* 98, no. 2, January 22, 1930.
Carstairs, John Paddy. "Looking at Hollywood." *Bioscope* 86, no. 1273, February 25, 1931.
"Cash Prizes for Live Showmen." *Bioscope* 84, no. 1250, September 17, 1930.
Chaine, Pierre. "A la poursuite du temps perdu." *Pour vous*, no. 232, April 27, 1933.
Champfleury, R. "Vive la chanson!" *Soir*, October 3, 1930.
Chanan, Michael. *Repeated Takes: A Short History of Recording and Its Effects on Music*. London: Verso, 1995.
"Changes Forced by Sound." *Variety* 94, no. 9, March 13, 1929.
Chapple, Stanley. "In the Recording Studio." *Gramophone* 6, no. 67, December 1928.
Chartier, J. P., and R. P. Desplanques. *Derrière l'écran: Initiation au cinéma*. Paris: Spes, 1950.
"Chicago's Canned Applause Making 'Em Warm Up." *Variety* 94, no. 9, March 13, 1929.
Chion, Michel. *Audio-Vision: Sound on Screen*. Translated by C. Gorbman. New York: Columbia University Press, 1994.
———. *The Voice in Cinema*. Translated by C. Gorbman. New York: Columbia University Press, 1999.
Churchill, Douglas. "Hollywood Arranges for a Moment Musicale." *New York Times*, September 6, 1936.
"Cinema: The New Pictures." *Time* 16, no. 26, December 29, 1930.
Cinemetrics. "Articles." Accessed February 18, 2018. http://www.cinemetrics.lv/articles.php.
"Circuits 1/3 of Wired." *Variety* 99, no. 5, May 14, 1930: 13.
Clair, G. "Disques et cinema." *Le cinéopse* 11, no. 117, May 1, 1929.
Clair, René. "The Art of Sound." In Weis and Belton, *Film Sound*, 92–95. First published 1929.
Clarrière, Georges. "'Singing Fool' Receipts." *Bioscope* 82, no. 1216, January 22, 1930.
———. "The Western Peril." *Sight and Sound* 3, no. 12 (Winter 1934–35): 153–56.
"Classical Composers Banished from Films." *Los Angeles Times*, October 16, 1932.
Claus, Horst, and Anne Jackel. "*Der Kongress tanzt*: UFA's Blockbuster *Filmoperette* for the World Market." In *Musicals, Hollywood and Beyond*, edited by Bill Marshall and Robynn Stilwell, 89–97. Exeter: Intellect Books, 2000.
"Coast Music Survey." *Variety* 96, no. 5, August 14, 1929.
"Coast Music Survey." *Variety* 96, no. 10, September 18, 1929.
Coeury, André, and George Clarence. *Le phonographe*. Paris: Ed. Kra, 1929.
Cohen, Annabelle. "Film Music: Perspectives from Cognitive Science." In Buhler, Flinn, and Neumeyer, *Music and Cinema*, 360–77.
Cohen, Thomas. *Playing to the Camera: Musicians and Musical Performance in Documentary Cinema*. London: Wallflower, 2012.
"Color and Sound on Film." *Fortune* 11, no. 4, October 1930.
"Come-Back for 'Musicals'? A 'Whoopee' Experience." *Bioscope* 8, no. 1257, November 5, 1930.
Conway, Kelley. *Chanteuse in the City: The Realist Singer in French Film*. Berkeley: University of California Press, 2004.

Connor, Steven. *Dumbstruck: A Cultural History of Ventriloquism*. New York: Oxford University Press, 2000.
Cook, Nicholas. "Methods for Analyzing Recordings." In Cook et al., *Cambridge Companion to Recorded Music*, 221–45.
Cook, Nicholas, Eric Clarke, Daniel Leech-Wilkinson, and John Rink, eds. *The Cambridge Companion to Recorded Music*. Cambridge: Cambridge University Press, 2009.
Cornu, Jean-François. *Le doublage et le sous-titrage: Histoire et esthétique*. Rennes: Presses universitaires de Rennes, 2014.
Courant, Curt. "Aus der Tonfilmpraxis des Kameramanner." *Film-Kurier* 12, no. 205, August 30, 1930.
Cowan, Lester, ed. *Recording Sound for Motion Pictures*. New York: McGraw-Hill, 1931.
Crafton, Donald. *Shadow of a Mouse: Performance, Belief, and World-Making in Animation*. Berkeley: University of California, 2013.
———. *The Talkies: American Cinema's Transition to Sound, 1926–1931*. Berkeley: University of California, 1999.
Crisp, Colin. "Film Music in the Classic French Cinema, 1930–1960." Unpublished manuscript, n.d., ca. 1997.
Crooker, Herbert. "Tie-Ups, Tie-ins, Advertising and Exploiting F. N. Pictures." *Variety* 99, no. 11, June 25, 1930.
Currid, Brian. *A National Acoustics: Music and Mass Publicity in Weimar and Nazi Germany*. Minneapolis: University of Minnesota Press, 2006.
"Dallas Fans' Likes." *Motion Picture News* 41, no. 23, June 7, 1930.
Dammann. "'Die Million.'" *Licht-Bild-Bühne* 24, no. 114, May 13, 1931.
Danan, Martine. "A la recherché d'une stratégie internationale: Hollywood et le marché français des années trente." In *Les transferts linguistiques dans les médias audiovisuels*, edited by Yves Gambier, 109–30. Lille: Presses universitaires de Septentrion, 1996.
"Das Sprachproblem des Tonfilms: Deutsche Filme in Paris." *Film-Kurier* 12, no. 161, July 10, 1930.
Davidson, Jane. "Bodily Movement and Facial Actions in Expressive Musical Performance by Solo and Duo Instrumentalists: Two Distinctive Case Studies." *Psychology of Music* 40, no. 5 (2012): 595–633.
———. "Communicating with the Body in Performance." In *Musical Performance: A Guide to Understanding*, edited by John Rink, 144–52. Cambridge: Cambridge University Press, 2002.
Day, Timothy. *A Century of Recorded Music: Listening to Musical History*. New Haven: Yale University Press, 2000.
"The Dealers and Theme Song Sales." *Variety* 93, no. 6, November 21, 1928.
de B., R. "Les nouveautés d'écran." *L'illustration*, May 24, 1930.
de Grazia, Victoria. *Irresistible Empire: America's Advance through Twentieth-Century Europe*. Cambridge: Harvard University Press, 2006.
"'Der Jazzkönig.'" *Licht-Bild-Bühne* 23, no. 248, October 16, 1930.
Dibbets, Karel. *Sprekende film: De komst van de geluidsfilm in Nederland, 1928–1933*. Amsterdam: Otto Cramwinckel, 1993.
"Die Musiker und die Tonfilmfrage." *Film-Kurier* 12, no. 221, September 18, 1930.
"'Die Privatsekretärin.'" *Licht-Bild-Bühne* 24, no. 15, January 17, 1931.
Distelmeyer, Jan, ed. *Babylon in FilmEuropa: Mehrsprachen-Versionen der 1930er Jahre*. Munich: text and kritik, 2005.

Dixon, J. L. "How the 'Talkies' Work." *Radio Times* 24, no. 314, October 4, 1929.
Doherty, Thomas. *Pre-Code Hollywood: Sex, Immorality, and Insurrection in American Cinema, 1930–1934*. New York: Columbia University Press, 1999.
"Doings in Hollywood." *New York Times*, September 21, 1930.
Donnelly, K. J. *Occult Aesthetics: Synchronization in Sound Film*. Oxford: Oxford University Press, 2014.
Downey, George. *Technology and Communication in American History*. Washington, DC: American Historical Association, 2011.
"Dubbing's Comeback on Coast; Sound Men Assure Results as Desired." *Variety* 100, no. 4, August 6, 1930.
"Dubbing Tough Routine but Cheaper." *Variety* 100, no. 8, September 3, 1930.
"Ducking Musicals." *Variety* 99, no. 13, July 9, 1930.
Ďurovičová, Nataša. "Local Ghosts: Dubbing Bodies in Early Sound Cinema." In *Film and its Multiples*, edited by Anna Antonini, 83–98. Udine: Forum, 2003.
———. "Vector, Flow, Zone: Towards a History of Cinematic *Translatio*." In *World Cinemas: Transnational Perspectives*, edited by Nataša Ďurovičová and Kathleen Newman, 90–120. New York: Routledge/American Film Institute, 2009.
Dwyer, Tessa. "Mute, Dumb, Dubbed: Lulu's Silent Talkies." In *Politics, Policy and Power in Translation History*, edited by Lieben D'hulst, Carol O'Sullivan, and Michael Schreiber, 157–86. Berlin: Frank and Timme, 2016.
Dyer, Richard. "Entertainment and Utopia." In *Movies and Methods*, vol. 2, edited by Bill Nichols, 220–32. Berkeley: University of California Press, 1985.
———. *In the Space of a Song: The Uses of Song in Film*. London: Routledge, 2011.
"Eddie Cantor Discourses of Music Films." *New York Times*, October 25, 1931.
"'Einbrecher.'" *Film-Kurier* 12, no. 297, December 17, 1930.
"Eindrücke aus Film-Frankreich." *Film-Kurier* 12, no. 79, April 1, 1930.
Eisenstein, Sergei M., and Vsevolod I. Pudovkin, and Grigori V. Alexandrov. "A Statement." In Weis and Belton, *Film Sound*, 83–85. First published 1928.
Eisler, Hanns, and Theodor Adorno. *Composing for the Films*. New York: Athlone, 1947.
Elsaesser, Thomas. "Going 'Live': Body and Voice in Some Early German Sound Films." In *Le son en perspective: Nouvelles recherches/New Perspectives in Sound Studies*, edited by Dominique Nasta and Didier Huvelle, 155–68. Brussels: Peter Lang, 2004.
———. "The 'Return' of 3-D: On Some of the Logics and Genealogies of the Image in the Twenty-First Century." *Critical Inquiry* 39, no. 2 (Winter 2013): 217–46.
"Engaging Musical Screened." *Los Angeles Times*, January 4, 1932.
"English House Returns to Silence for Summer." *Variety* 95, no. 10, June 19, 1929.
Epstein, Jean. "Le cinéma pur et le film sonore." *La technique cinématographique* 17, no. 28, October 3, 1946.
"Europe Off Dubbing." *Variety* 98, no. 13, April 9, 1930.
"Exposure of Talker-Making by Film Fan Mags." *Variety* 95, no. 7, May 29, 1929.
Eyman, Scott. *The Speed of Sound: Hollywood and the Talkies Revolution, 1926–1930*. Baltimore: Johns Hopkins University Press, 1999.
"Faint Hearted Publishers." *Variety* 99, no. 11, June 25, 1930.
Fairservice, Don. *Film Editing: History, Theory and Practice: Looking at the Invisible*. Manchester: Manchester University Press, 2001.
Feld, Hans. "'Es lebe die Freiheit!'" *Film-Kurier* 14, no. 16, January 19, 1932.
Feuer, Jane. *The Hollywood Musical*. 2nd ed. Bloomington: Indiana University Press, 1993.

"'Fifty Million Frenchmen,' without Music!" *Motion Picture Herald* 102, no. 1, January 3, 1931.
"Film Houses Work for Song Selling." *Variety* 93, no. 6, November 21, 1928.
"Filmusicals." *Bioscope* 87, no. 1279, April 8, 1931.
Fischer, Lucy. 2003. *Designing Women: Cinema, Art Deco, and the Female Form*. New York: Columbia University Press.
Fleeger, Jennifer. *Sounding American: Hollywood, Opera, and Jazz*. Oxford: Oxford University Press, 2014.
Fonjallez, René. "Défense du cinéma muet." *Revue mondiale*, June 1, 1932.
"'Fool' Big in Belgrade; Talkers Help Music Sales." *Variety* 98, no. 5, February 12, 1930.
"'Fool' Tops Holland as Disk Sales Soar." *Variety* 96, no. 13, October 9, 1929.
"Foreign Competition." *Variety* 99, no. 5, May 14, 1930.
Fraenkel, Heinrich. "Can Industry Stay International?" *Motion Picture Herald* 102, no. 5, January 31, 1931.
Frank, Nino. "Théâtre, music hall, melodrama, opéra." *Pour vous*, no. 141, July 30, 1931.
Franklin, Harold B. "Talking Pictures—the Great Internationalist." *Journal of the Society of Motion Picture Engineers* 15, no. 1, July 1930.
"French Jazz Composers Lagging; American Tunes Best in France." *Variety* 98, no. 10, March 19, 1930.
"From Cinema Palaces to Country Stores." *Motion Picture News* 42, no. 24, December 13, 1930.
Furia, Philip, and Laurie Patterson. *The Songs of Hollywood*. New York: Oxford University Press, 2010.
Garncarz, Joseph. "Made in Germany: Multiple-Language Versions and Early German Sound Cinema." In *'Film Europe' and 'Film America': Cinema, Commerce and Cultural Exchange, 1920–1939*, edited by Andrew Higson and Richard Maltby, 249–73. Exeter: University of Exeter Press, 1999.
———. "The Star System in Weimar Cinema." In *The Many Faces of Weimar Cinema: Rediscovering Germany's Filmic Legacy*, edited by Christian Rogowski, 116–33. Rochester, NY: Camden House, 2010.
"German Film Industry in May: Berlin Chamber of Commerce Report." *Film-Kurier* 12, no. 139, June 14, 1930.
"German Musicians Protest Officially against Sound Pictures." *Variety* 99, no. 12, July 2, 1930.
"Germans See the End of U. S. Film over There." *Variety* 97, no. 1, October 16, 1929.
"Ghosting and Doubling in Talker Publicity." *Variety* 96, no. 1, July 17, 1929.
Giddins, Gary. *Bing Crosby, A Pocketful of Dreams: The Early Years, 1903–1940*. Boston: Little, Brown, 2001.
Gilbert, Morris. "Audibility of American Pictures Satisfies Curiosity of Parisians." *New York Times*, March 30, 1930.
Gilmore, Jonathan. *The Life of a Style*. Ithaca, NY: Cornell University Press, 2000.
Gitelman, Lisa. *Always Already New: Media, History, and the Data of Culture*. Cambridge: MIT Press, 2006.
Gitelman, Lisa, and Geoffrey B. Pingree, eds. *New Media, 1740–1915*. Cambridge: MIT Press, 2003.
"Giveaways in Lobbies." *Variety* 99, no. 2, April 23, 1930.
Gladish, W. "The Year in Canada." In Rayment, *Kinematograph Year Book*, 1929, 35.
Goldmark, Daniel. *Tunes for 'Toons: Music and the Hollywood Cartoon*. Berkeley: University of California Press, 2007.

Goldstein, Leo. "Recording Companies Finding Things Improving despite the Slump and Radio Competition." *Gramophone* 10, no. 114, November 1932.
Gomery, Douglas. *The Coming of Sound: A History*. London: Routledge, 2004.
———. "The Coming of Sound to American Cinema: A History of the Transformation of an Industry." PhD diss., University of Wisconsin, 1975.
———, ed. *The Will Hays Papers*. Cinema History Microfilm Series. Frederick, MD: University Publications of America, 1988.
Goossens, Eugene. "The Gramophone in America." *Gramophone* 8, no. 87, August 1930.
Grace, Harvey. "Dance Music: A Short Life and a Gay One." *The Radio Times* 25, no. 338, March 21, 1930.
Green, Abel. "The Theme Song." *Variety* 93, no. 11, January 2, 1929.
———. "Words about Music." *Variety* 95, no. 12, July 3, 1929.
Greene, Walter. "Old Reliables Wobble, New Names on Wing as Sound Alters Star Values." *Motion Picture News* 41, no. 11, March 15, 1930.
Griffith, D. W. "Pace in the Movies." *Liberty* 3, no. 28, November 13, 1926.
Gronow, Pekka, and Ilpo Saunio. *An International History of the Recording Industry*. London: Cassell, 1998.
H., Dr. F. "Das Musikproblem im Tonfilm: Los vom Schlager!" *Film-Kurier* 12, no. 195, August 19, 1930.
Hagener, Malte. *Moving Forward, Looking Back: The European Avant-Garde and the Invention of Film Culture, 1919–1939*. Amsterdam: Amsterdam University Press, 2007.
———. "Unter den Dächern der Tobis: Nationale Märkte und europäische Strategien." In *Tonfilmfrieden/Tonfilmkrieg: Die Geschichte der Tobis vom Technik-Syndikat zum Staatskonzern*, edited by Jan Distelmeyer, 51–64. Munich: text and kritik, 2003.
Hagener, Malte, and Jan Hans, eds. *Als die Filme singen lernten: Innovation und Tradition im Musikfilm, 1928–1938*. Munich: text and kritik, 1999.
Haines, Richard. *Technicolor Movies: The History of Dye-Transfer Printing*. Jefferson, NC: McFarland, 1993.
Hall, Chapin. "Hollywood Turns to Music in Films." *New York Times*, April 3, 1932.
Hall, Mordaunt. "Clever Dubbing." *New York Times*, April 16, 1933.
———. "A German Film Operetta." *New York Times*, October 13, 1930.
———. "Havens of Laughter." *New York Times*, October 18, 1931.
———. "Mr. Jolson in Black-Face." *New York Times*, September 13, 1930.
———. "Ufa's English Dialogue Film." *New York Times*, September 1, 1930.
Harlé, P. A. "La margarine peut-elle remplacer le beurre?" *La cinématographie française* 13, no. 658, June 13, 1931.
Haskell, Molly. *From Reverence to Rape: The Treatment of Women in the Movies*. New York: Holt, Rinehart and Winston, 1974.
Hays, Will. "Free Speech in Sound Pictures Endangered." *The Motion Picture* 5, no. 3, March 1929.
"Heavy Drop in Sales Abroad on American Films." *Variety* 93, no. 8, December 5, 1928.
"Here's Dope on 'Dixiana' Campaign." *Motion Picture News* 42, no. 5, August 2, 1930.
Herzog, Amy. *Dreams of Difference, Song of the Same: The Musical Moment in Film*. Minneapolis: University of Minnesota Press, 2010.
Heymann, Werner Richard. "Musik und Bild als einheitliches Kunstwerk." *Licht-Bild-Bühne* 23, no. 280, November 22, 1930.
———. "Musik nach Maß." *Film-Kurier* 13, no. 202, August 29, 1931.

Hirsch, Leo. "Film sonore et film muet." *La technique cinématographique* 4, no. 26, February 1933.
Hitchcock, Alfred. "Direction." In *Hitchcock on Hitchcock: Selected Writings and Interviews*, edited by Stanley Gottlieb, 253–61. Berkeley: University of California Press, 1995. First published 1937.
Hodges, Douglas. "More Pantomime with Less Talk for Universal Films." *Exhibitors Herald World* 100, no. 3, July 19, 1930.
Hoffman, Jerry. "Westward the Course of Tin Pan Alley." *Photoplay* 36, no. 4, August 1929.
"'The Hollywood Revue.'" *New York Times*, August 11, 1929.
"Hollywood stoppt die Versionen." *Film-Kurier* 13, no. 40, February 17, 1931.
Hourée, Arthur. "Essai d'esthéthique du sonore." *La revue musicale*, no. 151, December 1934: 45–62.
Huron, David. *Sweet Anticipation: Music and the Psychology of Expectation*. Cambridge, MA, 2006.
"In Frankreich: Große Tätigkeit im Dubbing." *Film-Kurier* 15, no. 93, 1933.
"In Hollywood Now." *Bioscope* 86, no. 1,277, March 25, 1931.
Indicator. "Atmosphere." *Gramophone* 6, no. 61, June 1928.
Internet Movie Database. "Advanced Title Search." Accessed September 15, 2018. https://www.imdb.com/search/title.
"Interview mit René Clair." *Film-Kurier* 12, no. 203, August 28, 1930.
J., E. "Musik zu 'Zwei Herzen im Dreivierteltakt.'" *Film-Kurier* 12, no. 64, March 14, 1930.
Jacobs, Lea. *Film Rhythm after Sound: Technology, Music, and Performance*. Berkeley: University of California Press, 2014.
———. "The Innovation of Re-recording in the Hollywood Studios." *Film History* 24, no. 1, 2012): 5–34.
Jelavich, Peter. *Berlin Alexanderplatz: Radio, Film, and the Death of Weimar Culture*. Berkeley: University of California Press, 2006.
"Jobbers Can't Wait, Send Back Film Songs." *Variety* 100, no. 8, September 3, 1930.
"Jolson-Brunswick Renewal." *Variety* 93, no. 3, October 31, 1928.
"Jolson Leads All International Disc Sellers with 'Sonny Boy.'" *Variety* 96, no. 4, August 7, 1929.
"Jolson's Talker Royalties." *Variety* 95, no. 8, June 5, 1929.
"Jump of U.S. Film Exports First Six Months Explained." *Variety* 96, no. 3, July 31, 1929.
Kalinak, Kathryn. *Settling the Score: Music and the Classical Hollywood Film*. Madison: University of Wisconsin Press, 1992.
Kann, George. "Foreign Troubles Mean Domestic Troubles, Too." *Motion Picture News* 41, no. 24, June 14, 1930.
Kassabian, Anahid. *Hearing Film: Tracking Identifications in Contemporary Hollywood Film*. London: Routledge, 2000.
Katz, Mark. *Capturing Sound: How Technology Has Changed Music*. Revised ed. Berkeley: University of California Press, 2010.
Keating, Carla Mereu. "'100% Italian': The Coming of Sound in Italy and State Regulation on Dubbing." *California Italian Studies* 4, no. 1 (2013): 1–24.
Kelber, Michel. "From Vigo to the New Wave, a Cameraman's Career." In *Projections* 6, edited by John Boorman and Walter Donohue, 229–53. London: Faber and Faber, 1996.
"Kidding Kissers in Talkies Burns Up Fans of Screen's Best Lovers." *Variety* 97, no. 3, October 30, 1929.
Kingsley, Grace. "Action Usurps Film Dialogue." *Los Angeles Times*, September 12, 1931.

Kivy, Peter. *Introduction to the Philosophy of Music*. New York: Oxford University Press, 2002.
Koenig, William. "Studio Problems." *Variety* 99, no. 11, June 25, 1930.
Kracauer, Siegfried. *From Caligari to Hitler: A Psychological History of the German Film*. Revised and expanded ed. Princeton: Princeton University Press, 2004.
Kraft, James. *From Stage to Studio: Musicians and the Sound Revolution, 1890–1950*. Baltimore: Johns Hopkins University Press, 2003.
Kreimeier, Klaus. *The Ufa Story: A History of Germany's Greatest Film Company, 1918–1945*. Berkeley: University of California Press.
L., J.-P. "Auteurs et producteurs allemands rendent homage à 'Sous les toits de Paris.'" *Comoedia* 25, no. 6562, January 7, 1931.
L., M. "'Der Kongreß tanzt.'" *Christian Science Monitor*, July 19, 1932.
Laing, Heather. "Emotion by Numbers: Music, Song and the Musical." In *Musicals: Hollywood and Beyond*, edited by Bill Marshall and Robin Stillwell, 5–13. Exeter: University of Exeter Press, 2000.
Lang, Harry. "He Didn't Know How!" *Photoplay* 38, no. 1, June 1930.
"Language the Chief American Film Barrier." *Motion Picture News* 41, no. 23, June 7, 1930.
Larkin, Mark. "The Truth about Voice Doubling." *Photoplay* 36, no. 2, July 1929.
Lastra, James. *Sound Technology and the American Cinema: Perception, Representation, Modernity*. New York: Columbia University Press, 2000.
Layton, James, and David Pierce. *King of Jazz: Paul Whiteman's Technicolor Revue*. Severn, MD: Media History Press, 2016.
Leclérc, René. "Marcel L'Herbier über Deutschelands Produktionsmethode." *Film-Kurier* 12, no. 205, August 30, 1930.
Leech-Wilkinson, Daniel. "Recordings and Histories of Performance Style." In Cook et al., *Cambridge Companion to Recorded Music*, 246–62.
Lehmann, R. "A propos de 'dubbing.'" *Pour vous* 133, June 4, 1931.
Levitin, Daniel. *This Is Your Brain on Music: The Science of a Human Obsession*. New York: Penguin, 1996.
Lewin, George. "Dubbing and Its Relation to Sound Picture Production." *Journal of the Society of Motion Picture Engineers* 16, no. 1, January 1931.
Lewis, Harold. "Getting Good Sound Is an Art." *American Cinematographer* 15, no. 2, June 1934.
Lewis, Howard T. *The Motion Picture Industry*. New York: D. Van Nostrand, 1933.
Lewis, Kevin. "'Broadway' Playback." *Cinemontage*, January 1, 2009. http://www.cinemontage.org/2009/01/broadway-playback/.
Lipscomb, W. P. "Saving the 'Talkie' from Talk! Who Will Face Pioneer Hazards?" *Bioscope* 85, no. 1265, December 31, 1930), 95.
"Living Music Defenders Get Votes." *Variety* 98, no. 7, February 26, 1930.
"Lobby Chain Stores—Publix." *Variety* 98, no. 4, February 5, 1930.
Loiperdinger, Martin. "German Tonbilder of the 1900s: Advanced Technology and National Brand." In *Film 1900: Technology, Perception, Culture*, edited by Annemone Ligensa and Klaus Kreimeier, 187–200. New Barnet, UK: John Libbey, 2015.
London, Kurt. *Film Music*. New York: Arno, 1970. First published 1936.
"Loss of Foreign Trade." *Variety* 93, no. 11, January 2, 1929.
"Loud Ballyhoo." *Variety* 94, no. 13, April 10, 1929.
Louvish, Simon. *Monkey Business: The Lives and Legends of the Marx Brothers*. New York: St. Martin's, 1999.

M. "Quelques minutes avec Jean Renoir. " *Ami du peuple du soir*, October 16, 1931.
M., L. "Il faut mettre au point la question du 'dubbing.'" *Pour vous* 129, May 7, 1931.
MacDonald, Carlisle. "Demand Talkies in Own Language." *New York Times*, April 17, 1930.
MacKenzie, Compton. "You Are Making Robots out of Your Actors." *The Radio Times* 27, no. 345, May 9, 1930.
Maltby, Richard. "On the Prospect of Writing Cinema History from Below." *Tijdschrift Voor Mediageschiedenis* 9, no. 2 (2006). https://www.scribd.com/document/191710426/Richard-Maltby-On-the-Prospect-of-Writing-Cinema-History-From-Below.
Mann, Fritz. "Language *Barrier* Leads to Conflict: Anti-German 'Talkie' Riots in Prague." *Bioscope* 85, no. 1252, October 1, 1930: 19.
Manovich, Lev. *Language of New Media*. Cambridge: MIT Press, 2001.
"Manufacturers Want That Screen Plug." *Variety* 96, no. 6, August 21, 1929.
Marks, Martin. *Music and the Silent Film: Contexts and Case Studies, 1895–1924*. New York: Oxford University Press, 1997.
Matthews, Herbert. "London Film Notes." *New York Times*, July 14, 1929.
———. "Post-haste from Paris." *New York Times*, June 2, 1935.
Massey, Anne. *Hollywood Beyond the Screen: Design and Material Culture*. Oxford: Berg, 2000.
Maxfield, J. P. "Technic of Recording Control for Sound Pictures." In *Cinematographic Annual, 1930*, edited by Hal Hall, 409–24. New York: Arno and *New York Times*, 1972.
McClean, Shilo. *Digital Storytelling: The Narrative Power of Visual Effects in Film*. Cambridge: MIT Press, 2008.
McCracken, Alison. *Real Men Don't Sing: Crooning in American Culture*. Durham, NC: Duke University Press, 2015.
McNary, Dave. "Martin Scorsese Backs Kodak on Film Stock Production." *Variety*, August 4, 2014. http://variety.com/2014/film/news/martin-scorsese-backs-kodak-on-film-stock-production-1201274982/.
Medina, Paul. "Das Ende der franzosischen Avantgarde?" *Film-Kurier* 12, no. 43, February 18, 1930.
Meisel, Will. "Der Tonfilmschlager." *Film-Kurier* 15, no. 137, June 14, 1933.
Mendoza, D. "Problems of Recording Music." *American Cinematographer* 13, no. 10, February 1933.
Merrick, Mollie. "It's In, So It Can't Be Out: Music Never Left Films, Say Picture Chiefs." *Los Angeles Times*, August 30, 1931.
Meyer, Leonard. *Style and Music: Theory, History, and Ideology*. Chicago: University of Chicago, 1989.
"M-G Off Dubbing." *Variety* 98, no. 3, January 29, 1930.
"Micky." *Die Filmwoche* 8, no. 12, March 19, 1930.
Miller, Douglas. "The Influence of the Talkies on the Film Industry." *Film-Kurier* 11, no number, June 1, 1929.
"M. Jacques Haïk nous donne son opinion sur l'avenir du film parlant français." *La cinématographie française* 11, no. 560, July 27, 1929.
"'Monkey Business.'" *Variety* 104, no. 5, October 13, 1931.
Moretti, Franco. *Graphs, Maps, Trees: Abstract Models for Literary History*. London: Verso, 2005.
Morienval, Jean. "Film français synchronisés U. S. A." *Le cinéopse* 13, no. 141, May 1931.
———. "Le doublage, ses nécessités et ses limites." *Le cinéopse* 14, no. 152, April 1932.

Morton, David. *Sound Recording: The Life Story of a Technology*. Baltimore: Johns Hopkins University Press, 2004.
Mosco, Vincent. *The Digital Sublime: Myth, Power, and Cyberspace*. Cambridge: MIT Press, 2003.
"The Motion Picture Industry in Continental Europe in 1931." *Trade Information Bulletin*, no. 797. Washington, DC: United States Government Printing Office, 1932.
"Motion Pictures and Trade." *The Motion Picture* 4, no. 4, April 1928.
Moussinac, Léon. "Un film 'parlant.'" *Le monde*, February 2, 1929.
Mühl-Benninghaus, Wolfgang. *Das Ringen um den Tonfilm: Strategien der Elektro- und Filmindustrie in den 20er und 30er Jahren*. Düsseldorf: Droste, 1999.
Müller, Corinna. *Vom Stummfilm zum Tonfilm*. Munich: Wilhelm Fink, 2003.
"Musical Pictures Again to Be in Vogue." *Washington Post*, September 7, 1931.
"Music Men Again on Top." *Variety* 100, no. 7, August 27, 1930.
"Music Sales and Radio." *Variety* 99, no. 5, May 14, 1930.
"Musik-Kritik zum 'Lied einer Nacht.'" *Licht-Bild-Bühne* 25, no. 123, May 28, 1932.
Naremore, James. *Acting in the Cinema*. Berkeley: University of California Press, 1988.
Neer, Richard. "Connoisseurship and the Stakes of Style." *Critical Inquiry* 32, no. 1 (Autumn 2005): 1–26.
"Neuf microphones dans chaque studio." *Comoedia* 25, no. 6637, March 23, 1931.
"New Product." *Exhibitors Herald World* 101, no. 3, October 18, 1930.
Nichols, Lewis. "Tin Pan Alley is Weaving Its Lyrics in New Ways." *New York Times*, June 8, 1930.
"Nine Versions of *King of Jazz* made by Universal." *Exhibitors Herald World* 101, no. 3, October 18, 1930.
"Non-film Songs Don't Class with Picture-Songs." *Variety* 98, no. 12, April 2, 1930.
North, C. J., and N. D. Golden. "The European Film Market—Then and Now." *Journal of the Society of Motion Picture Engineers* 18, no. 4, April 1932.
———. "Sound Film Competition Abroad." *Journal of the Society of Motion Picture Engineers* 15, no. 6, December 1930.
"Notes of the Berlin Screen." *New York Times*, November 15, 1931.
O., Elisabeth. "Dreht 'menschliche Filme'!" *Die Filmwoche*, October 8, 1930.
O'Brien, Charles. *Cinema's Conversion to Sound: Technology and Film Style in France and the U. S.* Bloomington: Indiana University Press, 2005.
———. "The 'Cinematisation' of Sound Cinema in Britain: The Dubbing into French of Hitchcock's *Waltzes from Vienna*." In *Je t'aime . . . moi non plus: Anglo-French Cinematic Relations*, edited by Lucy Mazdon and Catherine Wheatley, 37–49. New York: Berghahn Books, 2010.
———. "Dubbing in the Early 1930s: An Improbable Policy." In *'Splendid Innovations': The Translation of Films, 1900–1944*, edited by Carol O'Sullivan and Jean-François Cornu, London: British Academy, 2017.
———. "Film, Gramophone, and National Cinema: *Die Dreigroschenoper* and *L'opéra de quat' sous*." *Cinema et cie* 7 (Fall 2005): 35–47.
———. "A Multimedia Presentation on the Differences between the German and French Versions." *The Threepenny Opera*. Directed by G. W. Pabst. New York: Criterion Collection, 2007. First released 1931.
———. "Multiple Language Versions and National Cinema, 1930–1933; Statistical Analysis." *Cinema et cie* 6 (Winter 2005): 45–52.

———. "Sound-on-Disc Cinema." In *Early Cinema: Critical Concepts*, edited by Richard Abel, 42–51. New York: Routledge, 2013.

———. "*Sous les toits de Paris* and French Film, at Home and Abroad." *Studies in French Cinema* 9, no. 2 (2009): 111–25.

Observer. "'Maurice' Becomes—a Marionette!" *Bioscope* 85, no. 1261, December 3, 1930.

O'Callahan, Casey. *Sounds: A Philosophical Theory*. Oxford: Oxford University Press, 2007.

O'Connell, J. S. "Talkers 'Producers' Rattles' Says Pioneer: 'Sound Is No Improvement.'" *Motion Picture News* 41, no. 23, June 7, 1930.

"1,250 Kinos haben abgestimmt." *Film-Kurier* 13, no. 119, May 23, 1931.

"Operettas Out at First National." *Motion Picture News* 41, no. 24, June 14, 1930.

"Operettas with Songs Only Considered Okay for All Over the World." *Variety* 99, no. 10, June 18, 1930.

"Operettenfilme sind Triumpf: Das Publikum wird überfüttert." *Film-Kurier* 12, no. 207, September 2, 1930.

"Operettenfilm = Krise in USA." *Film-Kurier* 12, no. 199, August 23, 1930.

O'Sullivan, Joseph. "Music as the Narrator." *Motion Picture Herald* 103, no. 2, April 11, 1931.

Palmer, Olive. "Requirements of the Radio Singer." In *Music, Sound, and Technology in America: A Documentary History of Early Phonograph, Cinema, and Radio*, edited by Timothy Taylor, Mark Katz, and Tony Grajeda, 115. Durham, NC: Duke University Press, 2012.

Palmer, Rex. "Microphone Matters." *Gramophone* 8, no. 85, June 1930.

Panofsky, Erwin. "Style and Medium in the Moving Pictures." *Transition*, no. 26 (1937): 121–33.

"Paramount Cuts Down Footage to Increase Action." *Motion Picture News* 42, no. 15, October 11, 1930.

"Paramount Next to Ban Musicals as 'Sales Poison.'" *Motion Picture News* 42, no. 3, July 19, 1930.

"Paramount-Publix and CBS Like Radio-Keith with N.B.C.; Now Two Biggest Air Formations." *Variety* 95, no. 10, June 19, 1929.

"Paris Conference Ends with Electrics Dividing World." *Variety* 100, no. 2, July 23, 1930.

Paulin, Scott. "Richard Wagner and the Fantasy of Cinematic Unity: The Idea of the *Gesamtkuntswerk* in the History and Theory of Film Music." In Buhler, Flinn, and Neumeyer, *Music and Cinema*, 58–84.

Pfeiffer, Heinrich. "Motif und Handlung im Tonfilm." *Film-Kurier* 12, no. 51, February 27, 1930.

Philip, Robert. *Performing Music in the Age of Recording*. New Haven: Yale University Press, 2004.

"Picture Songs Pushing Trade into Heavy Overproduction." *Variety* 97, no. 10, December 18, 1929.

"Pictures on Way to Third Place in World's Industrial Importance." *Variety* 95, no. 12, July 3, 1929.

"Picture Title Plugs Dropped." *Variety* 98, no. 7, February 26, 1930.

"Plan of Dubbing Foreign Lines in English Versions Being Discouraged." *Motion Picture News* 42, no. 17, October 25, 1930.

Polzer, Joachim, ed. *Aufstieg und Untergang des Tonfilms: Die Zukunft des Kinos*. Berlin: Polzer, 2002.

"Prague Hails 'Fool.'" *Variety* 97, no. 9, December 11, 1929.

Prawer, Siegbert Saloman. *Between Two Worlds: The Jewish Presence in Austrian and German Film, 1910–1933*. New York: Berghahn, 2005.

"Producers Optimistic Again That the 40 Percent Foreign Revenue Will Return to Former Status." *Variety* 100, no. 5, August 13, 1930.
"Probleme der Tonfilmgestaltung." *Film-Kurier* 13, no. 5, January 7, 1931.
"Problems of Presentation." *Bioscope* 83, no. 1231, May 7, 1930.
"Publix Convinced on Music Sales Enlarging." *Variety* 97, no. 11, December 25, 1929.
"Publix Music Counters Have Edge on Stores." *Variety* 99, no. 5, May 21, 1930.
Quigley, Martin J. "Dubbing." *Exhibitors Herald World* 100, no. 1, July 5, 1930.
———. "Musical Pictures." *Exhibitors Herald World* 100, no. 12, September 20, 1930.
———. "The Truth about Hollywood: 'No Silent Pictures.'" *Bioscope* 82, no. 1,222, March 5, 1930.
Quirk, James. "Close Ups and Long Shots." *Photoplay* 38, no. 6, November 1930, 29–30.
"Radio, Over-Production, High Prices, Mechanicals—All Blamed for Slump." *Variety* 99, no. 10, June 18, 1930.
"Radio's Many Money Names." *Variety* 95, no. 1, April 17, 1929.
Rayment, S. G., ed. *The Kinematograph Year Book, 1929*. London: Kinematograph, 1930.
———, ed. *The Kinematograph Year Book, 1930*. London: Kinematograph, 1931.
———, ed. *The Kinematograph Year Book, 1931*. London: Kinematograph, 1932.
———. "Year Two of the Revolution: The Story of 1929." In Rayment, *Kinematograph Year Book, 1930*, 9–16.
Régent, Roger. "La musique enregistrée supprimera-t-elle les orchestras?" *Pour vous*, no. 57, December 19, 1929.
"René Clair's New Film." *New York Times*, May 10, 1931.
Renoir, Jean. *My Life and My Films*. Translated by Norman Denny. New York: Atheneum, 1974.
"Restricted Radio Use Continued of Show and Talker Musical Hits." *Variety* 96, no. 3, July 31, 1929.
Richard, A.-P. "Le film sonore entre le théâtre et le cinéma." *La cinématographie française* 12, no. 604, May 31, 1930.
Robson, David. "Architects and Sound." *Bioscope* 85, no. 1,257, November 5, 1930.
Rodowick, David N. *The Virtual Life of Film*. Cambridge: Harvard University Press, 2007.
Rossholm, Anna Sofia. *Reproducing Languages, Translating Bodies: Approaches to Speech, Translation and Cultural Identity in Early European Sound Film*. Stockholm: Almqvist and Wiksell International, 2006.
Rother, Rainer. "Zwischen Parodie und poetischem Wachtraum: *Die Drei von der Tankstelle*." In *Das Ufa Buch*, edited by Hans-Michael Bock and Michael Totëberg, 272–75. Frankfurt: Zweitausendeins, 1992.
Roux-Parassac, Emile. "En écoutant le parlant." *Le cinéopse* 13, no. 141, May 1931.
Rubin, Martin. *Showstoppers: Busby Berkeley and the Tradition of Spectacle*. New York: Columbia University Press, 1993.
Sabaneev, Leonid. *Music for the Films*. Translated by S. Pring. New York: Arno, 1978. First published 1935.
Sacks, Oliver. *Musicophilia: Tales of Music and the Brain*. New York: Knopf, 2007.
Salt, Barry. *Film Style and Technology: History and Analysis*. 1st ed. London: Starword, 1983.
———. *Film Style and Technology: History and Analysis*. 2nd ed. London: Starword, 1992.
———. "Statistical Film Analysis (Basic Concepts and Practical Details)." Cinemetrics. Accessed August 31, 2018. http://www.cinemetrics.lv/salt.php.
"Same Necessity as in America." *Variety* 100, no. 2, July 23, 1930.

"Same Scene in Two Films, Lubitsch's-Schwartz'; German's Made First." *Variety* 100, no. 9, September 10, 1930.
Sanjek, Russell, and David Sanjek. *The American Popular Music Business in the Twentieth Century*. Oxford: Oxford University Press, 1991.
"Sapène Center Entire French Situation." *Variety* 95, no. 8, June 5, 1929.
Sargent, Epes Winthrop. "The Photoplaywright: Scenes and Leaders." *Moving Picture World* 13, no. 6, August 10, 1912.
Sarris, Andrew. "The Cultural Guilt of Musical Movies: *The Jazz Singer*, Fifty Years Later." *Film Comment* (September–October 1977): 39–41.
Saunders, Thomas. *Hollywood in Berlin: American Cinema in Weimar Germany*. Berkeley: University of California Press, 1994.
Schallert, Edwin. "Ghosting Songs Now Favored." *Los Angeles Times*, January 19, 1930.
———. "Jazz King Will Turn Comedian." *Los Angeles Times*, December 1, 1929.
———. "Laugh Feature Brightens Sky." *Los Angeles Times*, October 12, 1931.
———. "Revues Stir Controversy." *Los Angeles Times*, March 9, 1930.
———. "Sound Waxes International." *Los Angeles Times*, February 17, 1929.
Scheuer, Philip K. "Eddie Cantor's Chief Asset: Eddie Cantor." *Los Angeles Times*, October 12, 1930.
———. "Jazz Spectacle Sets Pace in Novelties." *Los Angeles Times*, April 13, 1930.
———. "Musical Picture Quietly Undergoes Renaissance." *Los Angeles Times*, February 22, 1931.
———. "Picture-Lyric Trend Queried." *Los Angeles Times*, August 4, 1929.
———. "Theme Song Own Excuse." *Los Angeles Times*, February 2, 1930.
———. "A Town Called Hollywood." *Los Angeles Times*, September 20, 1931.
Schmuck, Adolph. "The Case for Mere Listening." *Disques* 2, no. 3, May 1931.
Segal, Mark. "The Future of Film." *Close Up* 7, no. 2, August 1930.
Seiter, William. "Motion Pictures Must Move." In *Cinematographic Annual, 1931*, vol. 2, edited by Hal Hall, 263–65. New York: Arno and the *New York Times*, 1972.
Shisler, Geoffrey. "Joseph Schmidt." Music and the Holocaust. Accessed March 28, 2017. http://holocaustmusic.ort.org/places/camps/josef-schmidt/.
"Silent and Sound Facts Revealed by German Exhibs." *Variety* 97, no. 9, December 11, 1929.
"Silent Film Versions of U.S. Talkers Apt to Aid Foreign Films Abroad." *Variety* 94, no. 4, May 8, 1929.
Silverman, Sid. "'The Broadway Melody.'" *Variety* 94, no. 5, February 13, 1929.
———. "International Show Business." *Variety* 95, no. 12, July 3, 1929.
———. "Rehabilitation of Flesh-and-Blood in Film Houses Gains Momentum, Survey Shows." *Motion Picture Herald* 102, no. 3, January 17, 1931.
———. "The Smothering Talker." *Variety* 94, no. 11, January 2, 1929.
———. "'29 and Talkers—1930 and Wide Film." *Variety* 97, no. 12, January 8, 1930.
"Slams Talkers; Says Audiences Want Orchestras." *Motion Picture News* 42, no. 3, July 19, 1930.
Slowik, Michael. *After the Silents: Hollywood Film Music in the Early Sound Era, 1926–1934*. New York: Columbia University Press, 2014.
———. "Diegetic Withdrawal and Other Worlds: Film Music Strategies before *King Kong*, 1927–1933." *Cinema Journal* 53, no. 1 (Fall 2013): 1–25.
Smith, Jacob. *Vocal Tracks: Performance and Sound Media*. Berkeley: University of California Press, 2008.

Smith, Jeff. *The Sounds of Commerce: Marketing Popular Film Music*. New York: Columbia University Press, 1998.
Snyder, Bob. *Music and Memory: An Introduction*. Cambridge: MIT Press, 2001.
"Song Plugger Going?" *Variety* 93, no. 4, November 7, 1928.
"Sound Eliminates Much Export." *Variety* 93, no. 6, November 21, 1928.
"Sound or Silent Future." *Variety* 95, no. 10, June 19, 1929.
"Sound Rapidly Replacing Silents Abroad, Gov't Finds." *Motion Picture News* 41, no. 6, February 8, 1930.
Spadoni, Robert. *Uncanny Bodies: The Coming of Sound Film and the Origins of the Horror Genre*. Berkeley: University of California Press, 2007.
"Special Metro Song Discs in Loew's Lobbies." *Variety* 96, no. 4, August 7, 1929.
Spring, Katherine. *Saying It with Songs: Popular Music and the Coming of Sound to Hollywood Cinema*. Oxford: Oxford University Press, 2013.
Stein, Barry, Terrence Sanford, Mark Wallace, J. William Vaughan, and Wan Jiang. "Crossmodal Spatial Interactions in Subcortical and Cortical Circuits." In *Crossmodal Space and Crossmodal Attention*, edited by Charles Spence and Jon Driver, 25–50. Oxford: Oxford University Press, 2004.
Steiner, Fred. "What Were Musicians Saying about Movie Music during the First Decade of Sound? A Symposium of Selected Writings." In *Film Music I*, edited by Clifford McCarty, 81–107. New York: Garland, 1989.
Steiner, Max. "Scoring the Film." In *We Make the Movies*, edited by Nancy Naumberg, 216–38. New York: Knopf, 1937.
Stenhouse, C. "A British Eye on Paris." *Close Up* 6, no. 6, June 1930.
Stevens, A. E. "Bad Sound Is Due to Bad Prints." *Bioscope* 85, no. 1257, November 5, 1930.
Stilwell, Robynn J. "Sound and Empathy: Subjectivity, Gender, and the Cinematic Soundscape." In *Film Music: Critical Approaches*, edited by K. J. Donnelly, 167–87. Edinburgh: Edinburgh University Press, 2001.
Stone, Christopher. "Film Notes." *Gramophone* 8, no. 92, January 1931.
———. "Listener's Corner." *Gramophone* 11, no. 123, August 1933.
Stuart, Georges. "Dans une vieille rue de Paris . . . à Epinay." *Soir*, February 15, 1930.
———. "Le retour au bon sens." *Soir*, July 19, 1930.
Suisman, David. *Selling Sounds: The Commercial Revolution in American Music*. Cambridge: Harvard University Press, 2009.
Sullivan, Jack. *Hitchcock's Music*. New Haven: Yale University Press, 2006.
Swigart, Bill. "Studio Music." *Variety* 97, no. 12, January 8, 1930.
"Swing Away in Buenos Aires from Am. S. and D. Talkers—Going for Silents." *Variety* 99, no. 12, July 2, 1930.
"Talking of the Talkies." *Photoplay* 38, no. 1, June 1930.
"Ted Lewis' Walloping Hit in Paris w. All English Lyrics Songs." *Variety* 100, no. 5, August 13, 1930.
"Theme Song Interjection into Pop Music Industry Keeps Trade Topsy-Turvy." *Variety* 96, no. 2, July 24, 1929.
"They Say . . ." *Motion Picture News* 41, no. 24, June 14, 1930.
Thiele, Wilhelm. "Des lois que régissent l'opérette filmée." *Comoedia* 24, no. 6,285, April 2, 1930.
Thomas, Hans Alex. *Die deutsche Tonfilmmusik von den Anfängen bis 1956*. Gütersloh, Germany: Bertelsmann, 1962.

Thompson, Emily. *The Soundscape of Modernity: Architectural Acoustics and the Culture of Listening in America, 1900–1933*. Cambridge: MIT Press, 2002.
Thompson, Kristin. *Exporting Entertainment: America in the World Film Market, 1907–1934*. London: British Film Institute, 1985.
Thorburn, David, and Henry Jenkins, eds. *Rethinking Media Change: The Aesthetics of Transition*. Cambridge: MIT Press, 2003.
"Tonfilmschlager mit 1.8 Millionen." *Film-Kurier* 12, no. 15, May 15, 1930.
Toulet, Emanuelle, and Christian Belaygue, eds. *Musique d'écran: L'accompagnement musical du cinéma muet en France, 1918–1995*. Paris: Réunion des Musées Nationaux, 1994.
Trask, C. Hooper. "Audible Films Inspire German Producers." *New York Times*, November 23, 1930.
———. "German Film Notes." *New York Times*, February 22, 1931.
———. "Screen Notes from Germany." *New York Times*, May 10, 1931.
Trumpener, Katie. "The René Clair Moment and the Overlap Films of the Early 1930s: Detlef Sierck's 'April, April!'" *Film Criticism* 23, no. 2/3 (Winter/Spring 1999): 33–45.
Tsivian, Yuri. "Film Statistics: Give and Take." Cinemetrics. Accessed February 18, 2018. http://www.cinemetrics.lv/dev/fsgt_q1a.php.
———. "What Is Cinema? An Agnostic Answer." *Critical Inquiry* 34, no. 4 (Summer 2008): 754–76.
Turk, Edward. *Hollywood Diva: A Biography of Jeanette MacDonald*. Berkeley: University of California Press, 2000.
"Ufa Casting Chief in London." *Bioscope* 87, no. 1285, May 20, 1931.
"Un enquête à Londres: L'avenir du film parlant." *Pour vous*, no. 28, May 30, 1929.
"Une visite aux studios Salabert." *La technique cinématographique* 4, no. 34, October 1933.
"Universal Takes Lead in Foreign Version Films." *Universal Weekly* 31, no. 5, March 8, 1930.
Valentine, Maggie. *The Show Starts on the Sidewalk: An Architectural History of the Movie Theatre, Starring S. Charles Lee*. New Haven: Yale University Press, 1994.
"'The Vagabond Lover.'" *Gramophone* 7, no. 83, April 1930.
Vasey, Ruth. *The World According to Hollywood, 1918–1939*. Madison: University of Wisconsin Press, 1997.
"Vaudeville Coming Back." *New York Times*, September 10, 1931.
"Vaudfilm Back Abroad." *Variety* 100, no. 2, July 23, 1930.
Vinneuil, F. "'Monkey Business.'" *Action française*, October 23, 1931.
Von Hessert, Ria. "Wie soll man in Tonfilm singen?" *Film-Kurier* 15, no. 35, February 9, 1933.
Vuillermoz, Emile. "Le film musical." *Excelsior*, April 14, 1932.
W., H. H. "Musikalische Charakterisierung als Element der Film-Komödie." *Film-Kurier* 12, no. 239, October 9, 1930.
Wahl, Chris. *Multiple Language Versions Made in Babelsberg: Ufa's International Strategy, 1929–1939*. Translated by Steve Wilder. Amsterdam: Amsterdam University Press, 2016.
———. *Sprachversionsfilme aus Babelsberg: Die internationale Strategie der Ufa, 1929–1939*. Munich: text and kritik, 2009.
Waldman, Harry. *Paramount in Paris: 300 Films Produced at the Joinville Studios, 1930–1933*. Lanham, MD: Scarecrow, 1998.
"Warners Curtailing Theme Songs in Pcts." *Variety* 99, no. 13, July 9, 1930.
"Warners Plan Music Counter Chain." *Variety* 98, no. 13, April 9, 1930.
Warwick, H. Gibson. "Concert Hall or Studio?" *Gramophone* 6, no. 61, June 1928.

Wedel, Michael. *Der deutsche Musikfilm: Archäologie eines Genres 1914–1945*. Munich: text and kritik, 2007.

——. "Vom Synchronismus zur Synchronisation: Carl Robert Blum und der frühe Tonfilm." In Polzer, *Aufstieg und Untergang des Tonfilms*, 97–112.

Weinberg, Herman G. "Old Wine in New Bottles." *Sight and Sound* 8, no. 29 (Spring 1939): 21–22.

Weis, Elizabeth, and John Belton, eds. *Film Sound: Theory and Practice*. New York: Columbia University Press, 1985.

Welch, David, and Roel Vande Winkel. "Europe's New Hollywood? The German Film Industry under Nazi Rule, 1933–1945." In *Cinema and the Swastika: The International Expansion of Third Reich Cinema*, edited by D. Welch and R. Vande Winkel, 1–24. London: Palgrave MacMillan, 2007.

"West Coast No More a Gold Coast, Declare All the Film Songwriters." *Variety* 100, no. 3, July 30, 1930.

Wierzbicki, James. *Film Music: A History*. New York: Routledge, 2009.

Williams, Alan. "Historical and Theoretical Issues in the Coming of Recorded Sound to the Cinema." In *Sound Theory/Sound Practice*, edited by Rick Altman, 126–37. New York: Routledge/American Film Institute, 1992.

——. Introduction to *Film and Nationalism*, edited by A. Williams, 1–22. New Brunswick, NJ: Rutgers University Press, 2002.

Williams, J. D. "Americans in a Quandary." *Bioscope* 82, no. 1217, January 29, 1930.

——. "Overhaul the Quota!" *Bioscope* 82, no. 1217, January 29, 1930.

Wilson, P. "Acoustic versus Electric." *Gramophone* 10, no. 119, April 1933.

——. "Cornucopiae: A Study in Gramophone Theory." *Gramophone* 5, no. 11, April 1928.

Wins, Hans Heinrich. "Kommt des Orchester im Lichtspielhaus." *Film-Kurier* 12, no. 195, August 19, 1930.

"Witmarks Line Up with Warners for Music Publishing Combo." *Variety* 94, no. 1, January 16, 1929.

Wölfflin, Heinrich. *Principles of Art History: The Problem of the Development of Style in Later Art*. Translated by M. D. Hottinger. New York: Dover, 1950. First published 1915.

"World War of Talking Pictures Seen Raging with Hollywood as the Pivot." *Motion Picture News* 42, no. 3, July 19, 1930.

Wurtzler, Steven. *Electric Sounds: Technological Change and the Rise of Corporate Mass Media*. New York: Columbia University Press, 2007.

Young, Paul. *The Cinema Dreams Its Rivals: Media Fantasy Films from Radio to the Internet*. Minneapolis: University of Minnesota, 2006.

"'Zwei Herzen' Ends Long Run Soon." *New York Times*, September 14, 1931.

"'Zwei Herzen im Dreivierteltakt.'" *Film-Kurier* 12, no. 64, May 14, 1930.

INDEX

acousmatic voices, 75–76
action shots, 12–14, 93, 105, *106*, 114, 145, 174, 178, 180–81
Adorno, Theodor, 23–24, 72, 166
Albright, Daniel, 1, 26
Altman, Rick, 7, 82, 84, 159
"Always," 129
American Society of Composers, Authors and Publishers, 133, 161n12
Anderson, John Murray, 28, 81
anempathetic sound, 76–77
Animal Crackers, 68, 104–14, 136
Applause, 28
Arliss, George, 137
Arm wie eine Kirchenmaus, 68, 155
Arno, Siegfried, 75–76
Ates, Roscoe, 137
Axt, William, David Mendoza, and Ballard MacDonald, 36

Bad Company, 127
Bakshy, Alexander, 66
Balázs, Béla, 4, 27–28
Balcon, Michael, 151–52
Barrymore, John, 121
Barrymore, Lionel, 171
Barsony, Rosa, 160
Barthelmess, Richard, 82
Battle of Paris, The, 58
Baxter, Peter, 132
Bazin, André, 48
Bedtime Story, A, 41
Belton, John, 170
Berlin, Irving, 36, 108, 129, 134
Berliner, Emile, 51
Berkeley, Busby, 23, 80, 135
Be Yourself, 67
Bie, Oscar, 144
Big Boy, 60, 69–70, 133

Big Broadcast, The, 67, 129, 147, 148
Big Pond, The, 37, 73, 84, 109, 126, 137
Blackmail, 35, 40, 82–83, 87n75
Blue Angel, The, 9, 97, 137. See also *Der Blaue Engel*
Bomben auf Monte Carlo, 37, 97
Boones, Martin, 25
Bordwell, David, Janet Staiger, and Kristin Thompson, 48, 182n3
Bow, Clara, 4
Brecht, Bertolt, 90
Brice, Fanny, 67
Broadway Melody, The, 25, 28–35, 37–38, 40, 58, 78, 81, 99, 127, 177
"Broadway Melody, The," 28–34, 36, 38
Brooks, Louise, 77–78
Brown, Nacio Herb, 36, 137
Buck, Gene, and James Hanley, 129–30
Buhler, James, David Neumeyer, and Rob Deemer, 35
"Build a Little Home," 80
Burkan, Nathan, 161n12
Burrows, James, 81
"But Not for Me," 136–37

cadence, 28–29, 32–33
Canary Murder Case, The, 75
Cantor, Eddie, 67, 80, 133, 136–37, 145
Canty, George, 98
Carroll, Nancy, 37
cartoons, 5, 20, 26, 61, 111, 113, 138, 145, 147. See also Disney; Looney Tunes; Merrie Melodies; Silly Symphonies
Casparius, Hans, 162n41
Chaney, Lon, 87n74
Chartier, J., and R. Desplanques, 158
Chasing Rainbows, 79, 100
Chevalier, Maurice, 37, 41, 57, 68, 73–74, 76, 81–82, 84, 109, 126, 137, 147
Chion, Michel, 75, 76

Christians, Mady, 68
cinemetrics, x, 12–14, 174, 178–79, 182n6, 182n8, 182n10, 183n12
Civjans, Gunars, 174, 179
Clair, René, 5, 8–9, 16n35, 21, 58, 65, 80, 95, 147
Cocoanuts, The, 28, 104, 106–9, 112, 113, 117nn84–85
Coeury, André, and G. Clarence, 72
Colombo, Russ, 70
Connor, Steven, 66
Correll, Hugo, 79, 157–58
Crafton, Donald, 7, 58, 66, 159
Crawford, Joan, 82, 84
Crawford, Robert, 36
"Crazy for You," 127
Crisp, Colin, 158
Crosby, Bing, 67, 70, 129, 134, 136–37, 147, 148

Dance of Life, The, 37, 60, 68
Dangerous Curves, 100
Daniels, Bebe, 128
"Das gibt's nur einmal," 156–57
"Das ist die Liebe der Matrosen," 37
Das Lied einer Nacht, 75, 76
Davidson, Jane, 72
Dean, Basil, 97
Der Blaue Engel, 97, 115n43, 127, 254. See also *Blue Angel, The*
Der Herr auf Bestellung, 75
Der Jazzkönig, 21–23. See also *King of Jazz*
Der Kongreß tanzt, 97, 150, 152–54, 156–57
Der Mörder Dimitri Karamasoff, 27
Der schwarze Husar, 68
Der Sohn der weißen Berge, 149
Der weiße Rausch, 27
dialogue shots, 12–14, 93–96, 105–7, 145, 165, 174–76, 178
Die Dreigroschenoper, 9, 90, 150–51
Die Drei von der Tankstelle, 27, 37, 68, 142–45, 158, 179
Die Privatsekretärin, 145–46
Dietrich, Marlene, 4, 127, 137
Die verkaufte Braut, 145
Die verliebte Firma, 76, 148, 150–51, 155
direct sound, 60, 80, 103, 112–14, 148, 150–60, 163n50, 165, 175
Disney, 20, 26, 43n15, 146. See also cartoons

Dixiana, 128, 136
Doherty, Thomas, 123
Donnelly, Kevin, 28, 159
downbeat cut, 28–29, 31–32, 73–74, 78
Downey, Gregory, 47
Dracula, 21, 101
dubbing, 3, 65, 81–84, 95, 115n28, 143, 148–50, 158, 165, 167. See also playback; postsynchronization
Duck Soup, 104, 114
Dyer, Richard, 15, 26

Eaton, Mary, 58, 59, 130
Eggerth, Martha, 27, 154, 159
Ehrlich, Cyril, 50
Ein blonder Traum, 151–52, 159
Einbrecher, 27, 145, 159
"Ein guter Freund," 27, 37
Ein Lied, ein Küß, ein Mädel, 75, 146–47, 159
Ein Lied geht um die Welt, 75
Eisenstein, Sergei, 27, 89
Eisler, Hanns, 23–24, 160, 166
Eisler, Hanns, and Theodor Adorno, 23–24, 166
Elsaesser, Thomas, 170
Elstree Calling, 21
"Everyone Says I Love You," 109, 137–38

Fairservice, Don, 154
"Falling in Love Again," 137
Feet First, 129
Feuer, Jane, 56
Fifty Million Frenchmen, 136
film operetta, 3, 19, 21, 23, 97, 121, 142, 146, 157, 159, 161, 161n7, 164, 166; German-made, 5, 9, 68, 144–45, 158, 160 (see also *Operettenfilm*)
First Auto, The, 100
Fleeger, Jennifer, 7
"Flieger, grüß' mir die Sonne," 6
"Florida by the Sea," 28
Flying Down to Rio, 135
Footlight Parade, 56, 57, 125
formal integration, 4–5, 18–19, 21, 23, 167
Forst, Willy, 27, 75, 148
Forty Second Street, 135
F.P.1 antwortet nicht, 6

Frank, Nino, 1
Franklin, Arthur, 25, 103
Fritsch, Willy, 68, 154
Frölich, Gustav, 76, 159
Furia, Phillip, and Laurie Paterson, 71

Garncarz, Joseph, 149, 167
Garrick, John, 128
Gaynor, Janet, 69
Gershwin, George, and Ira Gershwin, 134, 136
ghost music, 78–79. See also nondiegetic music; underscore
Girl Crazy, 28, 129, 136
"Girl of My Dreams," 35
Gitelman, Lisa, 51
Glennon, Bert, 106
Gloria, 76
Glorifying the American Girl, 5, 27, 41, 58–60, 129
"goat gland" films, 16n22
Goldwyn, Samuel, 133, 136
Gomery, Douglas, 7, 48, 122
"Goodnight Monsieur Baby," 41
Goossens, Eugene, 132
Grand Hotel, 177
Grant, Cary, 147
Gray, Allan, 6
Green, Mitzi, 136–37
Griffith, David Wark, 96–97, 114n3
Grünbaum, Fritz, 68, 155

Half Shot at Sunrise, 117n80, 136
Hallelujah, I'm a Bum, 148
Happily Ever After, 151
Happy Days, 21, 56–57
Harkenrider, John, 5
Harvey, Lilian, 67, 146, 152–53, 156–60, 163n46
Haskell, Molly, 67
Heerman, Victor, 107
Hell's Harbour, 100
Helm, Brigitte, 76
Herzog, Amy, 20
Hesterberg, Trude, 68
Heygate, John, 152
Heymann, Werner Richard, 37, 145, 159–60, 163n69

Hirsch, Leo, 1
Hitchcock, Alfred, 35, 82, 95
Hollaender, Friedrich, 160
Hollywood Revue of 1929, The, 21, 23, 60, 80–81, 119–20, 137, 159
Hook, Line and Sinker, 136
Hörbiger, Paul, 75
Horse Feathers, 104, 109, 114, 137
Huron, David, 28, 31

Ich bei Tag und Du bei Nacht, 140n58
"Ich laß' mir meinen Körper schwarz bepinseln," 27
Ich und die Kaiserin, 152
"I Got Rhythm," 28
"I Have to Have You," 37
"I Love You Now as I Loved You Then," 36
"I'm Daffy over You," 39, 109–10
I'm No Angel, 129, 133
Interference, 100
intertitles, 6–7, 13, 66, 90, 93, 97–99, 115n15, 115n16, 175. See also X versions
"Irgendwo auf der Welt gibt's ein kleines bißchen Glück," 152, 156, 160
I Sing for You Alone, 75
isomorphic cadence. See cadence
"I've Got a Feeling I'm Falling," 28, 129

Jacobs, Lea, 106–7, 179, 182n
Jannings, Emil, 97, 115n44, 127
Jazz Singer, The, 25, 65, 98, 100
Je t'adore, mais pourquoi, 75
Jolson, Al, 37, 41, 57, 60, 65, 67, 69–70, 73–76, 121, 127, 129, 133, 148
Judge, Arline, 136

Kalinak, Kathryn, 7, 20
Kearns, Allen, 136
Kelly, Kitty, 28
Kid from Spain, The, 67–68
Kiepura, Jan, 75, 76
King, Charles, 28, 33–34, 37, 40, 58, 79, 177, 182n7
King, Dennis, 57, 136
King Kong, 101
King of Jazz, 21–23, 28, 81, 119. See also *Der Jazzkönig*

Klitsch, Ludwig, 115n44, 143, 152
Korff, Arnold, 21–23
Kraft, James, 49

La chienne, 67
Ladies of Leisure, 100
Laemmle, Carl, Jr., 94
Lang, Fritz, 9
Lange, Arthur, 60
Lastra, James, 7
Lawrence, Gertrude, 58
Le chemin du paradis, 144, 158
Lee, Davey, 41, 74, 129
Leech-Wilkinson, Daniel, 70
Leise flehen meine Lieder, 27, 148, 154
Le million, 8
LeRoy, Mervyn, 94
Levant, Oscar, 37
Lewis, Howard, 90, 124
Lewis Ruth Band, 150
Liebe muss verstanden sein, 159–60
Liebeswalzer, 96, 144–45
"Little Pal," 73–74, 86n44, 129–31, 140n59
London, Kurt, 2, 24, 26, 71, 145–46, 158
Lonesome, 100, 129
Looney Tunes, 138
L'opéra de quat' sous, 80
Lost Squadron, The, 101
Love, Bessie, 28, 79, 127, 177
Love Me Tonight, 68, 81–82
Love Parade, The, 80
Lubitsch, Ernst, 5, 21, 106, 142, 146, 159, 166
Lucas, Nick, 70, 129
Lugosi, Bela, 21

M, 9
MacDonald, Jeanette, 80
MacKenzie, Compton, 72
"Makin' Whoopee," 137
Maltby, Richard, 122
Mammy, 67
Mamoulian, Rouben, 5
Marx Brothers, the, 90, 103–14, 136–38; Chico, 110–13, 137; Groucho, 107, 110, 112, 137; Harpo, 68, 76, 110–13, 137; Zeppo, 111–12, 137
Maxfield, J. P., 81

McCormack, John, 121, 136
Melford, George, 99
Melodie des Herzens, 16n18, 146, 158
Melody of the Heart, 146
Merrie Melodies, 138
metrical montage, 27–28
Mexicali Rose, 79
Meydam, Wilhelm, 157
Meyer, Leonard, 11–12
Millie, 38, 130, 137
Milliken, Carl, 122
"Mir ist so millionär zu Mut," 152
Monkey Business, 39, 76, 104–14, 117nn75–76, 117n84, 137
Morgan, Helen, 28
Morgan, Paul, 155
Moritz macht sein Glück, 75–76
Morocco, 100
Motion Picture Producers and Distributors Association, 121–22
Motion Picture Production Code, 91
Moussinac, Léon, 2
Müller, Corinna, 149
Müller, Renate, 156–57
Murder!, 75
Mussolini, Benito, 3

Naremore, James, 66
narrative integration, 4–5, 18–19
Nasrin, Mohsen, 182n8
Navarro, Ramon, 57
Neer, Richard, 10
"Nobody Loves Me Like that Dallas Man," 129, 133–34
"No Foolin,'" 129–30
nondiegetic music, 39, 78–79, 89, 99–103, 111–12, 146–47, 174, 176–77, 186. *See also* underscore
Novis, Donald, 6

"Oh, How I Adore You," 137
Old San Francisco, 100
Oliver, Edna May, 137
Olsen, John, and Harold Johnson, 136
Once in a Lifetime, 56–57
Ondra, Anny, 82

On purge bébé, 101
On with the Show, 21, 60
Operettenfilm, 5, 9, 68, 144–45, 158, 160. See also film operetta
Our Dancing Daughters, 36, 100, 120

Pabst, Georg Wilhelm, 9, 150–51
Pagan, The, 100, 120
Page, Anita, 28, 177, 182n7
Palmer, Olive, 72
Palmy Days, 67, 137
Panofsky, Erwin, 26
Paramount on Parade, 21, 23, 119
Party Girl, 137
period style, 9–11
Phantom Broadcast, The, 75
playback, 65, 71, 81–82, 84–85, 148, 156–60, 163n53, 165. See also dubbing; postsynchronization; prescoring
"Please!," 129
Pointed Heels, 37, 100, 128
Pommer, Erich, 4, 21, 97
Porter, Cole, 134, 136
postsynchronization, 81–82, 84–85, 103–4, 112–14, 148–50, 155–58, 165. See also dubbing; playback
Préjean, Albert, 58, 80, 150–51
prescoring, 65, 81. See also playback
Prodigal, The, 134
Public Enemy, 99

Quatorze juillet, 8
Quick, 146, 150, 155
Quigley, Martin, 121
Quilian, Eddie, 136

Ramona, 120
Rea, Virginia, 72
Reaching for the Moon, 67, 134
Red-Headed Woman, 128
Regelly, Hélène, 78
Reisch, Walter, 6
Renoir, Jean, 67
Revelers, The, 72
revue film, 3, 19, 21–24, 119, 121
Ritchard, Cyril, 35

Robbins, J. J., 36, 124
Robeson, Paul, 72
Rodgers, Richard, and Lorenz Hart, 81–82
Roman Scandals, 68, 80
Rosse, Herman, 23
Rubin, Martin, 23
Ruggles, Charlie, 58, 147

Sabaneev, Leonid, 102, 176
Salt, Barry, 48, 92, 95, 173, 179
Sapène, Jean, 122
Sarris, Andrew, 2, 23
Say It with Songs, 41, 73–74, 78, 127, 129–31
Schipa, Tito, 75
Schmidt, Josef, 75, 86n46
Schneider, Magda, 75
Schuster, Friedel, 156
Scorsese, Martin, 169, 171n10
Scotto, Vincent, 58
Selznick, David, 25
Show Boat, 126
Show of Shows, The, 21, 119, 137–38
Silly Symphonies, 20
Silverman, Sid, 3
Singing Fool, The, 36–37, 39–42, 67, 74, 118, 120–21
singing shots, 12 14, 29, 68, 89, 102, 105–6, 109, 134–36, 145, 165, 174–77, 179, 181
"Singin' in the Rain," 36, 138
Skelly, Hal, 68
Slowik, Michael, 7
Smiling Lieutenant, The, 146–47
song form, 5, 24–25, 39, 78
"Sonny Boy," 36–37, 39–42, 74, 121, 133, 137
sound film patent conference, 7–8
"Sous les ponts de Paris," 58
Sous les toits de Paris, 8, 58, 80, 95–96
Spadoni, Robert, 7
Spring, Katherine, 7, 109–10
Steiner, Max, 25, 79, 101
Stevenson, Robert, 151–52
Stolz der dritten Kompanie, 158
Studio Murder Mystery, 75
Submarine, 53
Suisman, David, 123
Sunny Side Up, 69, 137

"Sunny Side Up," 69
Sunrise, 100
Sunset Boulevard, 67
"Swanee River," 37
Swanson, Gloria, 66

Tanned Legs, 37, 136
Technicolor, 5, 16n21, 23, 44n21
Testament of Dr. Mabuse, The, 9, 75
"That's the Song of Paree," 81–82
"There's Only One What Matters to Me," 4
"There's the One for Me," 6, 37
This Is the Night, 128, 147
Thompson, Emily, 54
Thompson, Kristin, 23, 48
Three Broadway Girls, 100–101
Tibbett, Lawrence, 57, 121, 134, 136
"Tomorrow Is Another Day," 69
Tonbilder, 51, 62n24, 143
Traub, Hans, 161n13
"True Blue Lou," 68
True to the Navy, 4
Trumpener, Katie, 26
Tsivian, Yuri, 12, 174
Tucker, Sophie, 72
Tuttle, Frank, 5
Twelvetrees, Helen, 128
Twentieth Century, 101

underscore, 25, 39–40, 103, 111–12. *See also* ghost music; nondiegetic music

Vagabond Lover, The, 70, 75
"Vagabond Lover, The" 27
Valentine, Maggie, 124
Vallee, Rudy, 27, 70–75
Vasey, Ruth, 91
ventriloquism effect, 75–76, 86n47
Viktor und Viktoria, 76, 146–48, 156–57, 160, 176

Violinsky, Sol, 110
von Sternberg, Josef, 9, 97, 100, 115n43, 127, 137, 154
Vorobiyova, Kira, 182n8
Vuillermoz, Emile, 20

Wahl, Chris, 96, 149, 161, 167
Walzerkrieg, 27, 154, 157–58
Waters, Ethel, 72
Weary River, 82
Webb, Millard, 5
"Wedding of the Painted Dolls," 81
Weill, Kurt, 160
Weintraub Syncopators, 154
West, Mae, 129, 133
Wheeler, Bert, and Robert Woolsey, 136
"When My Dreams Come True," 108–9
"When the Folks High-Up Do the Mean Low-Down," 134
Whiteman, Paul, 81, 121
Whoopee!, 133, 136–37, 145
"Why Am I So Romantic?" 68, 108–9, 112
Wierzbicki, James, 99, 103
Winston, Carl, 97
Winston, Sam, 97
Wir schalten um auf Hollywood, 21
"With You, With Me," 37, 136
Wonder Bar, 67
Wurtzler, Steven, 7, 125

X versions, 98–99, 116n52. *See also* intertitles

"You Brought a New Kind of Love to Me," 37, 76, 109, 126, 137
"You Were Meant for Me," 38, 41

Zanuck, Darryl, 41, 45n77
Ziegfeld Follies, 5, 56, 59
Zwei Herzen im Dreivierteltakt, 27, 144–45, 158

CHARLES O'BRIEN is Associate Professor of Film Studies at Carleton University. He is author of *Cinema's Conversion to Sound: Technology and Film Style in France and the U.S.* (Bloomington: Indiana University Press, 2005).

www.ingramcontent.com/pod-product-compliance
Lightning Source LLC
Chambersburg PA
CBHW070315230426
43663CB00011B/2134